# AIRSHIPS

HENRY BEAUBOIS

# AIRSHIPS

## AN ILLUSTRATED HISTORY

DRAWINGS BY CARLO DEMAND

TRANSLATED AND ADAPTED BY MICHAEL AND ANGELA KELLY

MACDONALD AND JANE'S

*First published in Great Britain 1974 by*
*Macdonald and Jane's (Macdonald & Co. (Publishers) Ltd.)*
*49/50 Poland Street, London W1A 2LG*

ISBN 0356 08103 6

Printed in Switzerland

# CONTENTS

# FOREWORD

Unassumingly designated in French, and sometimes in American, by a simple adjective used as a noun, *dirigeable* or dirigible, these lighter-than-air craft were more nobly baptized 'Airship' or *Luftschiff* in English and German. The French name, however, more aptly describes the fact that a pilot could guide his flying-machine at will, by a combination of the laws governing static lift and those of dynamic lift; that is, the lifting power of lighter-than-air gases, and that of airflow over a surface. One of the pioneers of French aviation, Captain Ferdinand Ferber described dynamic lift more poetically: 'this flower born of speed'.

It was to take a century, and even more, before man's ingenuity succeeded in mastering the problems inherent in overcoming the technical obstacles to the application of these two aerodynamic laws. Two dates are significant. On 21 November 1783, the first flight starting from Paris was made in a *montgolfière* by Pilatre de Rozier and the Marquis d'Arlandes. The second date was 8 August 1884 when the first actual round trip, at the end of which the dirigible returned to its point of departure, was accomplished by Charles Renard and Arthur Krebs aboard *La France*, and this also took place in the vicinity of Paris. Between these two dates innumerable attempts, which included many setbacks but also some partial successes, were milestones along the road to final triumph in more than one country.

Terminology suited to the new aeronautics was borrowed from existing technologies and many of the words from the jargon of seafarers. Colonel Paul Renard, who worked closely with his brother Charles, clearly summarized the technical characteristics of an airship. He wrote: 'In order to exert full control over the direction of a dirigible, it must be given a net speed in relation to the ambient air and greater than that of the wind. To achieve this, the driving force must be as powerful as possible but with as little weight as possible. The balloon should have an elongated shape to minimize air resistance during forward movement and it should be constructed in such a way as to maintain that form. While the airship must be stable in the vertical and horizontal planes as well as at any given altitude, a rudder or some form of guidance system should be provided. The nacelle should be attached to the balloon by a permanent fastening.'

Speed, considered as a parameter, is conditioned by the power/weight ratio, given that the engine's effective power is in proportion to the cube of net speed. Accordingly, in order to double the speed, the power must be increased eightfold. However, no positive solution to this equation was forthcoming until the advent of the internal combustion engine working on 'petroleum spirit' as it was called at the beginning of this century.

It was much easier to determine the best shape for the hull: a fish, also entirely submerged in the fluid in which it freely moves, came naturally to mind. As far back as the beginning of the nineteenth century, a scientist, Marey-Nonge, stated that these machines could only be propelled through the air if they were given 'the cod's head and mackerel tail' form. So originated the fish-shaped, or pisciform dirigible, its largest circumference established a quarter of the length of the hull from the nose. Nevertheless, many dirigibles, including the first Zeppelins, had strictly cylindrical hulls and these proved eminently successful. All this brought a new factor into consideration: how to maintain the envelope's shape. This was achieved by means of several different systems which led to airships being classified as non-rigid, semi-rigid and rigid.

In order to produce a non-rigid dirigible, an envelope is constructed from supple material, gas-proofed against the lifting medium, which could be coal-gas, hydrogen or, as used today, helium. The envelope should be shaped in such a way that, once inflated with the gas inside at a slightly higher pressure than the outside air, it assumes the desired form. In order to compensate for gas venting which would otherwise be lost into the air, the envelope should be fitted with ballonets — which could be regarded as reservoirs in this instance —into which the surplus gas could be pumped by a mechanical device, thereby maintaining the envelope at its full capacity and at its original slightly higher pressure than the air.

A rigid airship is based on a skeleton built of light alloy, and occasionally of wood. This framework is made up from one-piece longitudinal formers called longerons, interconnected by transversal polygonal rings of the same material. Crosspieces and stretchers of 'piano wire' strengthen the entire framework. Inside the rigid structure there is a series of individual gas bags which are not under pressure. A tough woven material stiffened by diagonal slats and laced to the skeleton covers the whole framework, forming the envelope which was subjected only to external air pressure. Underneath these rigid airships a kind of 'keel', usually triangular in section, is also fitted. This keel was used as a catwalk between engine nacelles during flight or to enable the inspection of gas bags to be carried out. On some of the large commercial airships this keel has been adapted for passenger accommodation or for the crew's use between watches. It can also serve as a means to distribute the load, particularly of the engine nacelles built each side.

The semi-rigid dirigible is by way of being a compromise. Underneath a flexible envelope, the power unit is provided with a rigid keel which reinforces the envelope thus enabling the inside gas pressure to be reduced and the use of thinner and, consequently, lighter covering materials. This technique was successfully adopted in France, Germany and Italy.

In the first few decades of this century, envelopes for airships were, generally, of rubberized cotton. Today, they are made from synthetic materials proofed by various processes using a variety of plastics which also provide an effective heat barrier against the sun's rays.

Non-rigid airships were usually provided with an oblong motor nacelle of good aerodynamic form, placed as near as possible to the envelope as was compatible with safety when hydrogen gas was used. As well as reducing the passive resistance which was greater when the nacelle was suspended some distance below the envelope, this design feature also prevented 'tilting' or 'pitching' due to the motive power in the nacelle tending to drive it forward faster than the envelope and thereby altering the airship's trim. When the non-inflammable helium became available, the nacelle could be attached directly to the underside of the envelope as can be seen in small non-rigid airships of the kind used for publicity purposes today. Before the use of helium, nacelles were slung under the belly of the airship on fine steel cables called car supports which formed a rigid triangular suspension, the upper ends of the cables being attached by hemp 'goose feet' fastened to boxwood batons embedded in a bolt rope, making a kind of thick strengthened hem sewn into the material which formed the envelope. These goose feet are known to old mariners, being triangular pieces of canvas, the base sewn to the sail or awning and the apex provided with an edged hole to take a sheet or rope.

Engine power was distributed over several nacelles on rigid airships and, on the latest Zeppelins, there were four or five. These were in line or horizontally opposed in pairs and connected to the sides of the hull by struts. The command nacelle, with the captain, pilot and navigator was situated below the nose.

Directional stability was maintained by a tail unit, consisting of fixed fins, normally in the form of a cross, or arranged like the flights of arrows. These surfaces enabled the airship to hold a steady course even if the critical speed was exceeded. If such stabilizing fins were not fitted, the airship could not maintain horizontal flight as there would have been a tendency for the nose to pitch up then, subsequently, dive as forward speed was lost, just as a ship's bow pitches up when it meets a wave then goes down by the head.

In the horizontal plane, the airship was steered by a classic system of rudders moving on a vertical shaft. By turning the single or multiple rudder system to the left or right, the airstream acting on the surface will swing the nose in the same direction. To make slight changes of altitude or to provoke a change of attitude in the horizontal plane, single or multiple elevators in the tail unit made use of the same airstream. When the trailing edge of the elevators are inclined upwards from the horizontal, the effect of the airstream on these surfaces makes the nose rise so the aircraft climbs and by depressing the trailing edge of these surfaces the nose drops and the aircraft dives. These control surfaces acted in exactly the same way as on modern conventional heavier-than-air craft. Without this aerodynamic assistance, rising air currents and other meteorological phenomena made it practically impossible for a lighter-than-air craft to maintain a steady flight path at any altitude within their operational height limits.

**German wood engraving of 1489**
Apart from the lack of some form of lifting sphere, then unthought-of, this is a curious preview of the sail balloons which were to appear in designs of lesser or greater merit proposed three centuries later.

# VISIONARIES
# AND PIONEERS

## 1780-1850

The *montgolfière* was one of the earliest names given to the first 'ships of the air' in honour of the Montgolfier brothers. They were also called *charlière* or *robertine* after two engineers, Charles and Robert, the first crew of a 'flying globe' filled with hydrogen. From the time of these first flights, many inventive minds began to consider seriously the possibility of producing a lighter-than-air craft whose course could be guided by the will of man rather than at the will of the winds.

Hardly one month after the first recorded air voyage in a *montgolfière* by Pilatre de Rozier and the Marquis d'Arlandes, the savant Lavoisier addressed a meeting of the Académie royale des Sciences in Paris on 27 December 1783, outlining to his colleagues the necessary conditions to steer a dirigible. Shortly afterwards, innumerable ideas began to appear on paper, either as a result of scientific deliberation or merely vivid imagination. The diagrams and sketches with which each of these inventors sought to convey their ideas have endowed posterity and the modern-day collector with a series of well-documented plates, many of which are included in this book. There were balloons with sails, balloons with oars, fish balloons, powder balloons, rocket balloons, whirling balloons, balloons with pedals, balloons powered by a horse, or even harnessed to eagles. There were American steam-powered balloons, topped with a funnel, suggested in all good faith to gullible promoters. Within this vortex of sometimes absurd ideas there were, nevertheless, others evincing rational foresight, some even leading to concrete results which, incomplete as they were, merit recognition today. The whirling balloon, incidentally, was designed with a 'thread' round the cylindrical envelope so that, by its revolutions on a fixed axis, it had the effect of screwing its way through the air.

Since a ship moves over the sea by means of its sails, a galley by means of its oars, it was only logical for some of the early pioneers to imagine that the answer to their problem was merely to equip a flying machine with similar means of propulsion. Obviously, this reasoning was over-simplified, at least as far as the use of sails was concerned. As Comte de Milley wrote in his thesis presented to the Académie royale des Sciences on 21 January 1784 in Paris: 'Aerial and marine navigation differ in one essential respect: sea vessels move in one fluid which supports them and project upwards into another which is more than eight hundred times less dense. This enables them to use sails which increase the surfaces so that they receive a greater force from the propelling fluid to overcome the resistance of the supporting fluid. However, these means cannot be employed in aerial navigation because the body carried does not float on the fluid but remains immersed in the same way as a sunken vessel might float neither on the surface nor on the bottom and be carried along by a current. Here, sails would not only be useless but actually detrimental in that, giving a greater hold to the force of the current and being raised above the centre of gravity, they would capsize and carry the vessel down... An aerial balloon is the body simultaneously floating yet submerged in a fluid: sails would only be a hindrance, as any marine officer would confirm.' Indeed, any passenger during his first flight in a free balloon is always struck by the total absence of a relative wind while ascending. The text of Comte de Milley's thesis appears in the second volume of the well-known work by Faujas de Saint-Fond published in Paris, 1784, entitled 'The first sequel to the description of the balloon experiments of Messrs. Montgolfier'.

As a matter of fact, it was recognized fairly quickly that rigging an airship with sails was useless. So, although several ideas originally combined sails with light oars to be rowed by the aeronaut, attention was soon concentrated on oars alone. These were used as the prime unit of propulsion and a rudder mounted on the nacelle or the envelope completed the system.

Jean-Pierre Blanchard, the first aeronaut to cross the Straits of Dover in a balloon filled with hydrogen on the 27 January 1785, had already equipped his nacelle with a small rudder and two pairs of jointed wings worked alternately. In Britain, during 1784, his dirigible was fitted with a type of rotating fan, actually a rudimentary propeller with several blades. Although the results of his experiments were inconclusive, the balloon owned by the Académie de Dijon and crewed by Guyton de Morveau and M. de Virey did manage to make several changes of course and some turns in the eye of a fairly light wind during a flight on 12 June 1784. This spherical flying machine had a boat-shaped frame round the largest circumference, a 'prow' and a 'stern' to which was fitted a rudder and, towards the middle, a pair of long jointed oars worked from the nacelle, to which were attached two other oars having fairly small oval blades.

Between 1785 and 1787, a series of flights were made by two directors of a hydrogen plant at Javel, on the outskirts of Paris. The two men who manufactured this gas, then known as 'inflammable air' were Alban and Vallet. Their flying machine, also spherical, was built under the patronage of the Comte d'Artois, the future King Charles X, and whose name it carried. Their nacelle was provided with a pair of oars having blades similar to the sails of a windmill and which were moved horizontally. They could be changed to zero pitch when the airship was ascending or descending, not unlike the variable pitch airscrew. One of the first major and important advances in the design of the airscrew was a system that could change the 'pitch' or the angle at which the leading edge of the airscrew cut into the air.

**1783: Blanchard's flying ship**
Jean-Pierre Blanchard's varnished silk balloon had a nacelle incorporating parts of a previous prototype for a heavier-than-air flying machine, consisting of a small rudder and two pairs of wings which moved alternately. These were designed to control direction. For safety's sake, an open umbrella device under the envelope served as a parachute.
This engraving commemorates the attempted take-off, 2 March 1784, from the Champ de Mars in Paris and shows the frontage of the *Ecole militaire* unchanged to this day. *Sic itur ad astra* or 'Thus we climb to the stars' was Blanchard's favourite motto.

**1784: Guyton de Morveau and his balloon**
During a flight on 25 April 1784 at Dijon, Guyton de Morveau and the Abbé Bertrand attempted to steer their balloon by means of rudders round the holding net, and by manipulating two paddles.

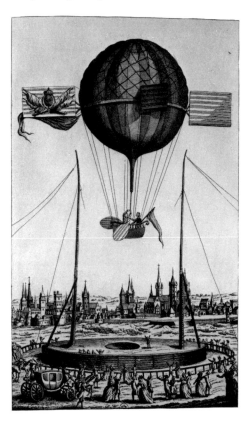

In fine pitch, the airscrew had less resistance to the air and, conversely, greater resistance in coarse pitch. Hence this arrangement for these oars. A third similar oar moving on a horizontal pivot was intended to propel the airship forward. This type of propulsion was common to small boats on the Seine at that time. According to accounts in the *Journal de Paris*, which may well have been coloured with journalistic enthusiasm, the results achieved by these paddles were most encouraging, as witnessed by the Royal family one day from the courtyard of the Château de Versailles.

Another design for a truly pilotable balloon well in advance of its time was produced in 1785 by a former colleague of Lavoisier, Lieutenant Meusnier of the Corps of Engineers. This elongated form given to the hull had already attracted attention in 1784, as seen in Bredin's design as well as the first envelope constructed in this shape by the Robert brothers which made two ascensions but without significant range. Meusnier, in his scientifically studied design, applied all the laws of airship stability after having proved the technical necessity for its elongation. Several features were so advanced that they were still incorporated in airship design a century later. An envelope provided with a gas-bag, in this instance supplied by two pumps operated manually, ensured that the external form was maintained and were also used to compensate for changes in altitude. The nacelle was suspended by a rigid triangulated system of bolt ropes sewn to the envelope while a set of three 'rotating' paddles were judiciously placed near the centre of resistance between nacelle and envelope. Their path described a spiral as they moved through the air like the modern airscrew. As a matter of fact, the airscrew or the screw which drives a boat can be described as the slice of a spiral or the thread as seen on a bolt or wood screw. These double-bladed propellers were to be operated by manual labour, the only source of energy so far available to power this dirigible which had a calculated volume of some 2,120,900 cubic feet, a length of 260 feet and a diameter of 135 feet at the beam. Meusnier's study even extended to certain devices for ground handling and mooring in the open or in a hangar. The excellent technical drawings and calculations, carefully preserved in the form of plates and tables, bear witness to the wide scope of this design which, for financial reasons, was never pursued. Having been promoted to the rank of general, this true instigator of the airborne operational base capable of being guided at will, died in battle at Mainz on 17 June 1793.

Before the political upheavals of the French Revolution swept all thoughts of aerial navigation into the background, an officer of the Dragoons, Baron Scott, conceived an ingenious design consisting of a large, oblong balloon having three gas bags inside a double envelope. One was placed in the nose and two in the tail so as to enable the longitudinal stability to be changed by an inclination towards the nose or rear end, as well as to control ascent or descent, with the result that the airship's flight followed an undulating path. His dirigible was fitted with a rudder and was to be propelled with oars. Entitled 'A Freely Guided Airship', Baron Scott's design was published in the form of an illustrated thesis in 1789 in Paris. It is interesting to see that, 120 years later, a German constructor, August von Parseval, also employed a double gas-bag with a controllable device for transferring the contents of one to another, to govern the vertical movement of the airship.

After the turn of the nineteenth century, the experiments in aviation by Jean-Pierre Blanchard and Vincent Lunardi, an attaché at the Neapolitan Embassy in London, were followed with interest in England. Here, Sir George Cayley, one of the greatest aeronautical geniuses of all time who, in 1809, had invented an aeroplane incorporating many of the aerodynamic characteristics still seen today, now believed that aerial navigation could best be achieved with an elongated dirigible. In 1816 Cayley designed an egg-shaped balloon to be powered by steam, developed soon after, and driven by twin five-bladed propellers placed transversally above a closed nacelle secured by triangulated rigging. As an alternative, he devised a system of superimposed wings, the forerunner of the biplane, in order to produce a guided glider. While studying the concept of a rigid dirigible, George Cayley was the first to see the need for separate gas-bags subdividing the inside of the skeleton whether it be in metal or, like the Schütte-Lanz from 1912 onwards, in wood. He specified that the frame-

### 1784: The Robert brothers' elongated balloon

The nacelle of this balloon was fitted with paddles in the form of two parasols. The Robert brothers rose up from the Tuileries on 19 September 1784 taking their brother-in-law, Collin-Hulin on a flight of 6 hours 40 minutes which ended at Beuvry near Arras, landing in front of a castle owned by the Prince de Ghistelles, another flying enthusiast who had recently piloted a montgolfière. Paddles were used in conjunction with the wind to steer their balloon and this proved effective, even to the point of making the aircraft describe an elipse.

### 1812: Jacob Degen's misfortunes

Jacob Degen was a Swiss clockmaker. Since 1806 he had made prolonged trials in Vienna of a flying machine with flapping wings. Equipping his invention with a small balloon, he took off but lacked directional control. This satirical illustration shows his unsuccessful public demonstration on the Champ de Mars, Paris, in 1812 when an angry crowd put an end to his futile attempts by wrecking his machine.

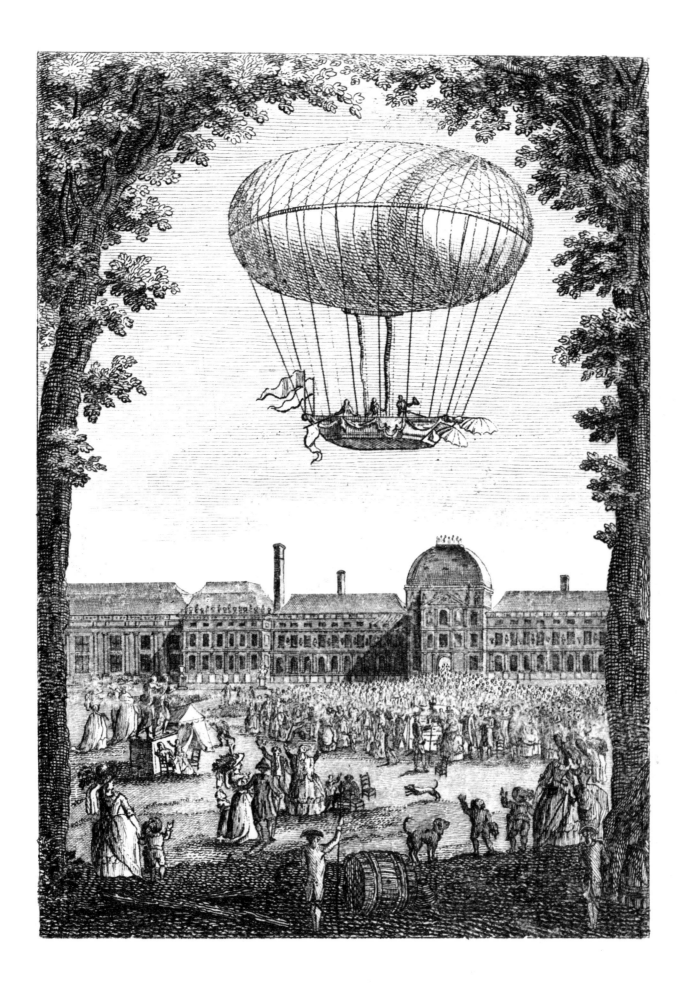

work should be constructed 'of small struts rigged and stayed inside with cross bracing made from cables or rope' so as to maintain the shape of the dirigible. These design features displayed an uncanny foresight on his part of the interior rigging of the German airships so many years later.

In 1832, when political peace had returned to France, Count Lennox, a former major with a considerable personal fortune, joined forces with Dr Le Berrier from Le Havre. Together they secretly built an elongated balloon in the quarries of Montmartre. Their ship was equipped with big paddles powered by sheer brute force. During the night of 24 August 1832, their airship flew over Paris and was able to change direction sufficiently for the Count, a fervent Bonapartist, to drop a wreath of everlasting flowers on Napoleon's column in the Place Vendôme. Few if any persons witnessed this gesture or flight in the dark skies.

Be that as it may, a new balloon ship, *L'Aigle*, was put into production, backed up by considerable publicity. The volume of its envelope was 70,000 cubic feet, containing a gas-bag of 7,000 cubic feet. Suspended by means of straps fixed to the holding net, the thirty foot nacelle was equipped with twenty oars each having a blade of about ten square feet in area with movable paddles to be rowed by seventeen able-bodied crew. At least, this was the idea on paper although, in practice, the lift from such a small volume would certainly have proved inadequate. However, there is some truth in the fact that Count Lennox had in mind another source of power he wished to keep secret. Provisions were also made for a small two-seater nacelle to be lowered by a winch below the airship. These seats were, no doubt, reserved for privileged enthusiasts with a somewhat different purpose in mind to the similar idea revived much later by some Zeppelins during wartime operations.

Count Lennox' balloon ship was inflated in a hangar built in the Cours-La-Reine. On 17 August 1834, *L'Aigle* was transported to the Champ-de-Mars for its first air tests but, on the way there, a considerable amount of gas leaked out, the envelope folded up and suddenly slipped out of the net to fall to the ground some distance off.

Pierre Jullien, a modest French watchmaker, succeeded in producing a small, very elongated pisciform balloon, about twenty-three feet in length, which he exhibited in Paris in November 1850. Driven by two propellers powered by clockwork, a mechanism with which he was well acquainted, his miniature airship was successfully flown and steered even against the prevailing wind. The following year, Pierre Jullien achieved similar successful flights with a larger model, forty feet long. Encouraged by these small scale triumphs, this airminded watchmaker began construction of a full size airship, *Précurseur*, in 1852. This dirigible, highly advanced in its aerodynamic conception, was fitted with a tail unit having movable surfaces which were to become the standard system adopted in the next century. Unfortunately, *Précurseur* was never air tested, possibly because an adequate power unit was not yet available.

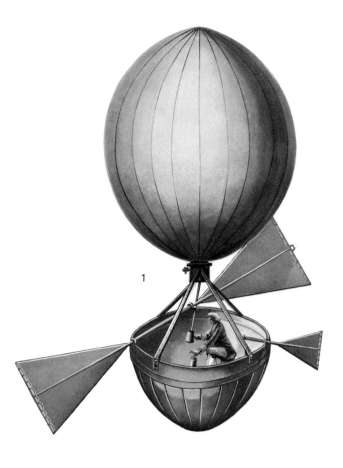

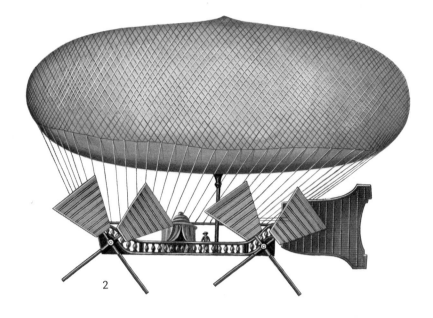

## 1 1783: Design for a flying sphere signed 'M. D.'

This hot air balloon was powered by the resultant gas from gunpowder exploded inside a barrel and then compressed in the lower hemispherical tank. It was steered by two inclinable oars and a rudder.

## 2 1784: Bredin's design

This elongated balloon was to be driven by two symmetrical pairs of paddle-wheels, operated by the physical force of the crew members, and guided with a large-surfaced rudder.

## 3 1783: An English flying machine from Martyn

Here is the first example of Man's dream to equip balloons with sails, and the nacelle carries a mainsail, jib and a rudder. Martyn's design also includes a parachute.

## 4 1784: A balloon by Jean-Louis Carra

A French physicist, Carra, submitted this design to the *Académie des Sciences*. Over a large, egg-shaped balloon towered a gas-bag bristling with metal spikes. A brass cable conducted the electricity captured by these spikes towards the nose of the nacelle which was fitted with two kinds of paddle-wheels, themselves operated manually. This design seems to have been an exercise in using the ambient electricity as power although the means of harnessing this power was not specified.

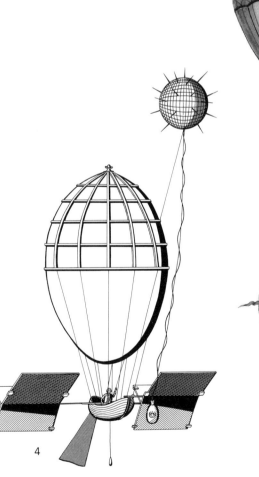

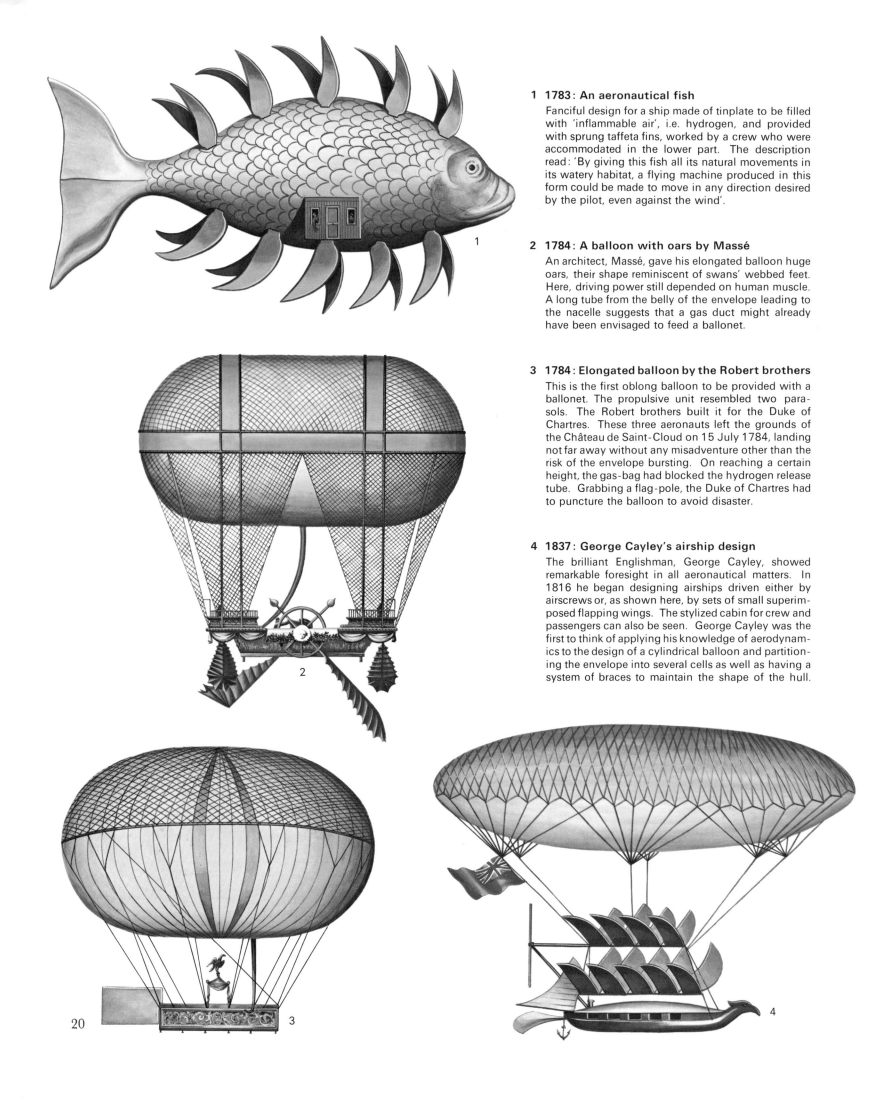

**1   1783: An aeronautical fish**

Fanciful design for a ship made of tinplate to be filled with 'inflammable air', i.e. hydrogen, and provided with sprung taffeta fins, worked by a crew who were accommodated in the lower part. The description read: 'By giving this fish all its natural movements in its watery habitat, a flying machine produced in this form could be made to move in any direction desired by the pilot, even against the wind'.

**2   1784: A balloon with oars by Massé**

An architect, Massé, gave his elongated balloon huge oars, their shape reminiscent of swans' webbed feet. Here, driving power still depended on human muscle. A long tube from the belly of the envelope leading to the nacelle suggests that a gas duct might already have been envisaged to feed a ballonet.

**3   1784: Elongated balloon by the Robert brothers**

This is the first oblong balloon to be provided with a ballonet. The propulsive unit resembled two parasols. The Robert brothers built it for the Duke of Chartres. These three aeronauts left the grounds of the Château de Saint-Cloud on 15 July 1784, landing not far away without any misadventure other than the risk of the envelope bursting. On reaching a certain height, the gas-bag had blocked the hydrogen release tube. Grabbing a flag-pole, the Duke of Chartres had to puncture the balloon to avoid disaster.

**4   1837: George Cayley's airship design**

The brilliant Englishman, George Cayley, showed remarkable foresight in all aeronautical matters. In 1816 he began designing airships driven either by airscrews or, as shown here, by sets of small superimposed flapping wings. The stylized cabin for crew and passengers can also be seen. George Cayley was the first to think of applying his knowledge of aerodynamics to the design of a cylindrical balloon and partitioning the envelope into several cells as well as having a system of braces to maintain the shape of the hull.

20

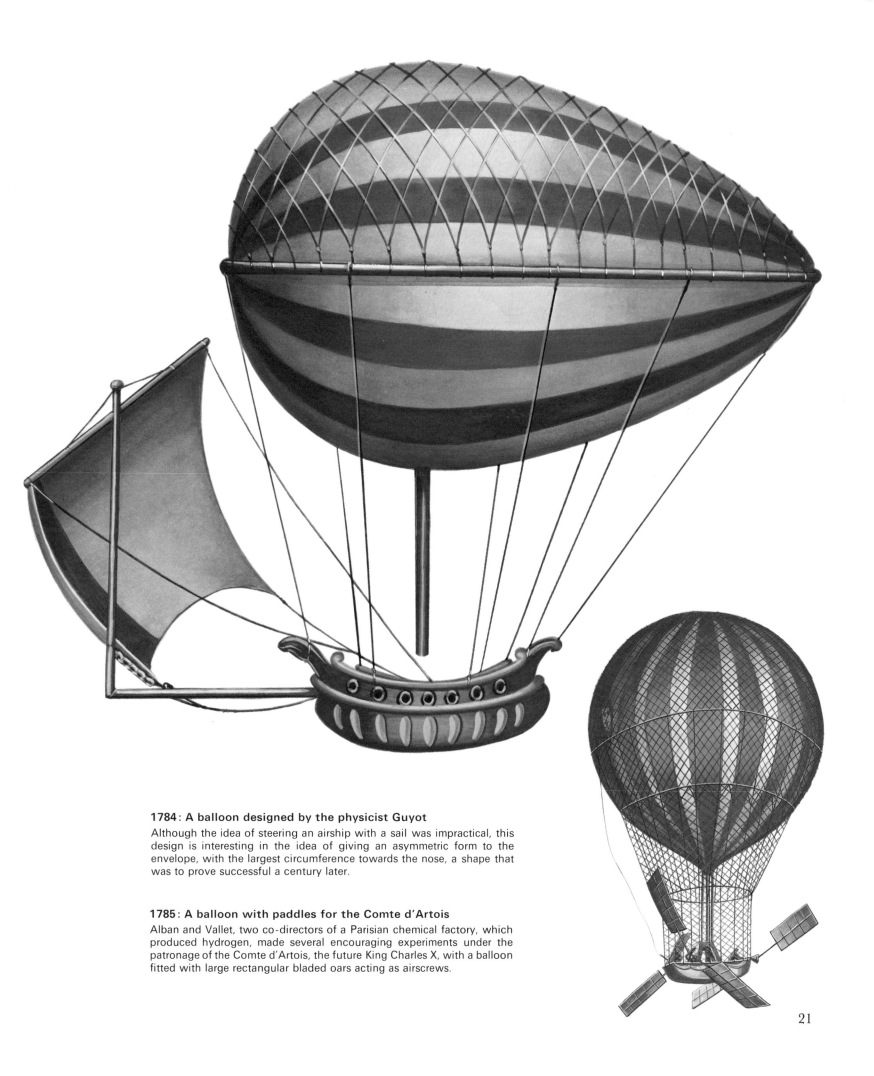

**1784: A balloon designed by the physicist Guyot**

Although the idea of steering an airship with a sail was impractical, this design is interesting in the idea of giving an asymmetric form to the envelope, with the largest circumference towards the nose, a shape that was to prove successful a century later.

**1785: A balloon with paddles for the Comte d'Artois**

Alban and Vallet, two co-directors of a Parisian chemical factory, which produced hydrogen, made several encouraging experiments under the patronage of the Comte d'Artois, the future King Charles X, with a balloon fitted with large rectangular bladed oars acting as airscrews.

21

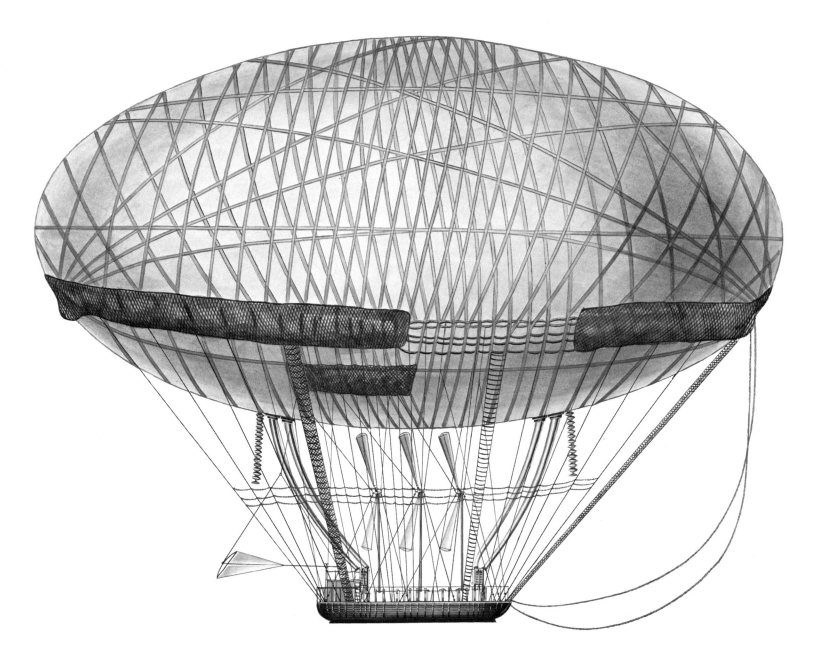

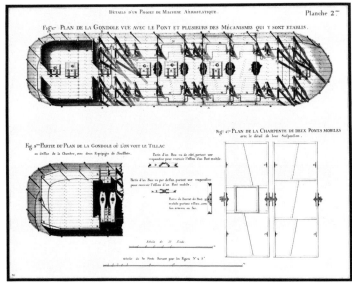

### 1785: A dirigible balloon design by General Meusnier

At that time a lieutenant in the Engineer Corps, Meusnier produced this rational design for a dirigible whose basic features remain valid to this day. The oblong envelope had an internal gas-bag to maintain its form and to control its vertical movement, propellers powered by hand-operated cranks, and a well-studied suspension system for the nacelle. His airship was to have a length of 277 feet, a diameter of 139 feet and a volume of 279,000 cubic feet.

A plan view of the nacelle for Meusnier's dirigible, showing the deck, the crank handles and other equipment carried aboard.

22

**1785: General Meusnier's controllable balloon**

This design depicts a long cable used as an anchoring device and a sort of tent or marquee on the upper part of the envelope. This could be spread out over the whole airship as a portable hangar guyed to the ground supported by slanting cables attached to a central pole.

Longitudinal view of the nacelle and the lower section of the envelope showing an arrangement of three 'rotating paddles' making up the steering gear, as well as the four tubes to feed gas into the internal gas-bag.

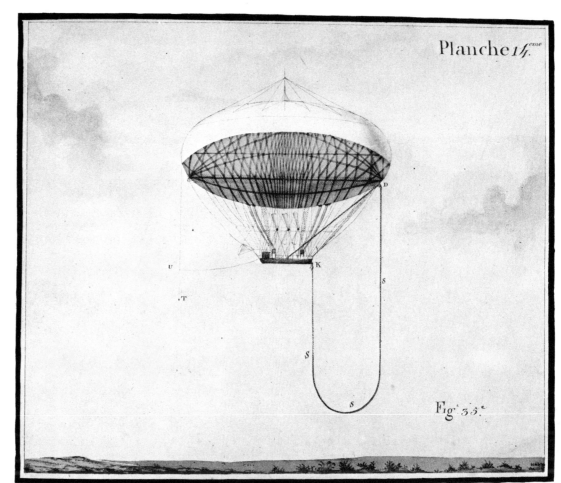

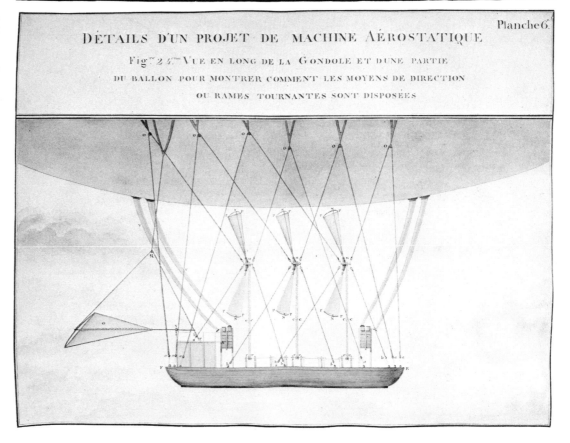

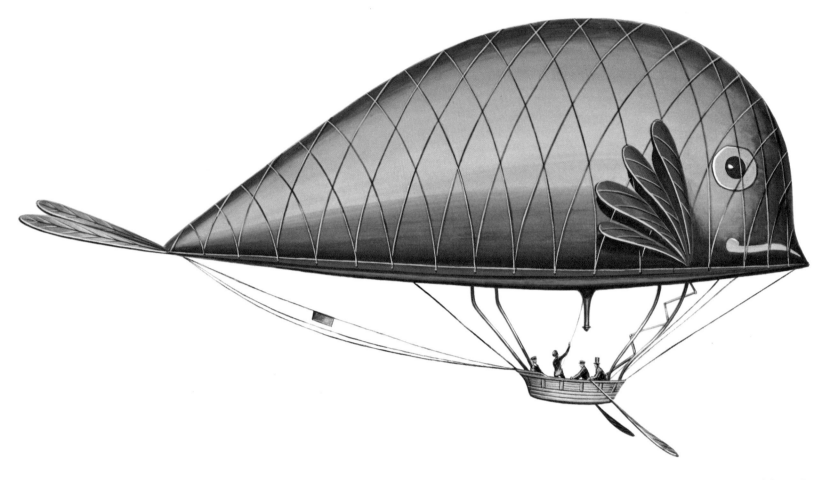

**1818: An airship by Pauley and Durs Egg**

Following on successful trials in 1804 and 1805 when they actually succeeded in changing course, S. J. Pauley and his colleague Durs Egg exhibited their dolphin-shaped airship in London. It was equipped with a pair of oars and had a sand-box sliding on a cable to keep the airship level fore and aft. A similar idea was actually used on the first Zeppelin built in 1900. These two Swiss gunsmiths were the first to produce an airship in Britain but, after watching its unspectacular performance, the Cockneys uncharitably dubbed it 'Egg's Folly'.

**1843: Airship scale model by Monck-Masson**

This working scale model of an elongated balloon with a well-proportioned steering gear was exhibited in London. Propelled by an airscrew driven by a clockwork motor, the model attained a speed of 5 m.p.h. during trials.

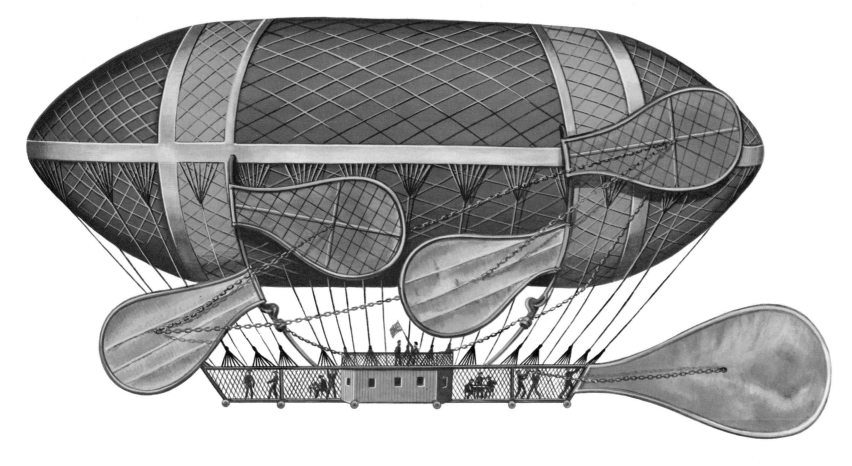

### 1834 : Count Lennox's 'Eagle'

This plate shows a guided balloon belonging to Count Lennox. It was 137 feet long, 39 feet in diameter, with a volume of 99,000 cubic feet, containing a gasbag of 7,070 cubic feet. *Eagle* was to be driven by a set of oars with movable paddles worked by a crew housed in a compartment of the nacelle theoretically designed to accommodate seventeen passengers. On the way to the Champ de Mars in Paris, where it was to have been flown on 17 August 1834, the envelope slipped out of its holding net and the flight never took place.

### 1835 : The Mackintosh design for a flying ship

Thomas Simmons Mackintosh had an extremely novel idea for his British airship. The steering mechanism was shaped like a fan: a team of eagles harnessed to each side of the envelope towards the nose was the source of power. The inventor quite seriously suggested that if eagles were unavailable, 'Stalwart pigeons might also do very well'.

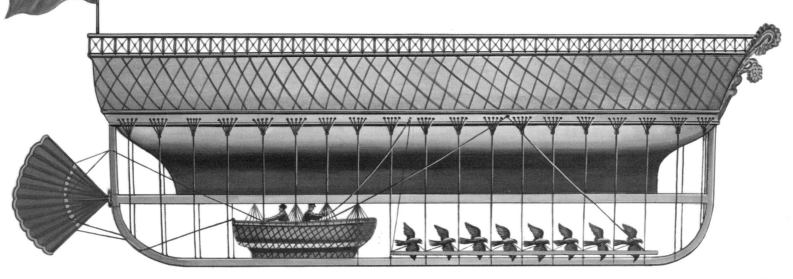

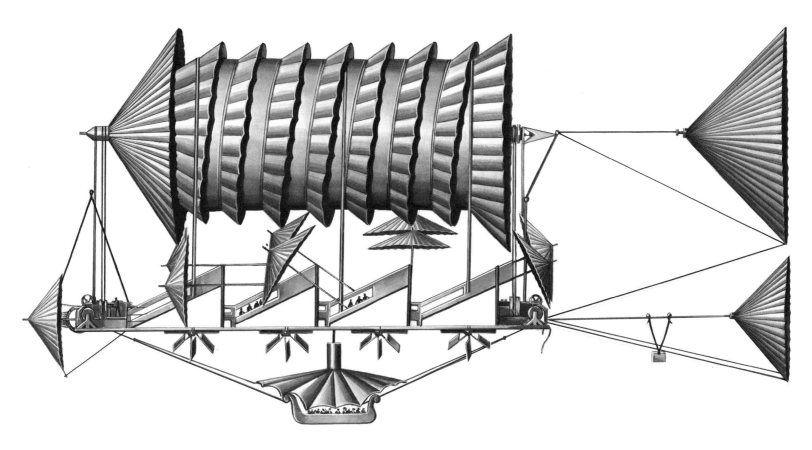

### 1835 : Design for a helicoidal dirigible by Pierre Ferrand

The rigid envelope of this balloon was supposed to serve as the propelling system, turning like a giant screw about an axis. An extraordinary system of rudders and other devices for steering can also be seen in this highly impractical design, the product of a feverish imagination.

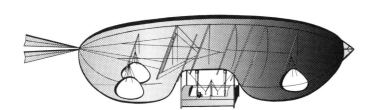

### 1789 : Fish balloon designed by Baron Scott

Baron Scott, an officer of the Dragoons, published his ideas in a paper entitled 'An airship to be steered at will'. Of elongated shape, his *aerambule* was equipped with a rudder and oars for propulsion and included fore and aft gas-bags like air sacs in fish. By compressing the gas, he hoped to 'tack' as a ship but in vertical movements according to the airship's ascending or descending position.

### 1850 : Pétin's flying ship

The news of this flying ship immediately captured the imagination of the Parisians. It was designed by a highly inventive hosier by the name of Ernest Pétin but although construction was completed it was never flown. This complicated machine had four enormous balloons with a total of 565,000 cubic feet and a huge timberwork frame with inclined planes attached to each side as climbing and diving vanes. The airscrews were to be driven by machinery . . . or by hand.

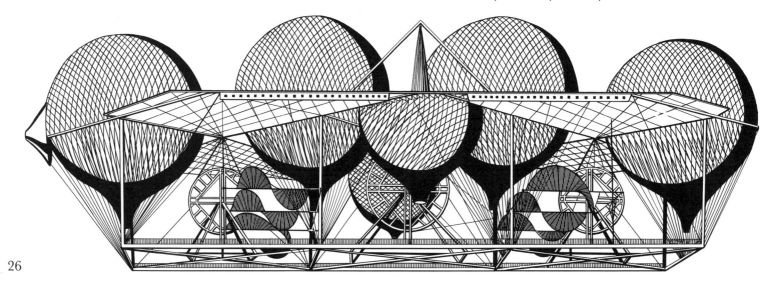

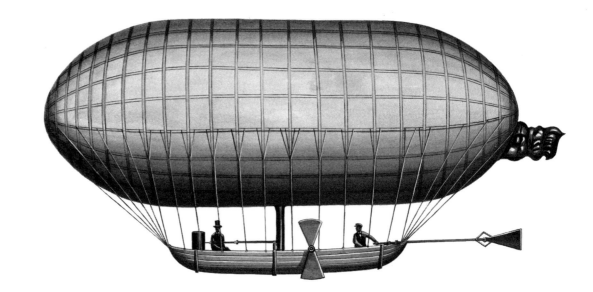

### 1850: Hugh Bell's dirigible

With a volume of about 17,700 cubic feet and 55 feet long, this elongated airship had a gasbag inside and was the first of this shape ever flown in Britain. A small rudder was carried on the nacelle, also fitted with two airscrews with shafts at right angles. Bell's airship made two flights at Vauxhall in London but its motive power, human muscle, proved inadequate.

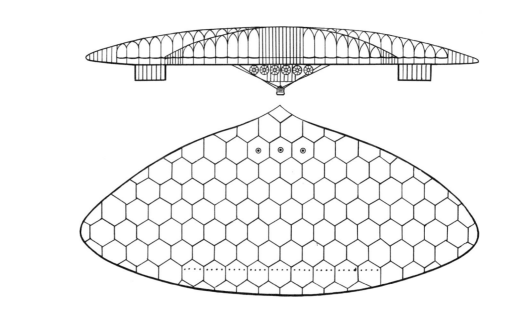

### 1855: Pline's design for a gliding airship

For the first time in history the name *aeroplane* was used to describe this flying machine which had a type of short wing and was to be driven by six propellers grouped together. The envelope was of a honeycomb structure for the gas.

### 1850: Jullien's mini-airship

A small clockmaker, Pierre Jullien, had some success at the Hippodrome in Paris with his scale model of a pencil-shaped dirigible. It measured 23 feet long, 43 cubic feet in volume and weighed only two and a half pounds. Well-designed, the model was fitted with elevators and rudders and the two airscrews were driven by clockwork. On 6 November 1850, it actually flew against the wind.

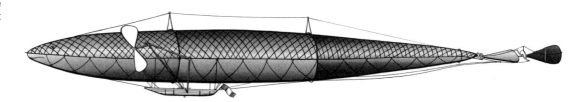

### 1852: 'Précurseur' by Jullien

Derived from the scale model built in 1850, Pierre Jullien's *Précurseur*, a full size airship with a length of 164 feet and a diameter of 26 feet, was aptly named. The small nacelle was suspended from a webbing net over the envelope while the tail unit with directional and pitch control vanes and the two airscrews, mounted near the centre of resistance, amply demonstrate Jullien's technical acumen. Unfortunately, *Précurseur* was never flown.

27

## 1904: Baldwin's 'California Arrow'

During the international exhibition in St. Louis, Missouri in 1904, an aviator called Roy Knabenshue successfully demonstrated a small airship for the first time in the United States. *California Arrow* was 50 feet long, powered by a 5 h.p. twin cylinder engine and had a varnished Japanese silk envelope.

# THE PIONEERS:
# SUCCESSES
# AND SETBACKS

## 1852-1913

In his quest for a suitable power unit, an eminent French engineer by the name of Henri Giffard turned his attention to the steam engine. Some less courageous individuals were aghast at the thought of placing a naked light beneath a swollen bagful of explosive gas. Undeterred, Giffard proceeded with this hazardous venture and succeeded, becoming the first aeronaut to pilot and control a flying machine driven by mechanical power. Giffard was also the first constructor to fit a keel between the envelope and the nacelle. This was a 60 ft. rod which helped to maintain the shape of the balloon and to which the rudder was fixed. On 24 September 1852, he rose up from the Hippodrome, near the Arc de Triomphe in Paris, and despite the strength of the prevailing wind succeeded in accomplishing 'various circular movements and lateral changes in course'. The actual speed of ten feet per second or 7 m.p.h., according to his calculations, excluded more ambitious manoeuvres. His next design, also rocket-shaped but even more tapered, had a volume of 109,550 cubic feet and was completed in 1865. Subjected to such violent jarring and yawing, due to the lack of a triangulated car suspension, it escaped from its holding net at take-off. In spite of this setback, Henri Giffard's experiments since 1852 had definitely proved the feasibility of using an engine as a source of power for flying machines.

More than twenty years were to pass before this power problem was tackled afresh. In the meantime, the Franco-Prussian war of 1870-1871 had broken out and free balloons had their hour of glory, providing a link between beleaguered Paris and the surrounding country; no fewer than sixty-six were launched from the French capital. As often happens in times of conflict, hostilities gave spur to various schemes, man's ingenuity being stretched to the limit, in this case to overcome his dependence on the winds. Of these many ideas, only one was developed and that only after hostilities were over. This flying machine was the brainchild of the renowned naval architect, Dupuy-de-Lôme, designer of early iron-clads. His efforts broke little new ground, as he had reverted to human muscle as the means to drive a huge propeller, eight men pulling hard, but ineffectually, on a winch. His first trials were carried out on 8 February 1872.

So far, there had been no great evidence of aeronautical activity in Germany but, towards the end of 1872, Paul Haenlein produced a pilotable balloon on the same lines as Giffard's airships. The age of muscle power as a driving force was over at last. Haenlein used a recent invention, an engine fuelled by coal gas. The actual gas from the envelope was used to supply an engine of four cylinders, horizontally opposed in pairs. Haenlein's dirigible, only tested while moored, did develop an appreciable pulling power. It was not flight-tested as it lacked sufficient lifting power, due perhaps to the engine's consumption of the lifting gas! Half a century later, the power unit for the *Graf Zeppelin*, LZ 127, was also fuelled with *Blau Gas* but this was no longer used as a means for producing lift.

Two Frenchmen, Albert and Gaston Tissandier, who were to achieve considerable fame, turned to electrical energy for their experiments. Although their motor only developed 1 h.p., they did manage to keep their airship head to wind and even gained ground while making two flights in 1883 and 1884.

The second and final flight made by the Tissandier brothers' dirigible on 26 September 1884 was preceded, six weeks earlier, by an event which marked an immense bound forward in the long quest for guided flight by lighter-than-air craft, powered by a mechanical unit. On 9 August 1884, *La France*, designed and built by Capitaine Charles Renard and Capitaine Arthur Krebs, made the first round flight ever accomplished in an airship. Taking off from the aeronautical establishment at Chalais-Meudon, it made a perfectly controlled flight round the site of the future aerodrome of Villacoublay, landed and finally reversed into its hangar under its own power. Instead of the needle-shaped envelope of the airships built by Giffard, Dupuy-de-Lôme and Tissandier, *La France* had an assymetric, fish-shaped outline. Scientifically designed, it was equipped with a compensating gas-bag, triangulated car suspension, rudders for steering and a stabilizing tail plane with elevators. *La France* was powered by an 8-horsepower electric motor, designed by Arthur Krebs and, in 1885, by a Gramme electric motor developing 9 h.p. The actual speed was twenty feet per second or approximately 14 m.p.h. Several round trips were flown with the same success, one actually passing over the south-west suburbs of Paris.

Meanwhile, research was progressing in Germany and, at the turn of the century, the first rigid dirigible designed by Count Ferdinand von Zeppelin was to give his country a flying start. In the year 1897, however, there were to be two unsuccessful and even tragic experiments. Dr Wölfert, a theologian, for many years fired with enthusiasm for airships, employing the capital from a company he had founded for this purpose, managed to produce a rocket-shaped dirigible with a bamboo nacelle precariously suspended under the belly of the envelope and equipped with a Daimler engine developing 8 h.p. This was the first time an engine fuelled by 'essence of petroleum' had been fitted to a flying machine and it drove an aluminium twin-bladed propeller. The airship was parked in a hangar which belonged to the Military Balloon Corps at Tempelhof which, today, is the busy civil airport for Berlin. On 14 June 1897, accompanied by his mechanic Robert

*Le dirigeable à vapeur de Giffard au-dessus du parc de Châlais-Meudon (1852)*

**1852: Giffard's steam airship**
In this skyscape by Marcel Jeanjean, the painter has imagined the steam-powered airship designed by Giffard flying over the balloon park at Chalais-Meudon. In actual fact, no flight was made by a dirigible from here until over thirty years later in 1884.

Knabe, the airship took off with Dr Wölfert at the controls. Very shortly afterwards there was an explosion, the airship caught fire and the two unfortunate occupants fell to their death.

A few years before, in 1893, an Austrian engineer, David Schwarz, had drawn up plans for a dirigible having a cylindrical envelope with a conical nose made from sheet aluminium. The nacelle was also made from sheet aluminium and was attached to the hull by latticed spars. The petrol engine was a 12-horsepower Daimler, driving three metal propellers. Before any trials could be carried out, Schwarz died but his widow managed to carry on his work. At Tempelhof on 3 November 1897, a young mechanic by the name of Jaegels Platz was entrusted with the first air test. After a brief piloted flight, the airship crashed but Platz escaped with his life.

The French were still making headway. In 1898, a man who was destined to make a great impact on aviation came on to the scene. He was of small stature but with that driving force which often produces a compensating dynamism in men of below-average height. His name was Alberto Santos-Dumont, son of a rich Brazilian planter of French extraction. After his first flying experience in *Brazil*, a small spherical balloon of about 4,000 cubic feet, in 1898 he began work on his own airship with the help of carefully selected technicians. Santos-Dumont was a born engineer. He was also a great sportsman, daring yet with a cool head and possessed of boundless energy and perseverance. As a result of his public-spirited efforts, he was soon to acquire an extraordinary popularity and contribute, perhaps more than anyone else, to fostering a national interest in all forms of aerial navigation. 'Santos', as he became known to all, was no technician himself and his inventions often paid little heed to the accepted scientific standards. Thus, although he was the first to introduce the 'bolt rope' suspension, even on his earliest prototypes, his almost invariably rocket-shaped airships failed through lack of longitudinal stability. Nevertheless, empirical though they may have been, his wealth of ideas were to make an outstanding contribution to aeronautical engineering which was still in its early stages. Although some of Santos' dirigibles were merely partial modifications of earlier types, he can be credited with the design of a dozen of these aircraft, produced successively from 1895 to 1907.

Of all Santos' efforts in aircraft construction, two of the most noteworthy were the sixth and the ninth. His first model, flight tested on 20 September 1898, folded itself neatly in half because of an inadequate supply to the gas-bag. The last, and eighteenth on the list, was a twin-engined airship intended to make the Paris-London air crossing but, apparently, was never once flown. On 6 September 1901, the sixth in the series was launched. On 19 October, this airship won the prize of 100,000 francs, about $77,300 at that time, offered by that generous patron of the 'new science', Henry Deutsch de la Meurthe, a rich and philanthropic industrialist who was a deeply-involved amateur of aviation. He had stipulated that the prize should be awarded to the first airship to take off from the grounds of the

Aéro-Club de France at Saint-Cloud, make a circuit of the Eiffel Tower and return to its point of departure on the outskirts of Paris in half an hour. In the ninth, a tiny craft nicknamed the 'Flying Barrow', Santos could take off at will and fly where he pleased within, of course, the limitations of the aircraft's range. This truly captured the imagination and the enthusiasm of the Parisians. As for the fourth in his series, produced in 1900, it had no nacelle but merely a pole attached beneath the envelope, fitted with a bicycle saddle and a pair of pedals to start the motor. This weird contrivance may have been gingerly tested while still moored but it could certainly never have been flown.

There is no space in these pages to elaborate on the contribution by Alberto Santos-Dumont to the progress of aviation but his work on aeroplanes should be briefly mentioned. His biplane 'Canard', number 14a in the series, logged a flight of approximately 250 yards on 12 November 1906 under official scrutiny. The fuselage of his 'Demoiselle', a frail little aircraft, originally consisted of a bamboo rod between nose and tail. Subsequently produced in quantity, this aeroplane had an excellent safety record.

*

* *

Just after the turn of this century, a long pencil shape with a metal skin smoothly glided out of its hangar floating on the unruffled surface of peaceful Lake Constance near Manzell. It was 2 July 1900. A man of somewhat advanced years was at the controls for the first flight test. Count Ferdinand von Zeppelin was living his dream come true. In 1874 he had boldly written a paper on the possibility of using an airship to carry passengers, mails and freight. A patent taken out in 1895 under his name specified the details of its construction. His airship was to have a rigid frame, to hold individual hydrogen gas-bags, and the aircraft was to be powered by several engines.

And so that extraordinary generation of rigid airships was born. Count von Zeppelin was an ex-cavalry officer with some technical knowledge acquired at the university of Tübingen. Despite the scepticism of certain experts in this new field, he undertook the supervision of the entire production from his own design, devoting himself to the task with an inflexible obstinacy and expending all his own resources as well as those of the 'Society for the Progress of Aerial Navigation by Airships' which he had founded. After the first encouraging results, however, he was to encounter severe setbacks with subsequent aircraft shortly afterwards. His LZ 4 was destroyed by fire on the ground in 1908 provoking an unexpectedly generous response from the German public who spontaneously started a fund that raised a veritable fortune of 6,200,000 German marks, which would amount to billions of dollars today. This was collected in only a few days, thus assuring the future success of the Zeppelin.

During the same period, while Santos-Dumont continued his astonishing experiments, two other designers were to appear in this new firmament.

**1897: Schwarz and his metal airship**

An Austrian engineer, David Schwarz, was the first man to produce a practical design for a dirigible with a metal envelope. His airship, sheathed in aluminium foil and shaped like a cannon shell, was 135 feet long, 46 feet in diameter and had a volume of 130,700 cubic feet. The nacelle was rigidly fixed to the envelope by aluminium struts and fitted with a 12-horsepower Daimler engine. Flight-tested only after the death of David Schwarz by his mechanic Jaegels Platz, the airship suddenly lost height and crashed although its occupant, fortunately, escaped with his life.

Although their achievements are associated with French aviation history, neither Augusto Severo nor Ottokar de Bradsky were actually French, and they were both doomed to become martyrs to the cause of aeronautical progress. Severo was a Member of the Brazilian Parliament and had a dirigible built to his own specifications by the balloon pilot and constructor, Lachambre. Christened with the noble name *Pax*, it had a very audacious arrangement of two propellers, one being placed at the forward point of the envelope's nose and one at the stern. This seemed quite a rational and technically sound idea on paper, even if a complicated structure and ingenious devices were necessary to put it into practice. A reinforced beam was tucked into the belly of the airship and ran under the length of the hull where the nacelle was placed. At each end, this beam turned up until level with the longitudinal axis of the balloon. Directional control and stability, fore and aft, were to have been achieved with a complicated system comprising five other propellers driven by two Buchet engines. On 12 May 1902, *Pax* rose up from its moorings on a field at Vaugirard on the outskirts of Paris, carrying Augusto Severo and his mechanic Sachet. Only a few minutes later the airship caught fire, exploded and crashed into an avenue in Paris, killing the two-member crew.

Five months later, another tragedy occurred. With the help of his friend and collaborator Morin, an engineer, Baron Ottokar de Bradsky developed an airship based on their own technical ideas. Most attempts to create a machine which could be flown and guided by its occupants were based on the idea of the balloon as the hull, the designers' attention being mainly concentrated on technical systems to attach nacelle and propulsion unit and on developing the most efficient possible propulsion unit. Bradsky and Morin, on the other hand, had designed a cylindrical balloon without a ballonet: car suspension by steel cables was not triangular. The nacelle carried an airscrew to provide forward speed and a second airscrew as a means of achieving vertical movement. Taking off from the same point as *Pax*, the Bradsky airship crossed Paris without any apparent manoeuvrability then, after a sudden lurching yaw, the nacelle broke away from its suspension and crashed to the ground not far from Le Bourget.

## 1908: The Lebaudy 'République'

It was on 24 June 1908 that this airship took to the air for the first time. On 25 September of the following year it crashed, as can be seen in the photograph above, right. The four members of the crew lost their lives. The photograph above, left, shows the nacelle, built from covered steel tubing with two metal airscrews fitted to each side.

## 1909: The Lebaudy 'Liberté'

Despite these two unsuccessful attempts which filled French aviation circles with gloom, the remarkable successes of Lebaudy's dirigible soon restored confidence. The flight of this airship was to herald a fertile period of intense activity and significant development of the guided aircraft in France as well as in the neighbouring countries of West Europe, which was sustained for a decade. A few years later, the nations at war derived most benefit. It was the dawn of an age when industrial production was beginning to develop, albeit in a small way, into what aircraft producers would speak of today as a production line. After the amateurish attempts by Alberto Santos-Dumont, Count von Zeppelin showed the initiative.

Oddly enough, this line production in France owed its origins to two rich industrialists who had nothing whatsoever to do with aviation. They were two brothers, Paul and Pierre Lebaudy, owners of large sugar refineries. Their first airship was named after them and the Parisians, having seen the aircraft on several flights, dubbed it *Le Jaune* or 'The Yellow Thing' because of the envelope's protective lead chromate covering. This dirigible was, to all intents and purposes, the prototype of the semi-rigid lighter-than-air flying machine. The envelope was attached to a long boat-shaped steel tubular structure from which the nacelle was slung by car supports. The nacelle was also built on to a tubular steel framework and was fitted out with a 40-horsepower Mercedes engine driving two metal airscrews at the sides. This airship, *Lebaudy*, was actually designed by Henri Julliot, employed by the industrialist brothers as an engineer, in collaboration with the self-taught but very efficient Don Simoni.

The aircraft rose into the air for the first time on 13 November 1902. Over the following three years, *Lebaudy* made a number of flights including one with a range of over sixty miles. After its civilian career, it was then offered to the Army which accepted it gratefully like a trained and tried remount. The Army was later to receive three more airships directly derived from this prototype. Several improvements had been incorporated, such as the addition of a cruciform tail unit to stabilize flight in both planes, a sophistication not included on the first model. Each of them had a characteristic elegance of line, the profile of the envelope slightly sway-backed because of the weight of the nacelle. They were named *Patrie*, *République* and *Liberté*. Unforeseen circumstances led to *Patrie* and *République* ending their careers in accidents, leaving *Liberté* to carry the Lebaudy flag.

Now recognized as a patron of aviation, Henry Deutsch de la Meurthe commissioned the construction of a non-rigid airship from the Surcouf workshops which had already built the *Lebaudy*. The new dirigible was called *Ville de Paris*. After conclusive flight tests in 1906 and 1907, it was also presented to the French army.

This was an age when amateurs from all walks of life produced designs for the new lighter-than-air flying machines which, notwithstanding their lack of feasibility, did attract considerable attention in France. For example, *Aviateur* (sic), built by an inventor called Monsieur Roze, was a rigid dirigible with twin envelopes which failed to take off when tested in 1901. On the other hand, a small hybrid airship, designed by Malécot, was successfully flown between 1907 and 1908. Slightly heavier than air, it was provided with supporting planes or wings projecting from the largest circumference of the body.

In the Anglo-Saxon countries, the first attempts to follow the course already charted in the skies over Continental Europe were being made. Formerly an experienced parachutist, Thomas Scott Baldwin produced a small dirigible in the United States. As pilot, he chose a certain Roy Knabenshue, some ninety pounds lighter than himself, to demonstrate his airship at an international exhibition held at St. Louis in the state of Missouri during 1904. Some twenty years later, this city's name was to become known the world over after Charles Lindbergh's transatlantic flight in his Ryan monoplane *The Spirit of St. Louis*. Baldwin's tiny flying 'skiff' was equipped with a small engine of 5 h.p. which had been built by one of the leading manufacturers of the time, whose name was to become a byword in aviation circles, Glenn H. Curtiss. This small airship had been first successfully flown at Oakland, on 3 August 1904. Four years later, with Curtiss aboard, Baldwin took delivery of a more sophisticated airship, built for the Signal Corps, which was paid for in cash after acceptance trials. It was to be the first American military dirigible.

Before taking off from the New World, one reckless adventure should not be overlooked. This was the first attempt to cross from one continent to the other in an airship, the idea of a somewhat eccentric, if far-sighted, rich journalist called Walter Wellman. With the help of Melvin Vaniman, an engineer, Wellman had a large airship built in France, having a volume of 353,200 cubic feet. Aboard *America*, as it was called, his initial intention was to cross the North Pole, after taking off from Spitzberg. Two attempts in 1907 and 1909 having failed, he transferred the whole ship and its overhauled equipment to Atlantic City on the American coast. Powered by two engines and an original system for maintaining trim, *America* and her crew took off on 15 October 1910. The ship remained airborne for only sixty-four hours before making a forced landing on the ice floes. This is the only reliable information on record concerning this unfortunate and somewhat foolhardy enterprise. Luckily, the crew had time to take to the lifeboat carried aboard and they were later picked up by a British steamer.

As a lighter tailpiece to this historical episode, there was a deep-sea captain among the crew, Murray Simon. With him he had brought his mascot, a cat christened 'Kiddo'. This was quite in the tradition of seafaring men as, apart from the superstitious attachment to a lucky mascot, a cat was a practical deterrent against mice and rats which made their floating homes in the holds of ships. When Kiddo's presence aboard *America* was discovered, Vaniman ordered the stowaway to be sent home immediately and actually tapped out a wireless message to Atlantic City requesting a launch to put out and take the cat off. Therefore, the first wireless message

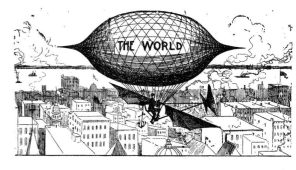

**1896: 'The World' of Carl Myers**
An American professor, Carl Myers, built a workshop to develop his flying machines at Frankfurt in New York State. Between 1896 and 1903 the professor experimented with small airships powered by pedals. Albeit aerodynamic in shape, the envelope bore an odd resemblance to a lemon. Underneath, a light metal chassis carried a saddle on which the professor energetically pedalled away to drive the airscrew. Equipped with mobile aerofoils to control direction and changes in height, these airships achieved surprisingly encouraging results. Another example is shown on the opposite page.

from the air to the ground over a distance of several miles concerned a cat. However, Kiddo was not separated from his master even during the forced landing and was rescued with the crew. This was the last seen of *America*; the wreckage was never recovered.

Across the Atlantic, Britain was to take the lead when, nine years later, the ocean was crossed in both directions by the rigid airship R34. By a curious coincidence, a stray cat was hidden in the bowels of the airship but, this time, all unknown to the crew.

It could be said that British constructors learned most about aviation during the war years. In the peaceful years leading up to the war, the United Kingdom had twice been obliged to call on the assistance and more advanced experience of the French in flying matters. The first British airship, commissioned for the Army, had an envelope made from goldbeater's skin. King Edward VII asked that it should be named *Nulli Secundus*, somewhat optimistically, even taking into account the tendency to exaggeration and dramatisation in bestowing names on all manner of things at that period. Unfortunately, trials undertaken in 1907 far from justified the name. Between 1909 and 1912, several air tests were successful with very small aircraft identified by the letters of the Greek alphabet, and so called *Beta*, also known as the 'Baby', *Gamma*, *Delta* and *Eta*. These also carried out manoeuvres with the Army.

At about this time, a young dentist of modest means but who was a fervent sportsman was about to make aeronautical history. In 1910, his second small dirigible, *City of Cardiff*, succeeded in flying from the Welsh town of Cardiff to Paris. As a result, Mr E.T. Willows and Mr Goodens, his mechanic, became the first flying crew to cross the Straits of Dover in an airship headed for the Continent.

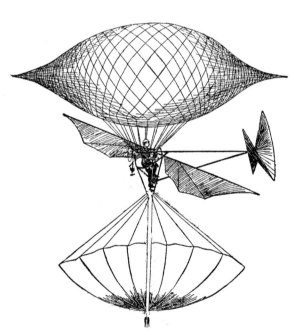

Germany and France, both well ahead of world competition, were spurred on by patriotic fervour and rivalry, which was often stimulated by campaigns in the press. Italy was to become the first nation to use an airship for military operations during the war against Turkey in Tripoli during 1911 and 1912. From 1905, the Italians had been quietly working on the design for a pilotable aircraft with an experimental machine produced by the Count Schio.

It was only in 1908 that the *Brigata Specialisti* of the Corps of Military Engineers, staffed by two extremely able officers, Captain Crocco and Captain Ricaldoni, designed and constructed the I, followed by the IA, a non-rigid airship with a curious form of transversal rigidity and an envelope divided into small compartments. Powered by an engine of 100 h.p., the yield in terms of forward speed was considerable for the period, being approximately 35 miles per hour. The following year, an engineer of high repute, Enrico Forlanini, had a big-bellied semi-rigid airship built and named *Leonardo da Vinci*. This type of cellular envelope and the semi-rigid bellied shape were to be the main features of such lighter-than-air craft constructed in Italy during the Great War and for some time afterwards.

In Germany, while a steady succession of Zeppelins issued from the workshops of Friedrichshafen, several other constructors were making themselves known. Major August von Parseval developed the non-rigid dirigible while Major von Gross, in association with an engineer, Nikolas Basenach, concentrated on building semi-rigid aircraft. Major von Parseval's first effort in 1906 could not truly be said to have any aesthetic form whatever but looked rather like the bent, black sausage the French call *boudin*. When moored, four limp flaps hung down from the nacelle. These were the blades of a 'soft' propeller not unlike those of a small, modern household electric fan. In fact, they were pieces of strong canvas attached to a light frame. When subjected to the centrifugal force under the power produced by the engines, they stretched out into four propeller blades with a certain rigidity. The decrease in weight was an advantage and the thrust from the blades was apparently not affected. Although an original solution, this device had naturally a short life and was replaced by semi-rigid blades braced with stiffeners so that their radial position was maintained and the best angle of attack was automatically assumed. The arrangement of two gas-bags, one in the nose and one near the tail, in order to keep the airship in good trim while making sideways movements, was continued for some time. These ballonets were joined by a forked tubular feed with a regulating system so that the contents of one gas-bag could be transferred to the other when necessary to balance the airship.

The first of the Gross-Basenach airships was built in 1908. Based on a design which had already proved its airworthiness, this type incorporated a longitudinal keel initially fitted close to the belly of the hull, as in the Lebaudy aircraft, but on subsequent models separated from the hull and made in three parts with a tail unit at one extremity. Production was limited to a mere half dozen, as compared with the twenty-seven airships produced by Parseval. Several Parseval dirigibles were sold overseas and one, produced in Great Britain, was still in service when the Armistice was signed in 1918.

These two new aircraft constructors constituted no great challenge to the output of the Friedrichshafen plant. On the other hand, in 1911, another company founded by a Dr Schütte and an engineer called Heinrich Lanz started producing rigid airships having a better aerodynamic form than the Zeppelins, and their example was only followed by the designers at Friedrichshafen in 1916. These new airships differed from the Zeppelins in that they featured a spiral framework of wood. The use of wood facilitated line production and, at the time, it was easier to work. Equally important, it ensured against any possible infringement of patents held by Count von Zeppelin. In all, twenty-two Schütte-Lanz were built and several took part in military operations with the German fleet at sea during the War.

Two other dirigibles were built in Germany in 1911, although neither left their mark on aviation history. The Suchard-Brücker was intended for an Atlantic crossing, which was never actually attempted, while the other

Alberto Santos-Dumont
seen by the cartoonist Sem.

was the powerful Siemens-Schuckert, designed for military service. Technical details of both are included with their illustrations in this book.

While, with very rare exceptions, this second wave of constructors delivered their airships to the German military services or foreign governments, Zeppelins were spreading out across the skies of Germany and, from 1910, began proving that regular civil air passenger services could be run with comparative safety for the first time in the history of the world. On 10 November 1909, the first air transport company or airline was founded at Frankfurt-on-Main. The technical director of DELAG or, under its full name, the *Deutsche Luftschiffahrt A.G.*, was Dr Hugo Eckener, who had worked closely with Count von Zeppelin for three years and whose name was henceforth closely associated with all the Zeppelins produced.

The first dirigible to be put into service with DELAG was the LZ7, named *Deutschland*, making its first flight on 19 October 1910. After its premature crash in a forest, it was replaced by the LZ8, *Ersatz Deutschland* which, first flown by the airline on 30 March 1911, was destroyed at its moorings on 16 May of the same year. Another airship was then brought into service, *Schwaben* or the LZ10, piloted by Dr Eckener himself.

Its days were ended after one year's service by a fire which broke out after a landing. However, these successive accidents did not discourage the DELAG company. In 1912, the LZ11, christened *Viktoria Luise* after the Kaiser's youngest daughter, was delivered to the airline. Three years later, it was requisitioned by the German army. The LZ13, *Hansa*, and *Sachsen*, the LZ17, were the last two ships in service with DELAG. These, too, were mobilized by the military services. For passenger traffic, all these Zeppelins had been comfortably fitted out with a central keel structure built as a huge cabin with windows down each side. Twenty or so passengers could sit at their ease, in well upholstered seats, at tables where they were served with meals. This first airline had an impressive operational record, despite the initial loss of some airships, but without any loss of human lives or injuries. The figures from June 1910 to the 31 July 1914 speak for themselves: 1,588 flights, 107,835 miles flown, making a total of 3,176 hours with 34,028 passengers carried, 10,197 of whom were fare-paying.

At Lunéville, on 3 April 1913, the French were surprised to receive an unexpected visit from a military Zeppelin, the LZ16 from the aerodrome at Metz, which had strayed off course during a routine flight. As on the opposite banks of the Rhine, French airship constructors were beginning to proliferate. A member of the famous dynasty of balloonists, Louis Godard, built *Belgique* for Robert Goldschmidt, a well-known sportsman. The Lebaudy brothers continued to produce semi-rigid airships one of which, *Morning Post*, was delivered to the British Government by air. In the meantime, three new companies were set up: the Astra, Clément-Bayard and Zodiac, which all began producing a series of non-rigid aircraft from 1908 onwards. All three companies were simultaneously engaged in the construction of aeroplanes, then in their first stages of development.

Once again, the name of Henri Deutsch de la Meurthe comes to the fore. In association with the qualified pilot Henri Kapférer, now in charge of the Edouard Surcouf airfield workshops, he was the moving force behind the Astra company. They supplied several airships called 'cruisers' to the French military air force and even sold one to Imperial Russia. Following the DELAG example, Astra then founded the *Compagnie Générale Trans-aérienne* in Paris on 25 March 1908 to organize tourist flights. There was a certain showmanship involved, recalling the air circuses of later years, in the use of these airships to develop a keen national interest. A delighted public were at last able *to fly* and during a tour of principal cities, the names on the envelopes were changed according to the towns visited, such as *Ville de Bordeaux, Ville de Paris, Ville de Lucerne* or *Ville de Nancy*, and so on.

In 1911, the Astra firm achieved considerable technical progress by developing the design principles put forward by a Spanish engineer, Leonard Torres Quevedo. This design was aimed at giving the envelope the necessary rigidity and consisted of an inside framework made up from individual parts which were held together under the inside pressure and from which most of the car supports suspending the small nacelle were attached, thereby appreciably reducing head resistance. This trefoil section or clover-leaf form was to become a familiar sight. The success of the Astra-Torres association was demonstrated in the long life of those units flying regularly in France, as well as the one in Great Britain. Adolphe Clément, who added to his name 'de Bayard', owned a large company manufacturing the new horseless carriages or small automobiles. Extending his commercial interests to aviation, he built and sold his first airship to Russia. The second was delivered by air to the British Government with the generous backing of a national newspaper, the *Daily Mail*, and others were acquired by the French Air Force. The best-known of these was *Adjutant Vincenot*. Not only did this dirigible capture the long-distance flight record for France, bettering that of the Zeppelins, but it also had a long and distinguished life on active service.

On the eve of the First World War, the Zodiac corporation undertook the construction of the only French rigid airship. The patents covering the design had been registered in 1873, prior to those of Count von Zeppelin, and were the property of a great patriot of Alsatian origin by the name of Joseph Spiess. The skeleton of the Spiess dirigible, like those built by Schütte-Lanz in Germany, was made of wood. After several short but successful trials in 1913, Joseph Spiess presented the airship to the French Government who accepted it without any great show of enthusiasm. In this case, as in many others in the history of technical development, the achievement was not recognized at its full value as those responsible for developments in military aviation were firmly opposed to the design principles of rigid dirigibles. They were wrong. Very soon, and from the other side of the River Rhine, the effectiveness of the rigid lighter-than-air craft as a weapon became plainly evident as soon as war broke out.

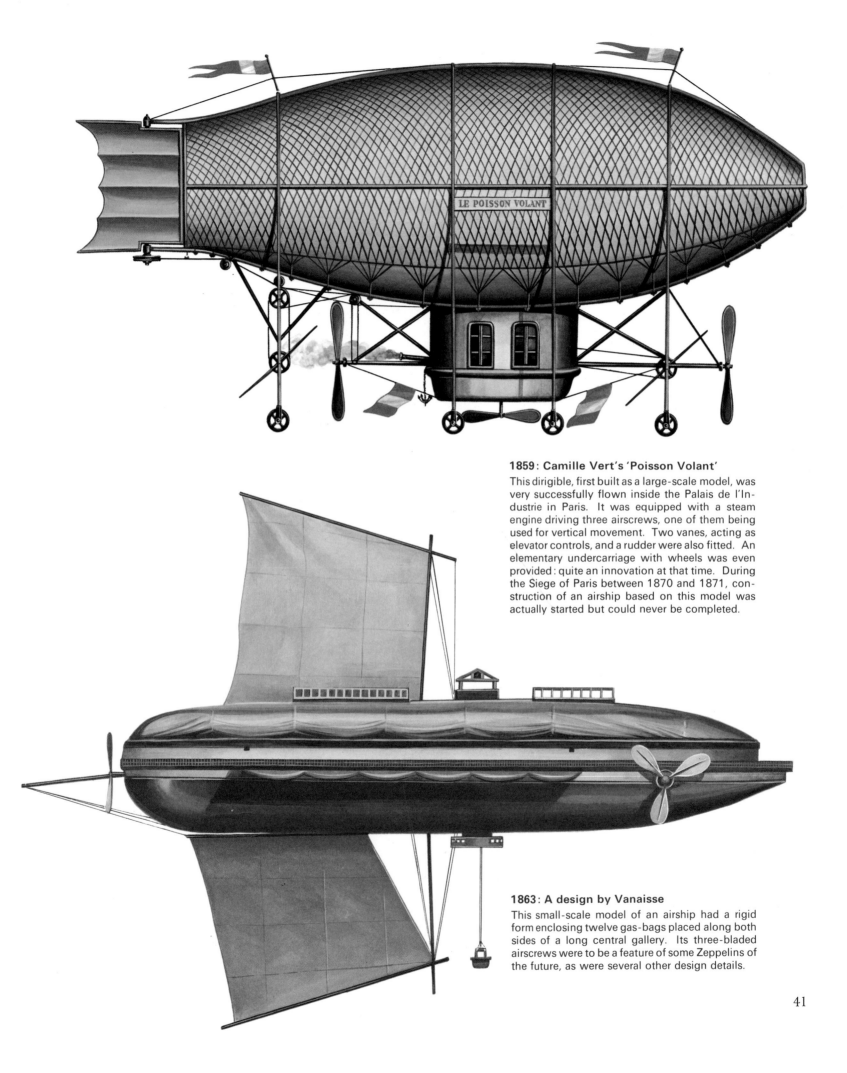

**1859: Camille Vert's 'Poisson Volant'**

This dirigible, first built as a large-scale model, was very successfully flown inside the Palais de l'Industrie in Paris. It was equipped with a steam engine driving three airscrews, one of them being used for vertical movement. Two vanes, acting as elevator controls, and a rudder were also fitted. An elementary undercarriage with wheels was even provided: quite an innovation at that time. During the Siege of Paris between 1870 and 1871, construction of an airship based on this model was actually started but could never be completed.

**1863: A design by Vanaisse**

This small-scale model of an airship had a rigid form enclosing twelve gas-bags placed along both sides of a long central gallery. Its three-bladed airscrews were to be a feature of some Zeppelins of the future, as were several other design details.

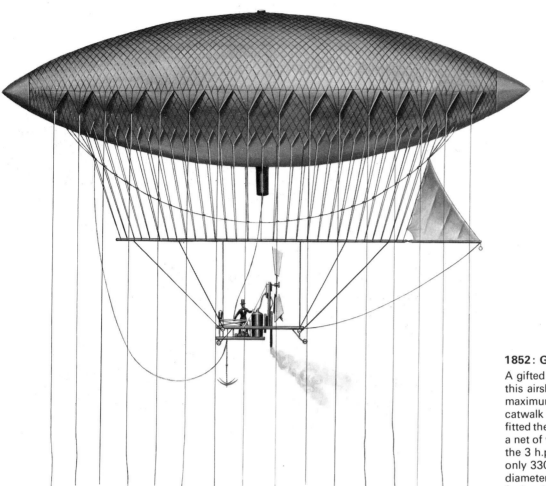

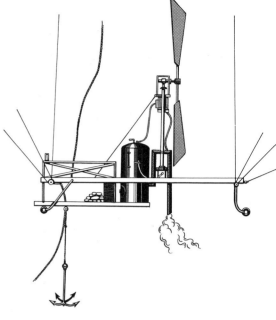

## 1852: Giffard's steam dirigible

A gifted inventor and builder, Henri Giffard constructed this airship of 88,000 cubic feet, 144 feet long with a maximum diameter of 39 feet. The nacelle was simply a catwalk attached to a boom 65 feet long to which was fitted the rudder, this beam itself joined to the envelope by a net of webbing. The picture above, to the right, shows the 3 h.p. coke-fired steam engine with a net weight of only 330 lbs. The three-bladed airscrew was 11 feet in diameter, driven at 110 r.p.m. The gas from the burning fuel and the used steam were exhausted through a funnel directed downwards. Changes of course and full circles in flight were successfully carried out.

## 1865: Delamarne's air-battleship

Prematurely christened *Espérance*, this airship of 70,500 cubic feet had a nose like a wind-cutter with the nacelle of similar shape. Three-bladed propellers were arranged symmetrically on each side of the envelope while the nacelle was also fitted with two airscrews for normal flight and two for vertical power, which the three or four aviators carried aboard were extremely hard put to drive. Only the propellers for vertical movement demonstrated any appreciable efficiency during several trials.

## 1863: The Abbé Carrié's design

Quite a feasible design by Carrié for a rigid airship, its envelope having interior compartments as well as certain features later to be found on Zeppelins. Oscillating Venetian blind slats symmetrically placed on each side of the middle formed the propelling system but one can only guess as to the means to be used for power.

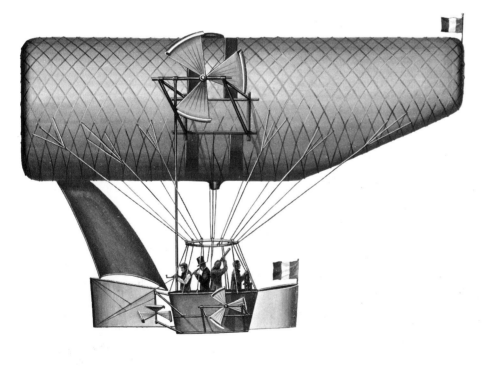

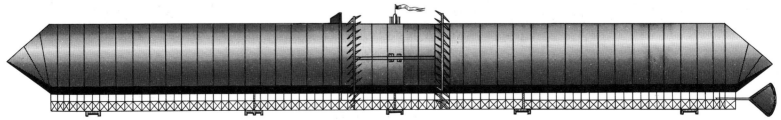

### 1850: Pennington's idea for a steam balloon

Incredible as it may seem, this American design was actually backed by the Aerial Steamship Company who published a prospectus declaring its intention to build the 230-foot long dirigible at a cost of $10,000 and offered $30 shares in the enterprise. Its name on the rudder, *New Era*, seems to have been a little over-optimistic.

### 1868: Marriott's design

Another American project for a steam-powered dirigible, *Aviator*, was also promoted by a corporation with a capital of $1 million, the Aerial Steam Navigation Co., founded by a San Franciscan publisher, F. Lederick Marriott. A combination of balloon and glider, this airship made its test flight In California over Lake Shell Mound.

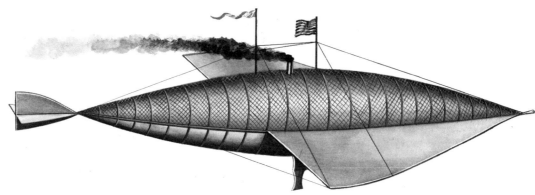

### 1878: Ritchell's flying bicycle

A small airship was produced by Professor C. E. Ritchell of Hartford in the State of Connecticut. The four-bladed airscrew was driven by means of two pedals, very similar to a bicycle. Apart from rising to a height of almost 200 feet and being airborne for over one hour on 12 June 1878, no other details of its capabilities are known.

### 1872: Haenlein's airship

Paul Haenlein, a German from Mainz, built this dirigible in Austria, basing his design on a patent registered in 1865. With a volume of 85,000 cubic feet, 165 feet long and 30 feet in diameter, this airship incorporated a ballonet. Under the envelope, a long structure maintained the shape of the envelope and distributed the forces acting on it. A coal gas fired engine developed 3.6 h.p. and drove a huge twin-bladed propeller, and the engine drew its fuel from the gas in the envelope. Although only tested while moored by a cable, quite good results seemed to be obtained.

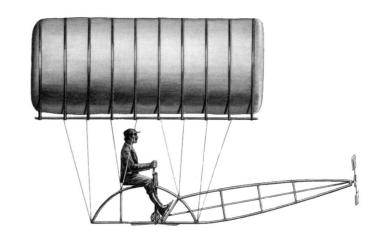

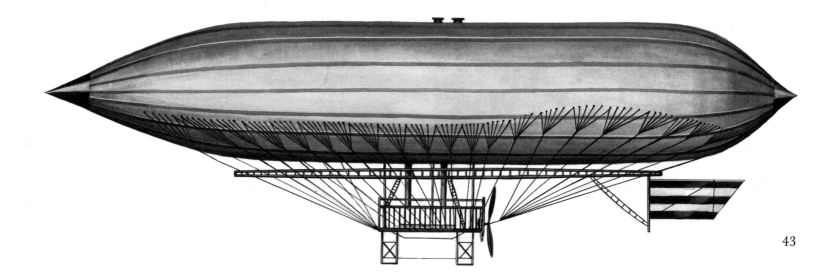

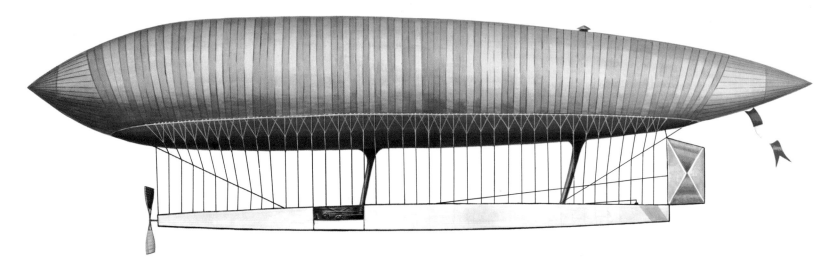

### 1884: 'La France', designed by Renard and Krebs

This airship was the first to have accomplished a round flight, taking off from one place and returning to land at its departure point. *La France* was crewed by its designers, Capitaine Charles Renard and Capitaine Arthur Krebs for its maiden flight over the balloon park at Chalais-Meudon on 9 August 1884. The bamboo nacelle, now housed in the *Musée de l'Air*, was 108 feet long, had a large canvas-covered propeller in the nose and, at the stern, a fixed stabilizing vane behind which was the rudder. *La France* was 165 feet in length, 27.5 feet at its maximum diameter, with a volume of some 66,000 cubic feet.

The power unit for *La France* was a multipolar electric motor designed by Capitaine Krebs. It developed 8 h.p., weighed 211 lbs. with a speed of 3,600 r.p.m. but as a reduction gear was used the propeller's speed was only 50 r.p.m. Banks of batteries weighing nearly 900 lbs. powered the motor. The following year, a 9 h.p. Gramme bipole dynamo replaced the original power unit.

### 1897: Dr Wölfert's 'Deutschland'

The nacelle was made from bamboo, and an underfloor lifting airscrew was fitted. This was the first time an engine fuelled by a mineral spirit was ever used as a power unit for a flying machine. Dr Wölfert's airship was fitted with an 8-horsepower Daimler engine. The envelope had a volume of 28,000 cubic feet and a length of 90 feet. On 14 June 1897, Dr Wölfert and Knabe, his mechanic, were killed at Tempelhof when *Deutschland* burst into flames and crashed.

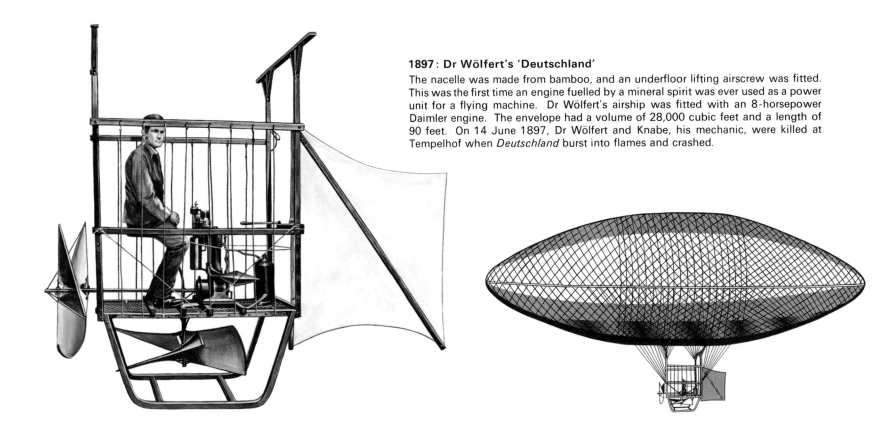

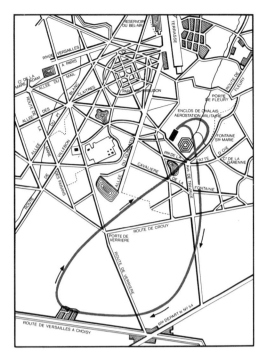

A map showing the route of *La France* on 9 August 1884.

These photographs show front and side views of *La France* and the proportion of men to airship gives a good idea of its size. After their first flight on 9 August 1884, Capitaine Renard and Capitaine Krebs sent a paper to the *Académie des Sciences* from which this extract is taken: 'Above Villacoublay, finding ourselves about four kilometers from Chalais-Meudon and entirely satisfied with the way our balloon was handling, we decided to turn back towards Chalais-Meudon and land there despite the small space between the trees. With only a slight angle to the rudder, about 11°, the balloon made a 180° turn to the right, describing a circle of about 1,000 feet.

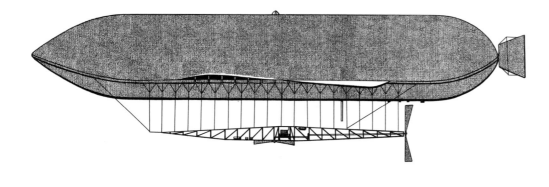

## 1902: Bradsky's airship

This balloon was cylindrical, both ends being conical, with a volume of 30,000 cubic feet, 85 feet in length and about 20 feet in diameter. At the rear end of the nacelle, a pusher airscrew was driven by a 16-horse-power Buchet engine. The nacelle itself was slung under the envelope by steel cables fixed to a light wooden framework centrally placed round the balloon, thus adding to the rigidity of the envelope. Two aerofoils with a total surface of about 800 square feet were also attached to this wooden frame, possibly with a view to giving extra lift. On 13 October 1902, the German constructor Ottokar von Bradsky with his French mechanic, Paul Morin, took off for the first flight but their airship crashed at Stains in the north-east of Paris. This accident which cost both their lives resulted from the rupture of the steel wires attaching the nacelle to the envelope.

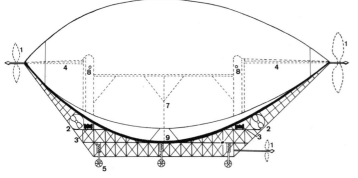

## 1902: Severo's 'Pax'

Longitudinal and cross sections of the internal structure of this dirigible showing the power unit transmission device contained in an inverted 'V' section cut out of the envelope.

A Brazilian member of Parliament, Augusto Severo, commissioned the building of this balloon which had a volume of 70,500 cubic feet, a length of 98 feet and a maximum diameter of 39 feet. Two airscrews projected from each end of the balloon, being linked by a beam running through the length of the envelope. These, as well as directional airscrews and another airscrew at the rear of the nacelle, compensating for changes in altitude, were driven by two Buchet engines, one of 16 h.p. and the other of 24 h.p. On 12 May 1902, *Pax* lifted off from Vaugirard in Paris but crashed soon afterwards in flames, killing Severo and his mechanic Saché instantly.

**Arrangement of Severo's 'Pax'**

1. tractor airscrew (front) pusher airscrew (rear)
2. directional airscrews
3. engines
4. airscrew transmission shafts
5. wheeled landing gear
6. inverted 'V' section
7. internal frame
8. engine transmissions
9. suspension

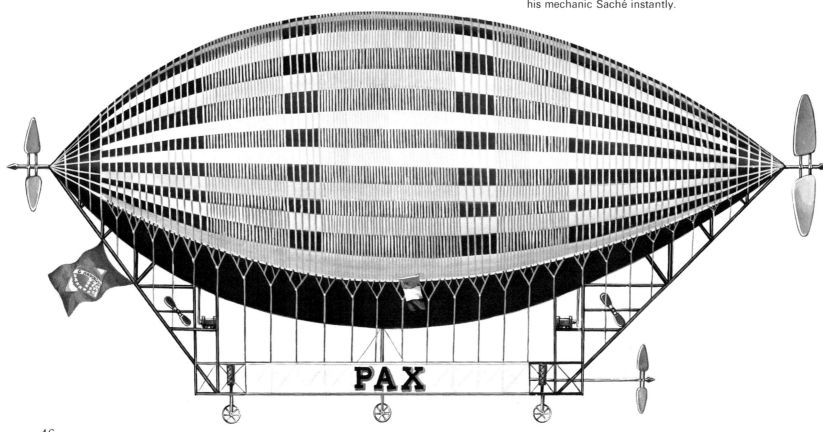

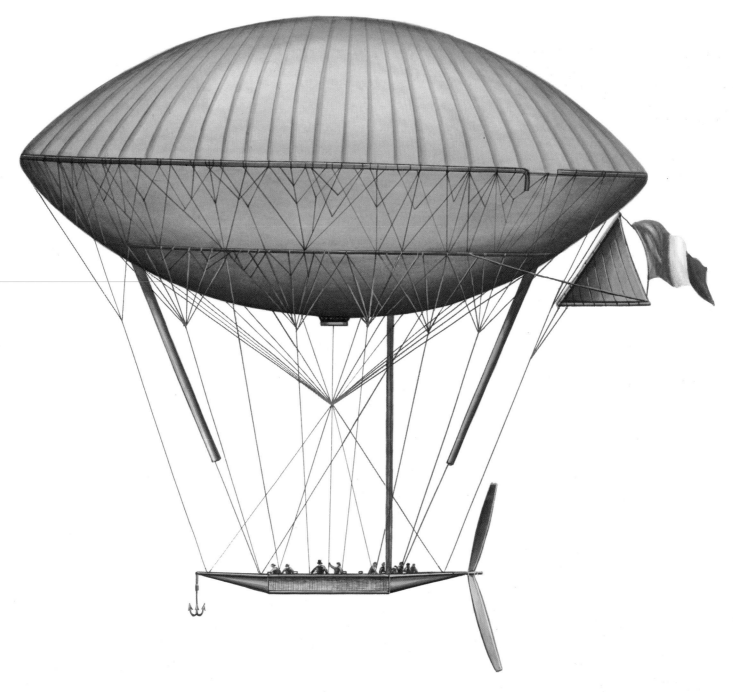

## 1872: An airship by Dupuy-de-Lôme

During the siege of Paris, the famous French naval architect Dupuy-de-Lôme designed this dirigible with the idea of establishing a means of communication beyond the besieging armies but it was only produced and tested in 1872. With a volume of 122,000 cubic feet, it was 118 feet long and 48 feet in diameter. To drive the airscrew, 30 feet across, a crank was installed to be operated by eight men but this system proved to be of insufficient power.

Opposite, the plan and elevation of the nacelle, which was made from wicker-work on a frame of thick bamboo. The plan view shows the crank that turned the huge propeller and the rod that braced its blades. This nacelle is now kept in the *Musée de l'Air* at Chalais-Meudon.

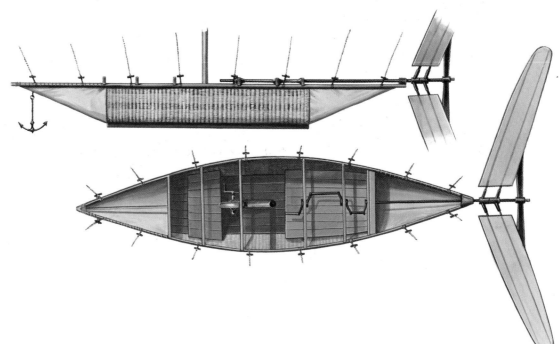

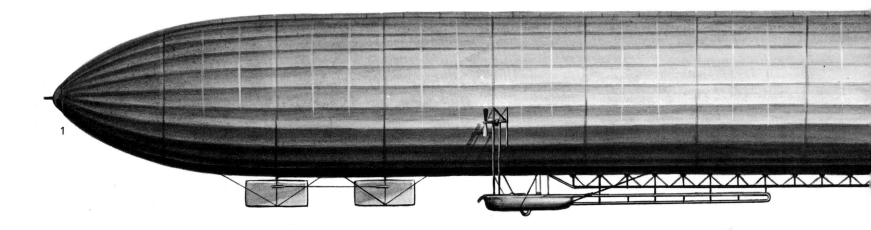

1

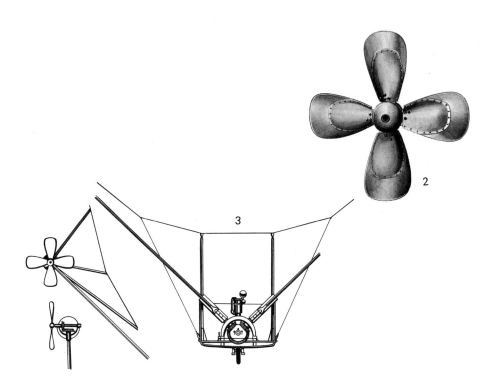

2

3

## 1 1900: The Zeppelin LZ1

First-born of a long line of airships built over forty years, the *Luftschiff* Zeppelin 1 was 420 feet long, 38 feet in diameter and had a volume of 399,000 cubic feet distributed between seventeen individual hydrogen gas bags inside an envelope stretched over an aluminium skeleton. Two nacelles were each provided with a Daimler engine of 14.2 h.p. driving two metal airscrews. Between the two nacelles, a free counterbalance weight on a cable was used to control the airship's fore and aft level. With Count Ferdinand von Zeppelin at the controls, the LZ1 took off on 2 July 1900 on its maiden flight.

2 This four-bladed airscrew, of very small diameter, the blades being only 3 feet 8 inches long, was made of aluminium, the metal being doubled over the greater part of its surface as a reinforcement.

3 Front-view technical drawing of the nacelle showing the two angled transmission shafts from the engines to each airscrew running in a tubular frame projecting out from the side of the airship's envelope.

## LZ1

1. Engine nacelles
2. Radiators
3. Sliding weight
4. Altitude vane/elevator
5. Rudder
6. Airscrew
7. Main ring-rib
8. Intermediate ring-ribs
9. Longitudinal frame
10. Cross-braced structure

4 General plan of the Zeppelin LZ1 showing the framework of jointless longerons with the connecting transversal hoops and, in the shaded sectional view, the criss-crossing of the stretchers bracing the skeleton.

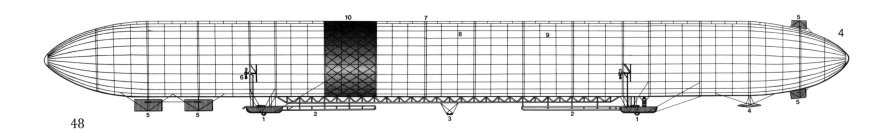

4

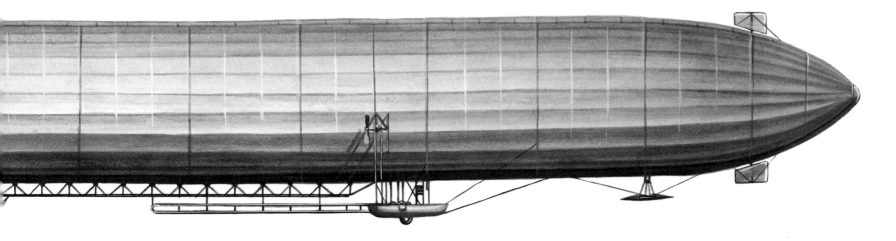

**5** Here is the engine-room telegraph, as on a ship, located in the command nacelle and transmitting orders to the mechanics in charge of each group of engines. From left to right the circular dial reads: 'Go ahead', 'Slow', 'Stop', and 'Go astern'.

**6** The very small rudders were operated by the lever, seen on the extreme right, by means of a system of gears. Later on, this lever was replaced by a wheel which could be handled with greater accuracy.

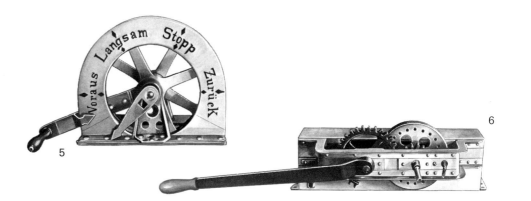

**7** The nacelle of the LZ1 was boat-shaped and equipped with a four-cylinder Daimler engine developing 14.2 h.p. and weighing 847 lbs. The engine was started by a crank handle and connected to angled drive shafts driving the airscrews. A wheel jutting out from the floor of the nacelle was provided to absorb the landing shock although the trials were actually carried out on Lake Constance where a floating hangar had been built, which could be turned according to the direction of the wind.

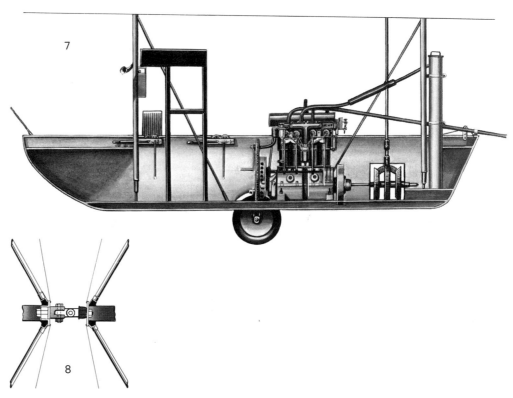

**8** A patent, registered by Count Ferdinand von Zeppelin on 3 November 1895, described a type of 'articulated flying train', the 'locomotive' being a cylinder, 377 feet long and with a diameter of 35 feet 6 inches, powered by two Daimler engines each developing 11 h.p. and weighing 1,100 lbs. This traction unit was designed to pull two quite separate balloon-trailers, each with its own nacelle, one accommodating most of the passengers and the other carrying mail. The drawing shows the coupling device for the three sections of the 'train' which was braced from below by a long trellis-work framework carrying the nacelles. Two masts at right angles were provided with a weight moving obliquely to control the vertical movement of the airship train.

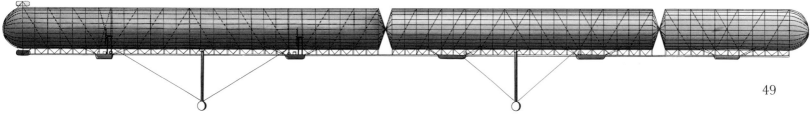

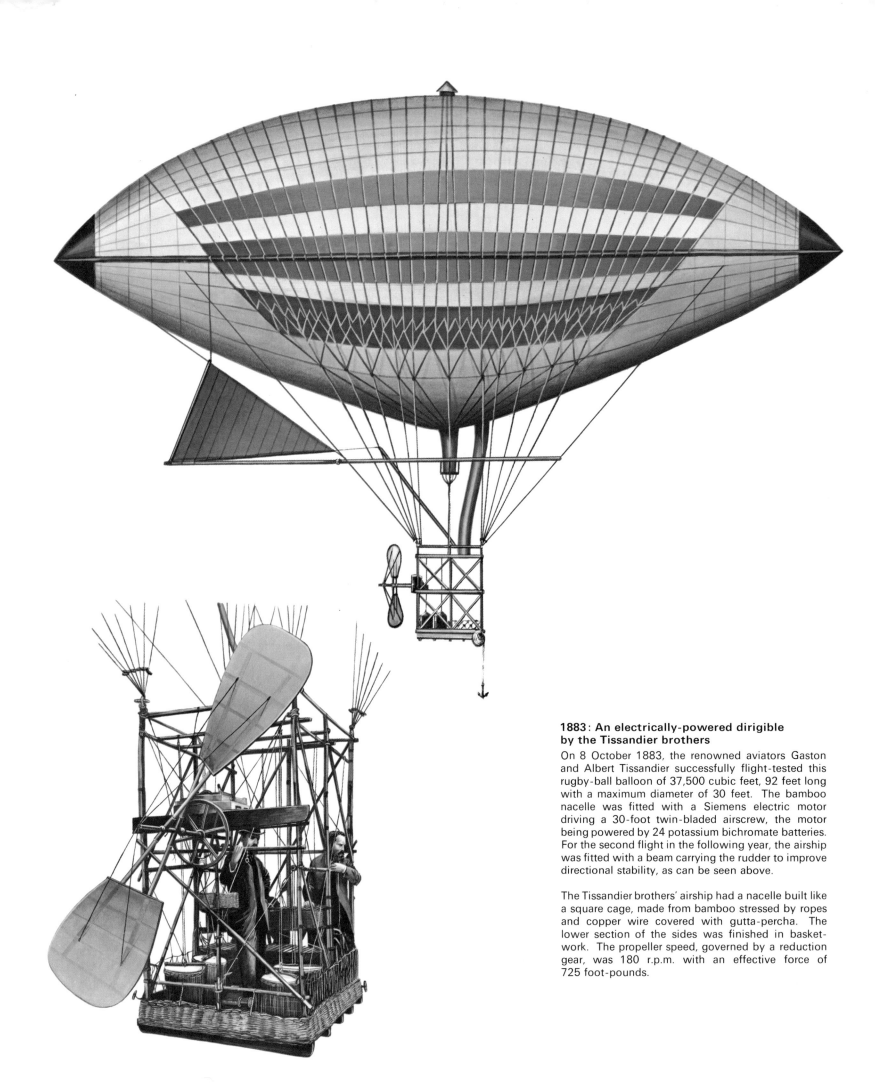

## 1883: An electrically-powered dirigible by the Tissandier brothers

On 8 October 1883, the renowned aviators Gaston and Albert Tissandier successfully flight-tested this rugby-ball balloon of 37,500 cubic feet, 92 feet long with a maximum diameter of 30 feet. The bamboo nacelle was fitted with a Siemens electric motor driving a 30-foot twin-bladed airscrew, the motor being powered by 24 potassium bichromate batteries. For the second flight in the following year, the airship was fitted with a beam carrying the rudder to improve directional stability, as can be seen above.

The Tissandier brothers' airship had a nacelle built like a square cage, made from bamboo stressed by ropes and copper wire covered with gutta-percha. The lower section of the sides was finished in basket-work. The propeller speed, governed by a reduction gear, was 180 r.p.m. with an effective force of 725 foot-pounds.

This photograph was taken in 1884 and shows the Tissandier brothers' dirigible before it was fitted with the stabilizing rudder beam.

1

### 1  1898: No. 1 in the Santos-Dumont series

A persevering pioneer of aerial navigation, Santos-Dumont made a test flight of this first small airship on 20 September 1898. With a volume of only 6,300 cubic feet, it was 82 feet long and 11½ feet in diameter. Owing to an insufficient flow from the gas-bag valve, the balloon folded in two and the photograph was taken as this started to happen. The gas-bag's hemispheric outline can be seen through the middle of the envelope.

### 2  1901: No. 5 in the Santos-Dumont series

With a volume of 19,500 cubic feet and a length of 179 feet, the envelope carried a 60-foot wooden frame, triangular in section, built by Santos-Dumont himself. A small nacelle was fitted towards the front end and a four-cylinder 16 h.p. Buchet engine in the middle drove an airscrew at the stern end, in front of the rudder.

### 3  1901: The Henri Deutsch de la Meurthe Grand Prix

Although only a montage, this photograph conveys the enthusiasm of the crowd as they cheered Santos-Dumont in the sixth of his series, while watching him circling the Eiffel Tower on 19 October 1901. Successfully completing the round flight, he won the coveted Grand Prix offered by Henri Deutsch de la Meurthe, this being the very acceptable sum of 100,000 francs in gold pieces.

### 4  1905: The nacelle of No. 14 in the Santos-Dumont series

Santos-Dumont in the nacelle of his fourteenth airship completed in 1905. Never flight-tested, No. 14 was very tapered in form and equipped with a 14 h.p. 'V' twin-cylindered Peugeot engine.

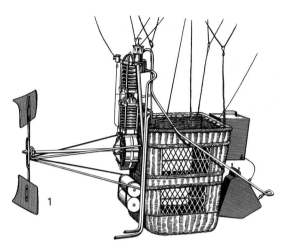

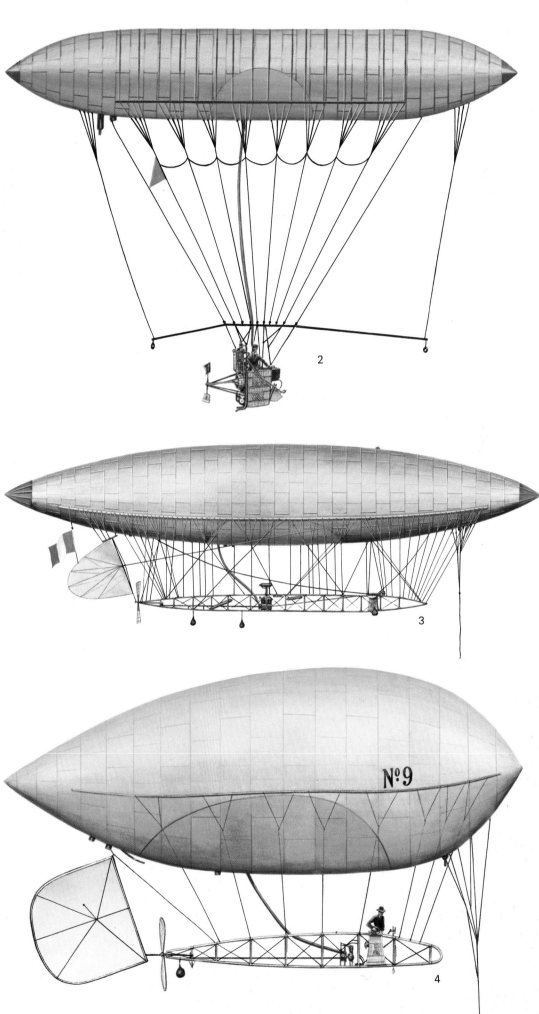

**1 1898: No. 1 in the Santos-Dumont series**

The nacelle of No. 1 was formerly on one of the free balloons used by Santos-Dumont and was equipped with a small De Dion-Bouton engine which Santos had modified by adding another cylinder in tandem. Developing 1¾ h.p., it drove a propeller with two square blades.

**2** This small dirigible was powered by a De Dion-Bouton petrol engine and flight-tested on 20 September 1898. The very light envelope in Japanese silk enclosed a ballonet and was fitted with a bolt rope suspension but, during trials, it folded in half owing to the insufficient flow from the ballonet valve (see opposite page).

**3 1901: No. 6 by Santos-Dumont**

This airship was 108 feet long, about 20 feet in diameter and had a volume of 22,320 cubic feet. Considerably more elaborate than his earlier models, it was driven by a 20 h.p. four-cylinder Buchet engine. This was the airship in which Santos-Dumont won the Henri Deutsch de la Meurthe Grand Prix of 100,000 francs by taking off from Saint-Cloud, circling the Eiffel Tower and returning to his point of departure within the specified time of thirty minutes.

**4 1903: No. 9 by Santos-Dumont: 'Baladeuse'**

This little sports airship was well-named, the French word *balader* meaning 'to go for a stroll or a joy-ride'. This was just how Santos-Dumont used it, once even landing in front of his apartment in the Champs-Elysées. *Baladeuse* was 50 feet long with a maximum diameter of 18 feet and a volume of 7,800 cubic feet and was powered by a three-horsepower Clément engine.

## 1906: 'Ville de Paris'

This dirigible was 113,000 cubic feet in volume, being enlarged to 127,000 cubic feet in 1908. It was about 200 feet long with a maximum diameter of 34½ feet and powered by a 70 h.p. Chenu engine. The stern stabilizing planes were made from four pairs of fabric tubes inflated with hydrogen.

(Left.) The nacelle from the front with three control wheels in the foreground. The dial on the left showed the pressure of the internal gas-bag and the dial on the right is that of a statoscope indicating ascent or descent.

(Below, left.) The front of the nacelle carried an airscrew, appearing somewhat distorted by the perspective in this picture.

(Below, right.) Henri Deutsch de la Meurthe, the great patron of aviation, seen in the nacelle of *Ville de Paris*.

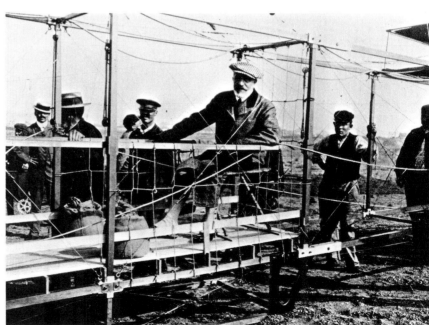

View along the nacelle. Léon Delagrange, who held one of the first aviation patents, is seated near the stern.

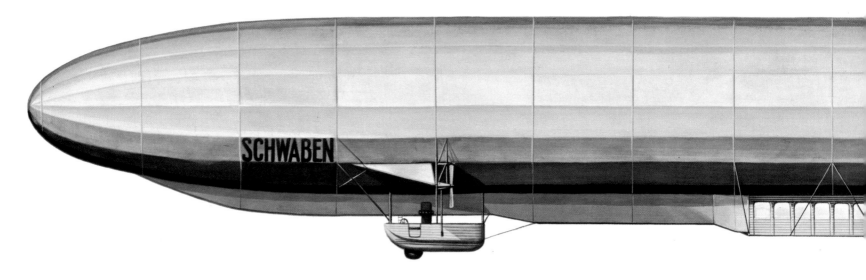

**1910: The Zeppelin LZ 10 'Schwaben'**

Tenth airship to leave the Zeppelin workshops at Friedrichshafen, *Schwaben* was the third of six put into service for domestic flights throughout Germany by DELAG, or the Deutsche Luftschiffahrt AG. This company, founded in Frankfurt-am-Main in November 1909, had as its Technical Director the same Dr Hugo Eckener whose name is so closely linked with the history of the Zeppelin. *Schwaben* was 433 feet long, 46 feet in diameter with a volume of 628,600 cubic feet and was powered by three Maybach engines each developing 145 h.p. On 26 June 1911, *Schwaben* made the first of 224 flights, carrying about 20 passengers on each trip, accommodated in a glass-windowed cabin built in the centre of the keel. With Dr Eckener as pilot, *Schwaben* was to carry a total of 4,354 passengers and cover 16,950 miles in the course of its career. On 18 June 1912, while moored at Düsseldorf, one of its ports of call, the airship was abruptly struck by a squall and caught fire, possibly from a spark caused by electrostatic discharge. Only six days before, *Schwaben* had carried the first German airmail, flying 200,000 souvenir postcards from Manzell, on Lake Constance, to Mainz.

**1912: The Zeppelin Z III**

This was one of the first rigid dirigibles produced for the German Army and was commissioned on 25 March 1912. Z III was 433 feet long, its diameter was 46 feet and 17 gas-bags made up its volume to 628,600 cubic feet. Four gas-bags can be seen in the part of the drawing with the envelope skin removed. Z III was fitted with three 145-horsepower Maybach engines, one behind the command nacelle and two in the next nacelle, the nacelles connected by a trellis-work catwalk. The airship had an average cruising speed of 47 m.p.h. Its tail unit consisted of a single rudder and double stabilizing vanes, the elevators being fitted directly above the nacelles. After 27 months' flying from its base at Metz-Frescaty, the Z III was taken out of service and scrapped on 1 August 1914.

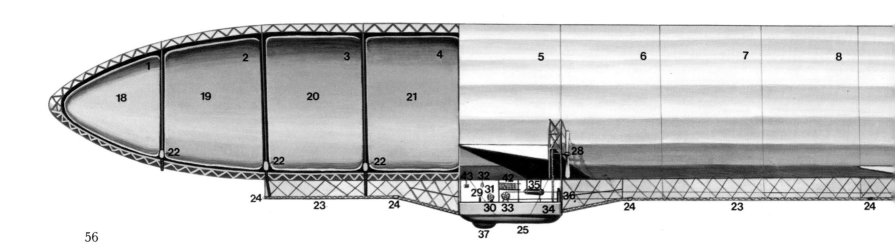

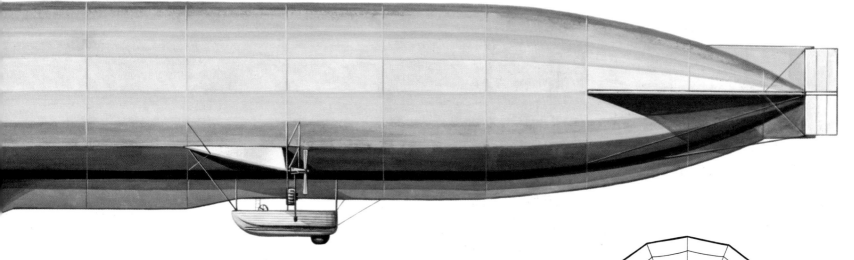

(Left) Technical rear view of *Schwaben* showing the wide tail unit with its rudders and elevators. The shafts driving the four-bladed airscrews on each side can also be seen. Two petrol tanks are mounted on top of the nacelle which is fitted with a pneumatic undercarriage to absorb landing shocks.

**Rear-view drawing for 'Schwaben'**

1. Gas-bags
2. Engine nacelle
3. Radiators
4. Airscrews
5. Transmission shafts
6. Altitude vane/elevator
7. Rudder
8. Stabilizing vanes

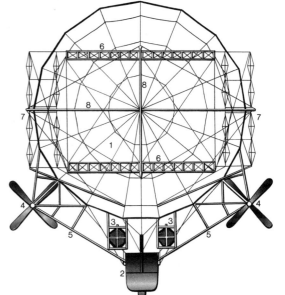

### Description of Z III, 1912

 1-17 Arrangement of gas-bags inside the en-velope
18-21 Cut-away drawing of the first four gas-bags
22. Water ballast bags
23. Keel, metal cat-walk
24. Storage for ground-handling equipment
25. Forward nacelle
26. Amidships nacelle
27. Stern nacelle
28. Airscrews
29. Helm
30. Altitude control
31. Command equipment for mechanics in rear nacelle
32. Six signalling bells
33. Conveyor belts for messages between nacelles
34. Engines
35. Oil tanks
36. Radiators
37. Pneumatic shock-absorbers for landing gear
38. Stabilizing vanes
39. Twin rudders between stabilizing vanes
40. Main rudder
41. Rudder cable
42. Control panel for valves and water ballast
43. Compass

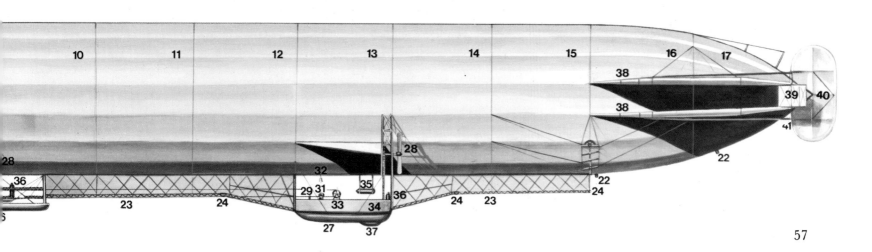

### 1907: 'Nulli Secundus'

The first dirigible to belong to the British Army had an envelope of gold-beaters' skin but no interior gas-bag. *Nulli Secundus* was 122 feet long, 26 feet in diameter with a volume of 532,000 cubic feet. The nacelle was attached to the envelope by webbing straps. Powered by an Antoinette 50-horsepower engine with a belt-drive for two airscrews mounted at each side, the airship as built made it first flight on 10 September 1907. It was subsequently modified.

Left, and left-hand page:

### 1901: Louis Roze and his dream airship

Undaunted by his total lack of aeronautical experience, the enterprising engineer Louis Roze tried out this astonishing mechanical contraption at Argenteuil, near Paris, in 1901. Two parallel, rocket-shaped hulls, 148 feet long, of cellular construction and with watertight communicating compartments, were combined with a rigid skeleton in aluminium, the covering envelope being two skins of varnished silk, all joined together by a kind of cage built of aluminium. This cage carried a 20-horsepower petrol engine, driving the propellers for vertical movement and one pusher airscrew, as well as a nacelle designed for eight persons. A test flight, bravely attempted on 4 September 1901, far from fulfilled its inventor's ambitious dreams.

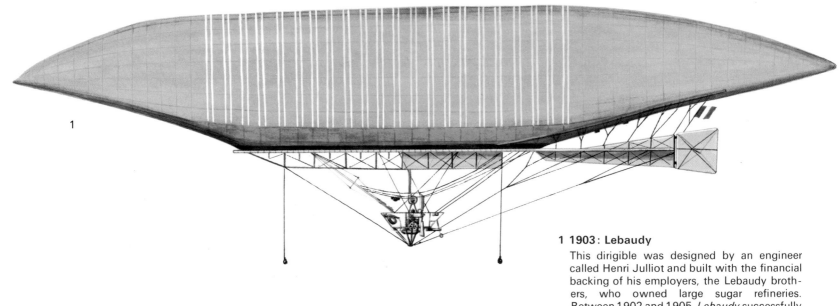

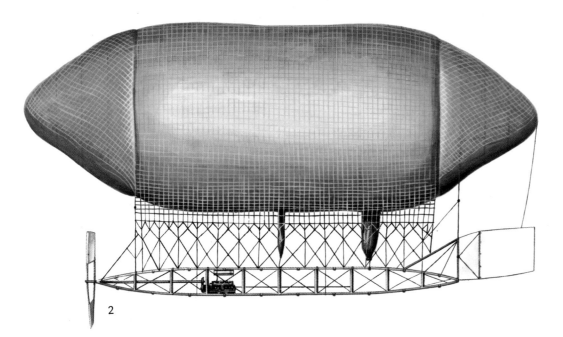

## 1 1903: Lebaudy

This dirigible was designed by an engineer called Henri Julliot and built with the financial backing of his employers, the Lebaudy brothers, who owned large sugar refineries. Between 1902 and 1905, *Lebaudy* successfully made a number of systematic flight tests. Its volume was 80,650 cubic feet, later increased to 116,538, its length was 164 feet and its girth 32 feet. The envelope was made from doubled rubberized fabric and to this skin was attached a platform made from steel tubing. At one end, the platform was extended to carry a cruciform tail unit and rudders and it also supported the boat-shaped nacelle which was sturdily constructed of steel tubing. A 40 h.p. Daimler-Benz engine drove two metal airscrews, mounted on each side through a bevel-gear transmission system at a speed of 1,200 r.p.m. Because it incorporated a metal support in the form of a chassis, 79 feet by 20 feet including the tail unit, the Lebaudy can be considered as the archetype of the semi-rigid dirigible.

## 2 1904: Baldwin's 'California Arrow'

Thomas Scott Baldwin built this small airship, about 52 feet long, and powered it with a two-cylinder 5-horsepower engine produced by that famous American aviation pioneer, Glenn H. Curtiss. Baldwin, an expert parachutist, was to build a total of thirteen dirigibles, all powered by Curtiss engines.

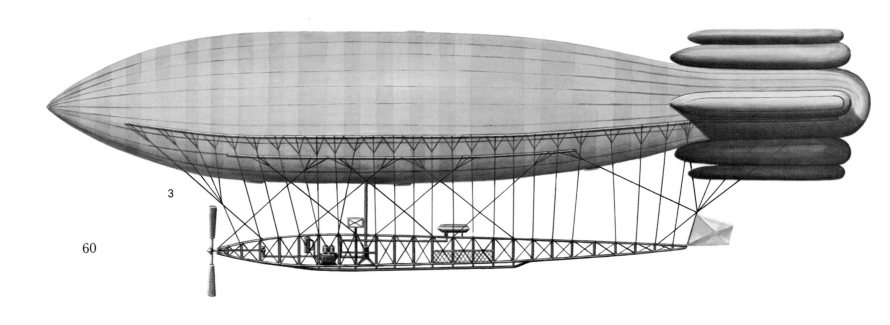

**1906: The Lebaudy airship 'Patrie'**

The army commissioned the building of the semi-rigid airship *Patrie* by the Lebaudy company and it was delivered in November 1906. On 26 November it flew from Chalais-Meudon to its home port at Verdun, covering the 150 miles in 6 hours 45 minutes. Three days later, a magneto broke down and the crew were forced to make an emergency landing. During the night, a violent storm wrenched the airship from its temporary mooring, the 200 handling personnel being powerless to hold it. With no crew aboard, *Patrie* was carried on the winds to Ireland where it lost an airscrew, then disappeared in the North Sea.

*Patrie* was similar in design to the preceding Lebaudy unit but had a volume of 114,800 cubic feet and was equipped with a 70-horsepower Panhard-Levassor engine.

**1906: The Lebaudy airship 'Patrie'**

The rigid steel tubular platform can be seen attached to the lower part of the envelope. This chassis carried the tail planes, the rudders and the nacelle made also from steel tubing.

**1902: Alberto Severo's 'Pax' in its hangar**

This photograph of the front of the airship in its hangar at Vaugirard shows one of the in-line airscrews and one of the triangular sections of the frame which supported the transmission shaft inside the hull. The small spherical balloon seen on the right was used as a lift by the crew responsible for rigging the envelope.

◁ **3 1906: 'Ville de Paris'**

This dirigible was produced by the aviator and builder Surcouf. The illustration clearly shows the tail stabilizing vanes consisting of four pairs of fabric sleeves inflated with hydrogen. A similar type of tail unit was used in later years on several French airships built by the firm of Clément-Bayard. Offered to the nation in 1908, *Ville de Paris* served in Verdun as a replacement for the military airship *Patrie*.

**1907: The Zeppelin LZ 3**     The LZ3, which made its first flight on the 8 October 1907, was 420 feet long and had a volume of 399,000 cubic feet, divided into 16 compartments. When the army took delivery of LZ3, which was its first airship and remained in service until 1913, the length was extended to 446 feet and another compartment was added, making the volume 430,800 cubic feet. Originally powered by two engines of 210 h.p., the LZ3 was subsequently equipped with engines of 230 h.p. This photograph of the LZ3 leaving its floating hangar on Lake Constance clearly shows the group of four elevators and the three rudders which moved between two fixed stabilizing vanes.

**4 1908: 'Nulli Secundus' II**     The original *Nulli Secundus* had a very short life. Flight-tested on 10 September 1907, it made a second ▷ flight of almost 19 miles on 3 October and was destroyed by a storm only one week later. The paradoxically named *Nulli Secundus* II, with a volume of 77,700 cubic feet, differed from the first in having a sort of triangular keel fitted under the envelope, giving it the appearance of a semi-rigid airship. With a speed that rarely exceeding 15 m.p.h., *Nulli Secundus* II had a short and undistinguished career.

## 1 1909: The Gross-Basenach M III

In certain respects, the semi-rigid airships designed by Major Hans von Gross and his engineer Nikolas Basenach were modelled on those made in France by Lebaudy. A rigid platform or chassis initially coupled to the envelope was soon replaced by a covered lattice girder to carry the tail unit, airscrews, fuel and ballast. On the M III, the initial M denoting military, this girder was made in three jointed sections. M III, which made its first flight on 31 December 1909, had a volume of 247,000 cubic feet, a length of 272 feet and a maximum diameter of 41 feet. Four Koerting engines developed a total of 300 h.p. Only four airships were built by the Gross-Basenach company, which ceased production in 1914, and these were used principally as training aircraft.

## 2 1908: Baldwin's airship

This small dirigible produced by Thomas Scott Baldwin was the first delivered to the U.S. Army. 95 feet long, with a maximum diameter of 20 feet, its volume was only 19,800 cubic feet. A 20 h.p. Curtiss engine was fitted in the 65-foot nacelle and the large rudder, with its central tail plane, bore the national colours. The U.S. Government in Washington had offered the sum of $10,000 to anyone who could produce a practical military method for controllable aerial navigation. After a demonstration at Fort Myers by Thomas Scott Baldwin, an agreement to purchase the airship on behalf of the Signal Corps was concluded there and then, on 18 August 1908.

3 The front view, on the extreme right, shows the huge airscrew and the triplane system for elevator control. The plan view on the right gives an accurate impression of the long, slender nacelle with its cross-bracing, carrying the nose propeller and, behind that, the elevator unit, the engine driving the airscrew by a long transmission shaft, and in the rear, the stern stabilizing vanes.

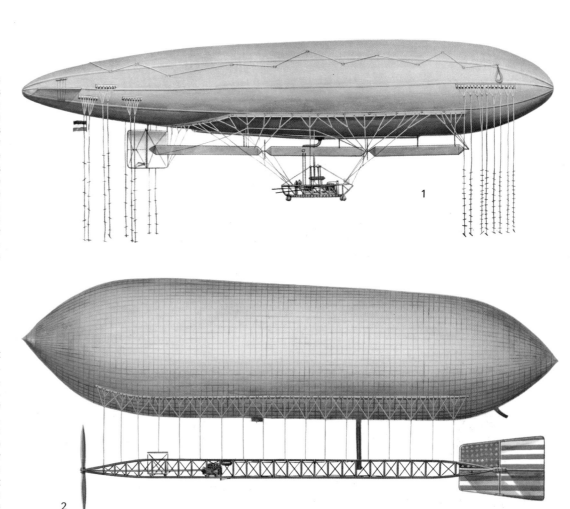

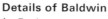

**Details of Baldwin**

| | |
|---|---|
| 1. Engine | 4. Rudder |
| 2. Valve | 5. Altitude vane/elevator |
| 3. Stabilizing vane | 6. Airscrew |
| | 7. Petrol tanks |

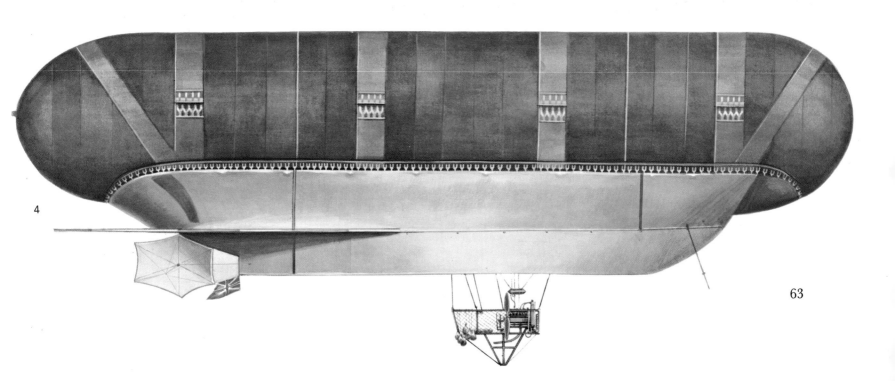

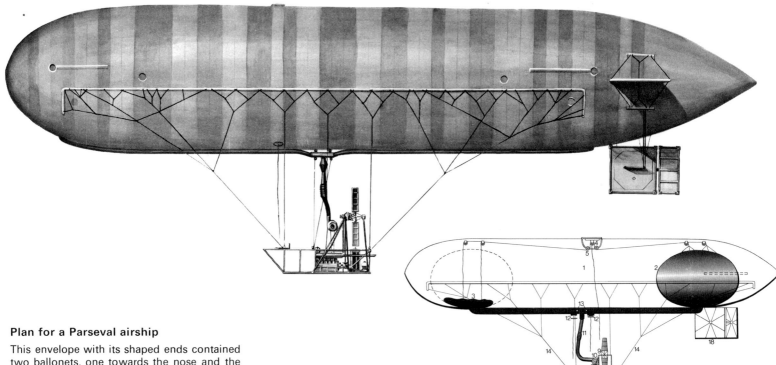

## Plan for a Parseval airship

This envelope with its shaped ends contained two ballonets, one towards the nose and the other at the stern. A control enabled one to be inflated while the other was deflated; here, dotted lines indicate the volume of the inflated ballonet. Their envelopes were balanced by a system of internal pulleys and the weight differential caused by one or the other being brought into play contributed to the action of the elevator control which was mounted forward of the stern point of the envelope. This drawing also shows the T-shaped duct to feed the ballonets and its extension fixed to the belly of the airship. A stabilizing vane is mounted in front of the rudder at the stern.

| | |
|---|---|
| 1. Envelope | 10. Pump |
| 2. Filled ballonet | 11. Gas conduit |
| 3. Partially empty ballonet | 12. Valves |
| 4. Valve | 13. Distribution device for ballonets |
| 5. Control cable for gas-bag valves | 14. Suspension cables |
| 6. Petrol tanks | 15. Pulley |
| 7. Tail-fin | 16. Nacelle |
| 8. Engine | 17. Helm |
| 9. Airscrew | 18. Rudder |

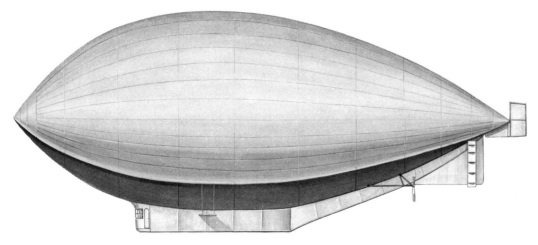

## 1909: Forlanini's airship 'Leonardo da Vinci'

In 1877, an Italian engineer, Enrico Forlanini, (1848-1930) produced a scale model of a steam-powered helicopter which was the first ever to be flown. In 1909 the Italian Government commissioned him to carry out trials with this semi-rigid airship of 115,300 cubic feet, 131 feet long and with a maximum diameter of 46 feet. Forlanini's airship was powered by a French engine, a 40-horsepower Antoinette, and a 2-horsepower auxiliary engine was also fitted to drive a pump for the gas-bag. This occupied the entire lower part of the envelope which was divided into seven compartments. The nacelle of steel tubing was entirely closed in and an integral part of a rigid framework composed of reinforced steel tubing beams which made up the keel. *Leonardo da Vinci* made its maiden flight on 22 August 1909.

## Various Parseval nacelles

This is a side view of the nacelle for the Parseval PL2, built in 1908 and flown for the first time on 13 August of that year. With a volume of 134,200 cubic feet and a length of 190 feet, it was powered by an 85 h.p. Mercedes-Daimler engine which had two blocks of two cylinders. The flexible four-bladed airscrew was chain driven through a gear-reduction unit. When handed over to the Army, PL2 was designated Military P1.

Extreme right:
The nacelle of Parseval PL2 seen from the stern. This diagram shows the 85 h.p. Mercedes-Daimler engine mounted on a bracket fixed to the floor of the nacelle, its petrol and oil tanks, the pump with its driving shaft and the airscrew with four 'soft' blades. These were panels of strong fabric cut to a suitable shape and weighted to assume the necessary rigidity when subjected to the centrifugal force. The drawback to this arrangement was that when the airscrew was stopped, the blades had a tendency to fall on to the transmission chain sprocket or to catch round the supporting frame when the centrifugal force was not sufficient to keep the blades extended although the airscrew was still rotating. In order to overcome these disadvantages, rigid blades in stiffened fabric were subsequently adopted, particularly on the PL5.

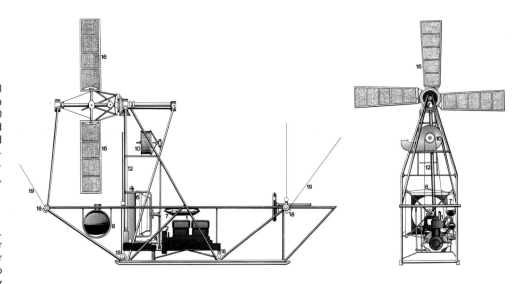

These numbers apply to all drawings

1. Engine
2. Control wheel
3. Control wheel with pump
4. Clutch
5. Clutch lever
6. Radiator
7. Oil tank
8. Petrol tank
9. Exhaust silencer
10. Pump
11. Airscrew chain drive
12. Transmission shaft
13. Pump transmission belt
14. Shaft
15. Airscrew blade pitch adjusting wheel
16. Airscrew
17. Helm
18. Pulleys
19. Suspension cables

This view of the nacelle on PL3 shows the two MAG engines, each developing 120 h.p. and symmetrically placed, one on each side of the nacelle. The drawing also shows the driving chains to the airscrews with four 'soft' blades; and the three-point device joining their shafts. In the middle is the control wheel for the rudder.

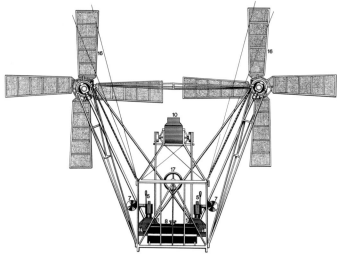

A side view of the nacelle for the Parseval PL3, an airship of 197,760 cubic feet with a length of 226 feet, which was built in 1909 and made its first flight on 19 February 1910. The two six-cylinder MAG engines weighed 880 lbs, developed 120 h.p. each, and were started by compressed air. Each engine drove one airscrew, 13 feet in diameter, with four 'soft' blades at 250 r.p.m. by a chain and reduction gear. The drawing shows the radiator behind the engine, and halfway up, the pump for feeding the gas-bags. The steering wheel can be seen towards the nose. Bought by the German Government, PL3 became Military P II.

▽

A longitudinal view of the nacelle for the Parseval PL5, a so-called 'sports' aircraft built in 1910. It was only 51,200 cubic feet in volume and about 130 feet long. Under the nose of the envelope, a wing acted as an elevator in conjunction with two interconnected gas-bags. PL5 was powered by two 33-horsepower engines, each driving an airscrew with four stiffened blades. The drawing shows the starting handle, the exhaust pipe, the radiator, the gas pump in front of the propeller shaft, the fuel tank on the floor of the nacelle and, towards the nose, the steering wheel.

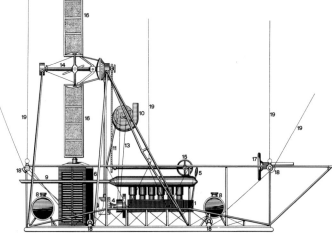

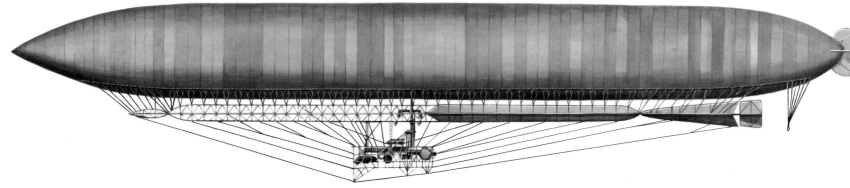

## 1910: 'Morning Post' by Lebaudy

In 1910, the *Morning Post*, a British national daily newspaper, appealed to its readers for funds to buy an airship for the government. So successful was their campaign that they raised a sum of £18,000 sterling. The Lebaudy brothers received the contract to build this dirigible which, like previous successful units produced by this company, was semi-rigid. Fitted with a long lattice-work keel made of steel tubing, carrying the tail unit, it was rigged on the nose and stern with mobile elevators, inversely interacting. The envelope contained three ballonets with a net volume of 353,000 cubic feet, was 338 feet long and 39 feet in diameter. The stern was fitted with a classic cruciform tail unit and the tubular steel nacelle carried two Panhard-Levassor engines developing a total of 270 h.p. This airship was also supplied with two inflatable floats and a drag anchor for its flight over the English Channel on the way to its base at Farnborough, not far from London. It was delivered on 26 October 1911 after a flight of 5½ hours with 8 people on board, and which covered about 230 miles.

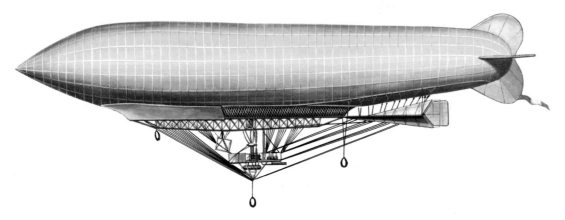

## Lebaudy's 'Liberté'

After the two ill-fated military airships *Patrie* and *République*, the Lebaudy brothers built another semi-rigid dirigible called *Liberté* which made its first flight on 2 January 1909. Its dimensions were identical to those of *République*, being 200 feet in length, 35 feet in diameter with a volume of 162,450 cubic feet, later increased to 229,545 cubic feet. It was originally powered by one Panhard-Levassor engine of 100-120 h.p. and later with two engines by the same manufacturer, each developing 50-60 h.p. After the accident to *République*, the metal airscrews were replaced by wooden ones fitted to each side of the nacelle. Whereas previous units were equipped with single ailerons for fore-and-aft control, this airship had double rectangular aerofoils which were deemed more efficient.

## 1911: The Zodiac 'Capitaine Ferber'

Following on the success of their other productions the Société Zodiac delivered a 'flying cruiser' to the army in 1911. It was 211,900 cubic feet in volume and named after that great military aviation pioneer, Capitaine Ferber, who had been killed while flying on 24 September 1909. This airship was 249 feet long and 41 feet in diameter at its largest circumference. Its two ballonets could be interconnected by means of a duct. The 115-foot long nacelle was built from nickel steel tubing and could be dismantled into five sections. Two Dansette-Gillet engines developing 90 h.p. apiece each drove two airscrews of 11½ feet in diameter. These airscrews were mounted to each side on upswept struts, transmission being a system of bevel gears and floating shafts. The motors also drove pumps to supply either the forward or stern ballonet or both at once. The system of rudders and vanes was identical to that used on the dirigible *Le Temps*. With six people aboard, *Capitaine Ferber* was able to attain a speed of 35 m.p.h.

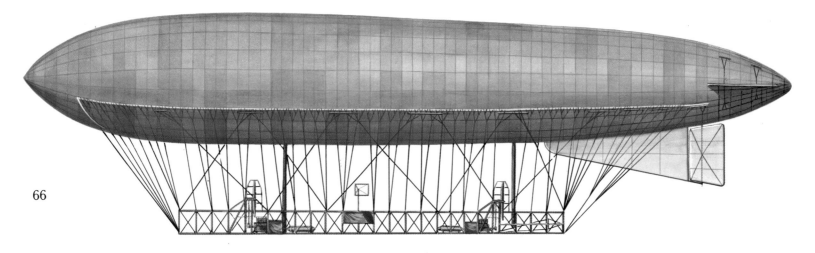

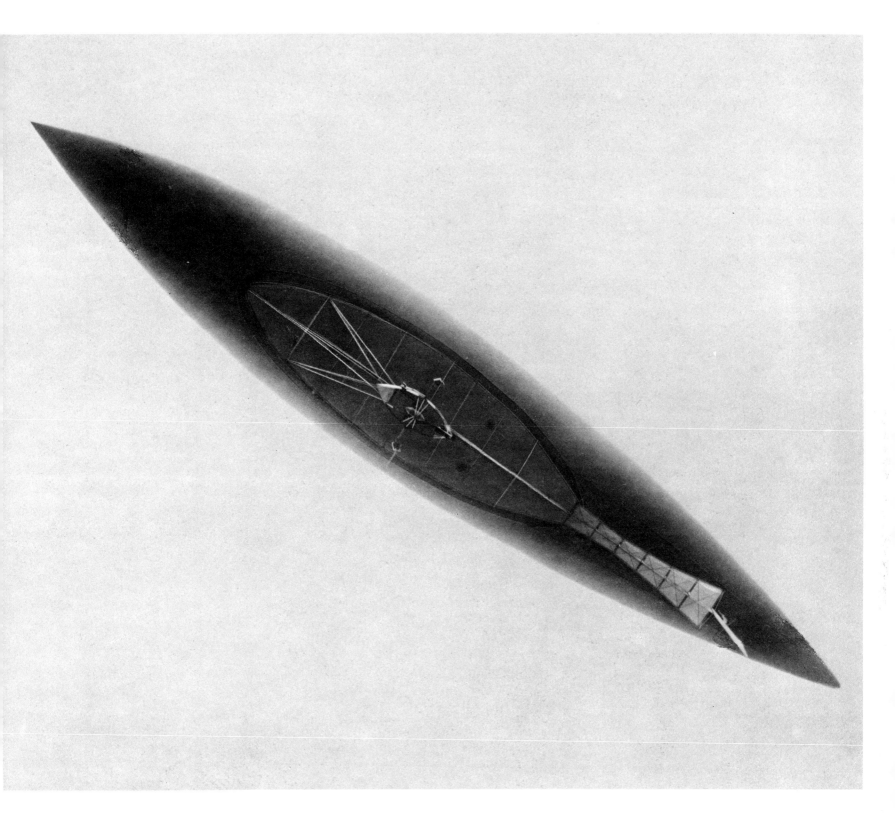

**Lebaudy's dirigible in all its glory**
This excellent photograph shows off the fine lines of the envelope, a long slim rocket still without
stabilizing vanes. The shape of the rigid frame supporting the nacelle by an arrangement of double
cables can be seen clearly, as can the athwartships airscrews. There is also the long reinforced
beam carrying the cruciform tail unit, its horizontal surfaces composed of several sections braced
diagonally. Behind, the rudder is at an angle, as for a turn.

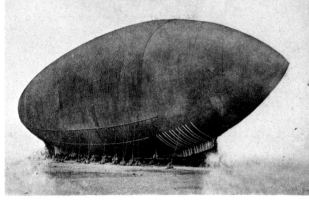

**1 1904: Thomas S. Baldwin's 'California Arrow'**

During the International Exhibition of 1904, the city of St Louis, Missouri, put on the first international competition for flying machines. Roy Knabenshue piloted the *California Arrow*, almost completing a round flight.

**2 1907: Wellman's airship 'America'**

*America* was built in Paris for an expedition to the North Pole. 193 feet long and with a maximum diameter of 52½ feet, its envelope was made from rubberized cotton and silk and, in its original form, had a volume of 275,450 cubic feet.

**3** The twin-bladed airscrews seen below were driven in pairs by two V-engines each developing 80-90 h.p.

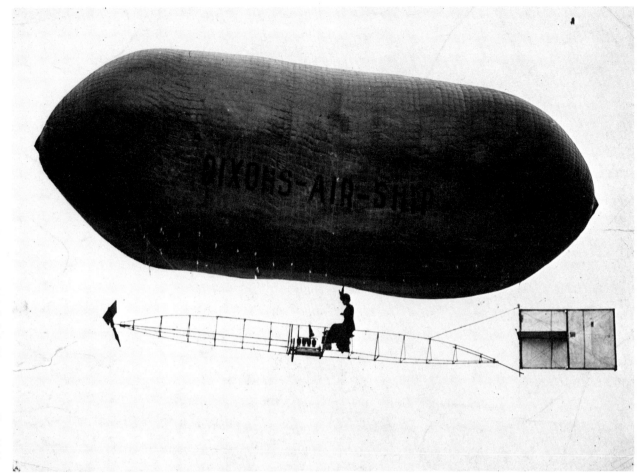

### Circa 1909: Mrs Dixon aboard Cromwell Dixon's Airship

Cromwell Dixon from Seattle, Washington, was the youngest ever American aviator, being only fourteen when he produced this small airship *Moon* in 1907. 24½ feet long, its airscrew was driven by pedals. Later, he fitted an engine on a reinforced beam. To thank his mother for having sewn together the envelope he sent her off for a flight, and this photograph commemorates the event.

### 1907: An American dirigible race

In September 1907, the city of St Louis, Missouri, organized a national race. Entries were mainly small airships of rather improvised design and some were downright dangerous, as witness the one which burst into flames and crashed into the ground.

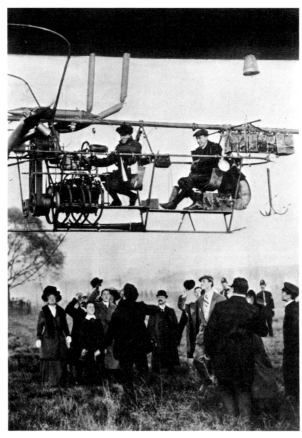

### 1910: 'City of Cardiff', No. 3 by Willows

Out of his own pocket, E.T. Willows, an Englishman, built a series of small airships. His third, *City of Cardiff*, flew from Cardiff to London in nine hours on 9 August 1910. On 4 November he left London at 15.30 hrs, landing at Douai in France at 02.00 hrs, then carrying on to Paris. Opposite, to the left, Willows and his mechanic Veden Kanig Goodens seen in the nacelle and, on the far left, *City of Cardiff* arriving in Paris.

### 1910: The Astra airship 'Colonel Renard'

The Astra dirigible, below, is shown lifting off at Issy-les-Moulineaux where the airship company had a large hangar. The biplane elevators can be seen and the picture shows the airship just after the crew had dropped ballast.

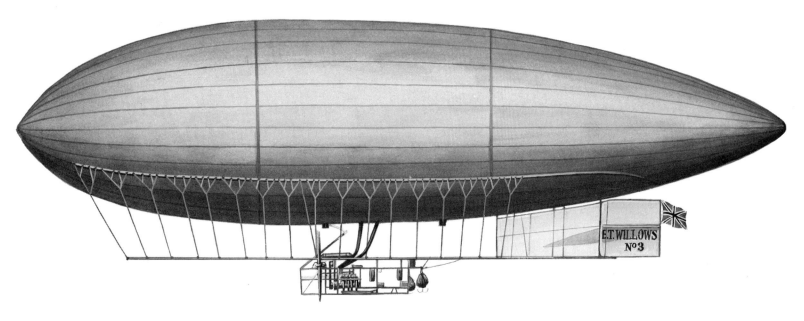

### 1910: Willows' third airship, 'City of Cardiff'

About 120 feet long, with a girth of 40 feet and a volume of 42,400 cubic feet, *City of Cardiff* was powered by a four-cylinder JAP engine of 35 h.p. with a belt-drive for two in-line airscrews. At the stern, a large fin was mounted in front of the rudder. In 1910, E.T. Willows and his mechanic Veden Kanig Goodens crewed the first British airship to cross the English Channel, flying from Cardiff to Paris after landing in London and Douai.

### 1908: Zodiac II

The Zodiac company, which was founded in 1908 to carry on and develop the workshops opened some ten years earlier by that famous aeronaut Maurice Mallet, used his plans to produce a dirigible for *Le Petit Journal*. 98½ feet long with a maximum diameter of 23 feet and a volume of 24,750 cubic feet, its asymmetric rocket-shaped envelope prominently displayed the paper's name, thus initiating the vogue for aerial publicity. It was powered by a 16-horsepower engine built by Pierre Clerget who, together with Count Henri de La Vaulx, was its diligent and indefatigable pilot. The well designed two-seater nacelle was made of pine in the form of a rectangular section reinforced beam with an elevator in the nose and, at the stern, a pusher airscrew, 7½ feet in diameter, driven through a reduction gear. A tail plane and a rudder were placed under the stern of the envelope. Often filled with coal-gas, Zodiac II was easily assembled and dismantled and could be carried in an ordinary trailer. It was, in fact, the prototype of the sporting 'autoballoons'. During the following year, Zodiac III was built, equipped with a 45 h.p. engine and, in 1912, another Zodiac model was produced and named *Le Temps*, after the newspaper whose nation-wide campaign had raised the necessary funds. Fitted with a 60 h.p. engine, it was used for training military airship crews.

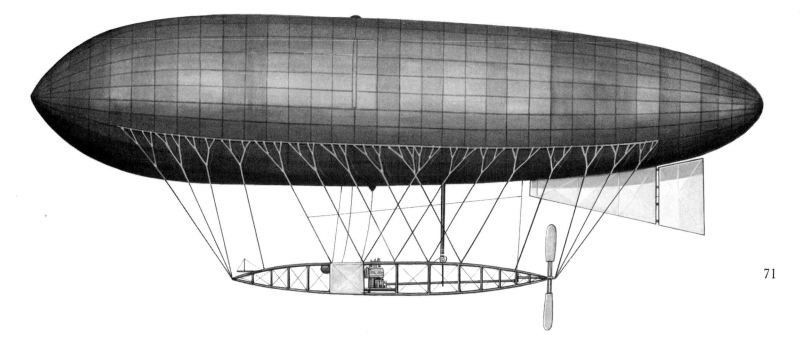

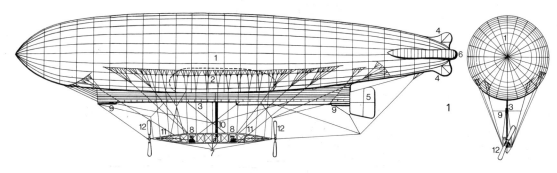

## Construction: 'Belgique'

1. Envelope
2. Ballonet
3. Keel
4. Tail-fin
5. Rudder
6. Horizontal stabilizing cylinder
7. Nacelle
8. Engines
9. Altitude vane/elevator
10. Pump with gas conduit
11. Transmission shafts
12. Airscrews

### 1 1910: 'La Belgique' by Louis Godard

Built in France in 1909 by the Louis Godard aircraft workshops, this airship made its maiden flight near Brussels on 28 June. In the following year, its original volume of 95,350 cubic feet was increased to about 141,000 cubic feet, its length then being 207 feet and its diameter at the largest circumference 36 feet. Its rocket-shaped metal nacelle, 74 feet in length and accommodating four persons, was originally equipped with two Belgian Vivinus 60 h.p. engines each driving its own airscrew at either end of the nacelle. These were replaced in 1910 by a single 120-horsepower Germain engine driving *La Belgique* at a speed of approximately 25 m.p.h.

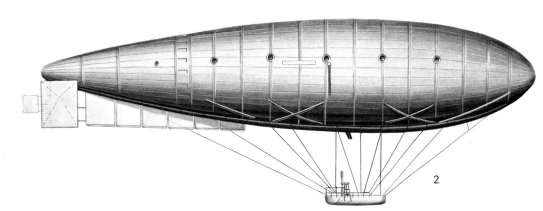

### 2 1909: The Italian dirigible 1 A

Captain Crocco and Captain Ricaldoni of the Italian Army initiated production of this dirigible displaying several original features. The fish-shaped envelope, which had a volume of 130,700 cubic feet, a length of 230 feet and a diameter of 36 feet, was divided into seven airtight compartments. In some respects, the 1 A resembled a rigid dirigible athwartships and a non-rigid, longitudinally. The keel could be dismantled, being made of seven fabric-covered steel tubular frames extending over the stern half of the hull, ensuring longitudinal stability. A 26-foot long, 5-seater nacelle was shaped rather like a motor-boat and a 120 h.p. Clément-Bayard engine drove two elevated airscrews, 8 feet in diameter, on either side of the nacelle. This Italian airship, with its high speed of 33 m.p.h. made its first flight on July 1909.

### 3 1910: Gross-Basenach M 1

This up-dated version of the Gross-Basenach unit produced the previous year was a semi-rigid airship having a triangular reinforced beam fixed to the envelope. This beam was equipped with an elevator at the nose and a tail fin in front of a rudder at the stern. It also carried two aluminium three-bladed airscrews, driven by belts and pulleys, at either side and above the nacelle. The envelope was 243 feet long with a diameter of 39 feet and a volume of 212,000 cubic feet, incorporating two gas-bags, one in the nose and one in the stern, like the Parseval units. Powered by two 75-horsepower Koerting engines, the Gross-Basenach M 1 had a cruising speed of 28 m.p.h.

These sectional and plan drawings show the reinforced beam running half the length of the envelope and, at its centre point, the two stayed brackets for the airscrews. At the nose are the two symmetrically positioned elevators and, at the stern, the rudder unit described above. Two semi-elliptical stabilizing vanes were also fitted towards the stern of the hull.

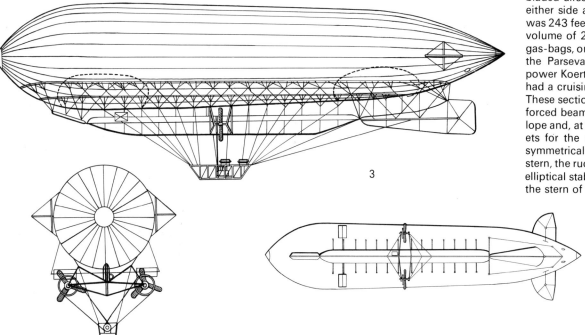

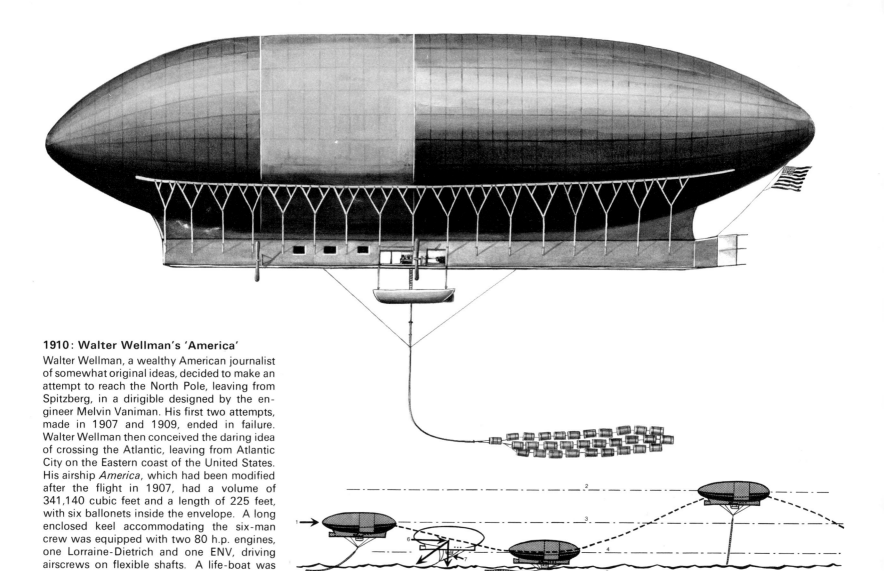

## 1910: Walter Wellman's 'America'

Walter Wellman, a wealthy American journalist of somewhat original ideas, decided to make an attempt to reach the North Pole, leaving from Spitzberg, in a dirigible designed by the engineer Melvin Vaniman. His first two attempts, made in 1907 and 1909, ended in failure. Walter Wellman then conceived the daring idea of crossing the Atlantic, leaving from Atlantic City on the Eastern coast of the United States. His airship *America*, which had been modified after the flight in 1907, had a volume of 341,140 cubic feet and a length of 225 feet, with six ballonets inside the envelope. A long enclosed keel accommodating the six-man crew was equipped with two 80 h.p. engines, one Lorraine-Dietrich and one ENV, driving airscrews on flexible shafts. A life-boat was slung under this keel, as was a buoyant, jointed balancing device consisting of a 295-foot long steel cable carrying several cylindrical tanks filled with a reserve supply of gasoline and, at its lower end, forty blocks of wood. This elaborate arrangement was intended to maintain as constant an altitude as possible. On 15 October 1910, *America* lifted off from Atlantic City, heading first to the East, then drifting South-East, remaining airborne for as long as 64 hours before coming down in the ocean. Thanks to the life-boat providently carried aboard, the crew were saved and picked up by the steamer *Trent* on 18 October.

### Fittings on 'America'

1. Closed-in nacelle
2. Life-boat with instruments, radio and provisions
3. Helm and compass
4. Engines
5. Airscrews with swivelling axes
6. Envelope
7. Non-inflammable fabric skin
8. Hatches
9. Main petrol tank
10. Suspension struts
11. Stabilizer

### Forces acting on the stabilizer fitted to 'America'

1. Wind speed of 35 knots
2. Maximum ceiling
3. Mean height of free lift
4. Minimum height of free lift
5. Sea level
6. Wind pressure
7. Resultant downward thrust

### Route followed by 'America' (15 to 18 October 1910)

1. 18.00 h. Saturday
2. 08.00 h. Sunday
3. 16.00 h. Sunday
4. 21.00 h. Sunday
5. 03.00 h. Monday
6. 12.00 h. Monday
7. Point where rescued 08.00 h. Tuesday

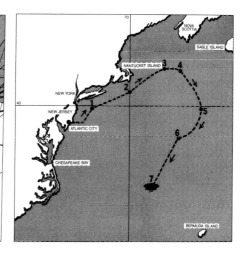

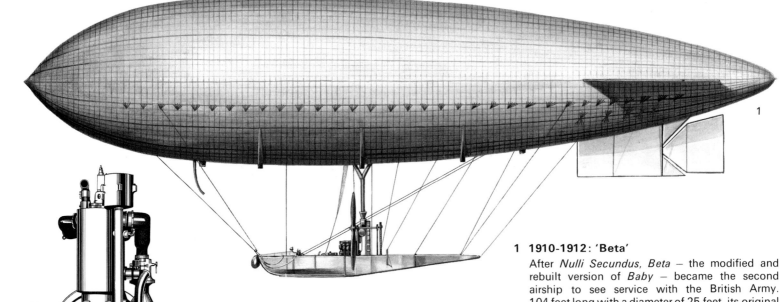

1

**1910-1912: The Green engine fitted to 'Beta'**
Developing 35 h.p., this was a four-cylinder in-line water-cooled engine weighing 158½ lbs. The cylinders were cast steel and the water-jacket made from copper. The ignition system included a high voltage magneto which can be seen clearly in this drawing. A camshaft drove overhead valves, the crankshaft was made from nickel-chrome steel running in white metal bearings and the engine was lubricated by oil under pressure.

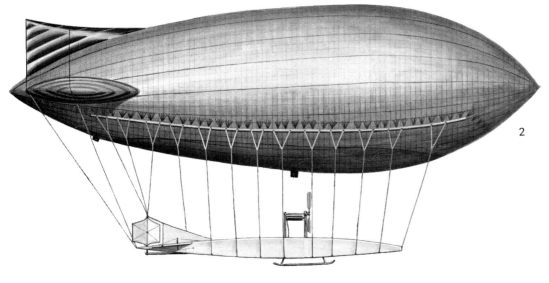

2

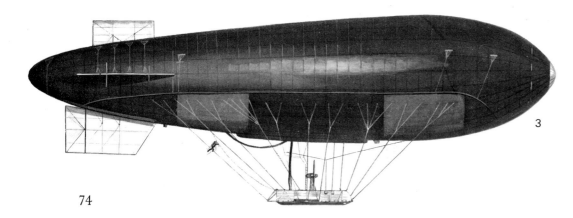

3

## 1 1910-1912: 'Beta'

After *Nulli Secundus, Beta* — the modified and rebuilt version of *Baby* — became the second airship to see service with the British Army. 104 feet long with a diameter of 25 feet, its original volume of 36,400 cubic feet was increased to 49,500 cubic feet in 1912. *Beta* was first powered by a radial 45-horsepower Clerget engine then by a 35-horsepower Green engine. Two airscrews were fitted above the centre point of the nacelle-keel which resembled an aircraft fuselage. From the first flight on 26 May 1910, 311 ascensions were made until its long career ended when it was taken out of service and scrapped in May 1916. With a maximum speed of 28 m.p.h., *Beta* goes down in history as the first dirigible ever moored to a mast erected on land, in February 1912.

## 2 1909: An airship nicknamed 'Baby'

This small British test dirigible first took to the air on 11 May 1909. It had a volume of only 24,000 cubic feet, a length of 84 feet and its largest diameter was 23½ feet. A tail unit, cruciform in shape when inflated, was attached to the stern of the envelope made from gold-beaters' skin. A system of bolt ropes from goose-feet on the envelope supported the nacelle which was fitted with two landing skids at the centre and at the stern, where rudder and elevator controls were also placed. *Baby* was powered by an 8-horsepower three-cylinder Buchet engine, driving the airscrew mounted above it by a belt and pulley. The official name of this small airship was *Beta* by which it became known after modifications in 1910.

## 3 1912: 'Delta'

The construction of the British airship *Delta* was started in 1910. Its first envelope was made from proofed silk, resistant to water but not to pressure so a rubberized fabric was used for the next envelope fitted in August 1912, the volume being 173,000 cubic feet. Rigged in a similar way to the modified *Beta*, this airship was also fitted with a tail unit having a tail plane and a fin underneath to which the rudder was attached. An upper fin was added later. A very short nacelle with a small closed cabin carried elevators and was equipped with two 50-horsepower Green engines driving two airscrews raised above its centre, giving *Delta* a speed of about 45 m.p.h. Provided with wireless equipment, *Delta* successfully cooperated with the Army on manoeuvres in 1912 and, at the beginning of the 1914-1918 war, was used on patrol over the English Channel.

The small British airship nicknamed *Baby*.

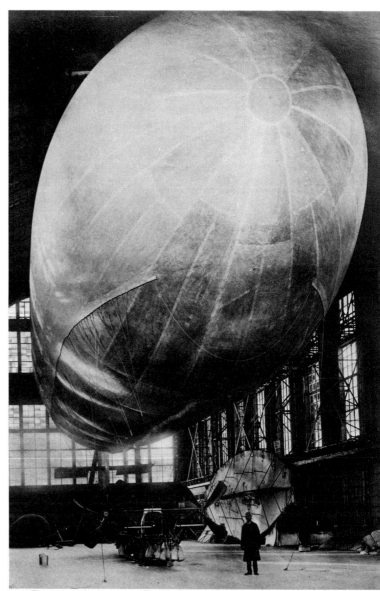

(Right.) The first airship ever constructed in Russia, *Dux*, in its hangar. 131 feet long, it had a volume of 98,900 cubic feet.

(Below.) *Beta* made its maiden flight on 3 June 1910, covering the distance between Farnborough and London in 4 hours 4 minutes. During its long career, it made numerous patrols over the Thames estuary and took part in reconnaissance flights over Dunkirk before being taken out of service and scrapped in May 1916.

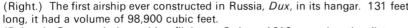

### 1908: The Clément-Bayard No. I

This airship was built in 1908 by the Astra company for export to Russia. 185 feet long, its largest diameter was 35 feet and its volume 123,600 cubic feet. It was driven at just over 30 m.p.h. by a 100-horsepower engine. On the extreme left of this page can be seen the cockpit with the steering wheel on the left-hand side and, on the right, the elevator control wheel as well as the instruments. The Clément-Bayard I is seen lifting off, to the left, by dropping ballast. During its final trials it crashed and was never rebuilt.

### 1912: The Clément-Bayard III

This dirigible was a flying cruiser built in 1912 with a length of 289 feet and a volume of 317,850 cubic feet, its largest diameter being 44 feet. The Clément-Bayard III was powered by two 125-horsepower engines.

### 1912: The Clément-Bayard airship 'Dupuy-de-Lôme' ▷

This airship of 346,000 cubic feet was built for the Army in 1912, and here it is seen in perspective from the top of its hangar. This picture shows one of its most interesting features: the large quadriplane stabilizing tail unit with rudders attached to each end. On 20 August 1914, *Dupuy-de-Lôme* carried out a bombing raid in Belgium, attacking German troops under canvas. Only four days later, it was shot down by French troops who mistook it for a German Zeppelin.

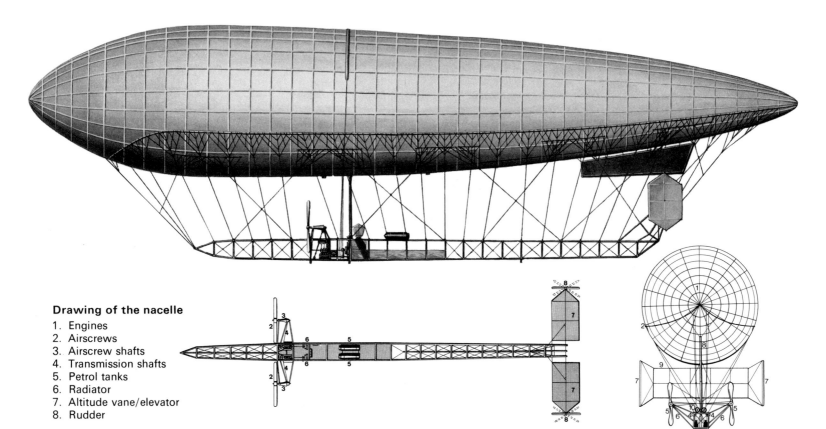

### Drawing of the nacelle

1. Engines
2. Airscrews
3. Airscrew shafts
4. Transmission shafts
5. Petrol tanks
6. Radiator
7. Altitude vane/elevator
8. Rudder

### Rear view

1. Envelope
2. Bolt-rope
3. Nacelle
4. Engines
5. Airscrews
6. Transmission shafts
7. Rudder
8. Tail-fin
9. Altitude vane/elevator
10. Petrol tanks

### 1910: The Clément-Bayard II

After building automobiles and, later, aeroplanes, Adolphe Clément-Bayard turned his attention to airships in 1908 and produced a number of different types until the outbreak of the First World War. Designed by the engineer Lucien Sabathier, the Clément-Bayard which took part in the French Army manoeuvres in Picardy in 1910 had a volume of 229,500 cubic feet, a length of 54 feet and a diameter of 43 feet. Its long metal nacelle was fitted out with two of the manufacturer's own 125 h.p. engines. With the help of the *Daily Mail*, a British committee bought the Clément-Bayard airship and presented it to their Government. Flown over to its new base at Wormwood Scrubs near London, with Adolphe Clément-Bayard aboard, on 16 October 1910, it made the first ever airship crossing from the Continent of Europe to the British Isles.

This rear view shows the position of the two large twin-bladed wooden airscrews driven by shafts fitted with bevel-gears from the two engines on the floor of the nacelle, on the top of which are the pumps for the gas-bags. For the fore-and-aft control, a long biplane structure was placed at the centre of the nacelle and an outsize tail unit for steering comprised three fixed tail planes, four fixed vertical fins and two ailerons. All these were mounted on the stern of the nacelle which was upturned, like a scorpion's tail, in order to avoid slipstream turbulence and so make for greater efficiency.

This plan of the steel tubular latticework nacelle shows, from front to rear, the position of the two airscrews on their triangular mountings, the cockpit, the two engines in the section covered with fabric, and the very large tail unit described above.

### 1911: The R1 by Maxim and Vickers & Sons

Vickers, the well-known arms manufacturer, and Maxim worked in the closest secrecy for three years building this airship. 510 feet long, 48 feet in diameter with a volume of 706,300 cubic feet, it was constructed along similar lines to the German Zeppelins. Each of the two nacelles was fitted with twin Wolseley engines developing 200 h.p., the forward nacelle having two four-bladed airscrews and the rear nacelle one two-bladed airscrew.

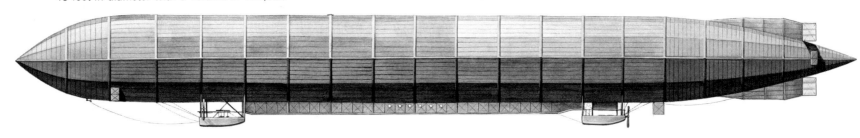

Dramatic end to the LZ10, *Schwaben*, at Düsseldorf on 18 June 1912.
(Right.) Rear view of the LZ4 which was destroyed by fire on 20 June 1908, after a brief career of only forty-six days.

(Below.) The LZ11, *Viktoria Luise*, flying over sailing boats taking part in a regatta at Kiel in 1912. Employed on pleasure cruises throughout Germany, this Zeppelin carried no fewer than 22,039 persons during 1,292 flying hours in the course of its career.

During manoeuvres with the German army in the autumn of 1909, two airships simulated an attack on a fortified position near Coblenz. This photograph, taken during the manoeuvres, shows a Zeppelin in the hangar, a Gross-Basenach in front of it and, in the air, a Parseval. At the end of November, the Gross-Basenach and Parseval left Cologne for Metz, then still on German territory.

(Left) Although only the nacelle and two aviators are visible, this is a Parseval being pulled on to the tarmac for take-off. The limp blades of the airscrew are a distinguishing feature of this type of airship.

## 1912: The Parseval PL VII

Before the outbreak of the First World War, the German constructor August von Parseval received many orders for airships from foreign governments, namely Austria, Russia, Japan and Great Britain. Ironically enough, one of his dirigibles, designated *HM Airship 4*, was even employed by the Admiralty against Germany during the 1914-1918 war. The Parseval PL VII was delivered to Imperial Russia and was 230 feet long, 40 feet in diameter with a volume of 236,600 cubic feet. The PL VII was powered by two 110-horsepower engines, each driving a pair of airscrews on either side and above the short, rocket-shaped nacelle. A tail plane was fitted across the longitudinal axis of the envelope near the stern pointed end of the hull and, below it, a large rudder was also placed. In the nose of the nacelle, just in front of the supply ducts for the gas-bags, a covered ladder provided access to a small longitudinal keel fixed to the belly of the envelope. This feature would appear to mark the transition to the semi-rigid formula later adopted by this constructor.

## 1912: The Schütte-Lanz SL1

Like the Zeppelins, the dirigibles produced by Schütte-Lanz were of the rigid type but in other respects they had little in common. The Schütte-Lanz skeleton was made up of a spiral wood framework glued together, its form was more aerodynamic and the position of its keel made it an integral part of the envelope. The SL1 was 688,650 cubic feet in volume, 430 feet long and 60 feet in diameter a third of its length from the nose. The envelope contained eleven gas-bags, each filled with about 70,600 cubic feet of hydrogen and interconnected so that their pressures could be equalized. The two steel tubular engine nacelles were attached by flexible mountings, each being fitted with a 270-horsepower Daimler engine driving a three-bladed pusher airscrew.

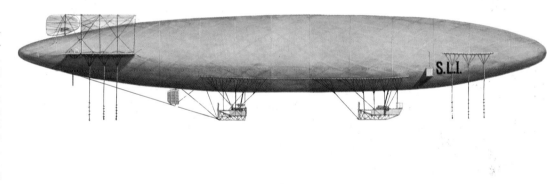

## 1912: The Astra 'Adjutant Réau'

On 13 January 1912, the French Army took delivery of this airship. Its pisciform envelope was 285 feet long, had a volume of 316,000 cubic feet and a maximum diameter of 53 feet. The stern carried the tail unit, a group of fixed fabric-covered planes. It was powered by two Brasier engines developing a total of 240 h.p. driving three airscrews through a reduction gear and clutch transmission system.

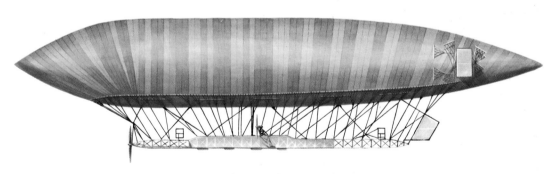

## 1912: The Astra-Torres I

A characteristic feature of this airship was its supple catenarian framework inside the hull. The envelope had a volume of 56,150 cubic feet, a length of 155 feet while the nacelle, underneath, measured only 18 feet. A 55-horsepower Chenu engine drove a 15-foot traction airscrew by means of a reduction gear.

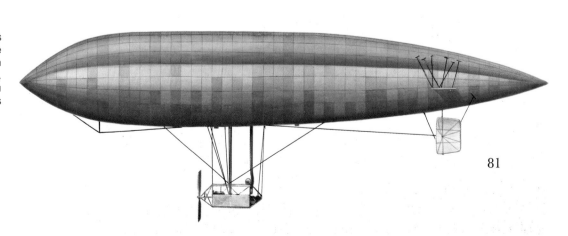

81

## 1913: The Clément-Bayard 'Adjutant Vincenot'

The military authorities took delivery of this airship during the first months of 1911. In July 1913, following prolonged trials, considerable modifications were carried out to the tail unit on the envelope and to the braced steel tubular nacelle, its original length of 180 feet being reduced to 85 feet. The dimensions of the envelope, being 289 feet in length with a maximum diameter of 44 feet and a volume of 353,150 cubic feet, remained unchanged. Two four-cylinder Clément-Bayard engines of 120 h.p. each drove a 20-foot diameter airscrew, giving the airship a speed of about 33 m.p.h. In its final form, the envelope was fitted with a vertical fin behind which was the rudder, two horizontal triplane tail units and four elevators.

In 1911, *Adjutant Vincenot* broke the existing world distance and flight duration records by covering just over 406 miles in 16 hours 15 minutes. Between 27 and 28 June 1914, it beat the Zeppelin record by twenty minutes, flying for 35 hours 19 minutes without landing. After taking part in many reconnaissance and bombing missions, it was shot down on 1 June 1916.

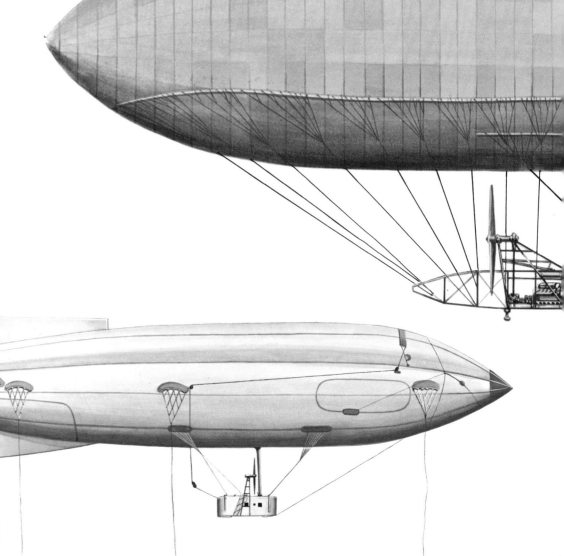

## 1913: Astra Torres XIV

As its name implies, this was the fourteenth airship built by the Astra company. Delivered to the British Admiralty in September 1913, it was officially designated H.M.A.3 and was used extensively on long-range coastal patrols during the First World War. H.M.A.3 was 253 feet long, the diameter of the lobes was 30 feet and its volume was 307,240 cubic feet. Two Chenu 200-horsepower engines enabled the airship to attain a speed of nearly 52 m.p.h. at Farnborough in December 1913, making it the fastest dirigible in the world at this time. During flight, the six-man crew could move the nacelle towards the nose or stern, thus giving the envelope a positive or negative position. At the stern, the envelope was fitted with two long fins, one above and one below, carrying two fixed horizontal symmetric planes and one rudder. So that the airship could be more easily handled on the ground, cables were attached to a semi-circle of short bolt ropes fixed to a set of six goose-feet.

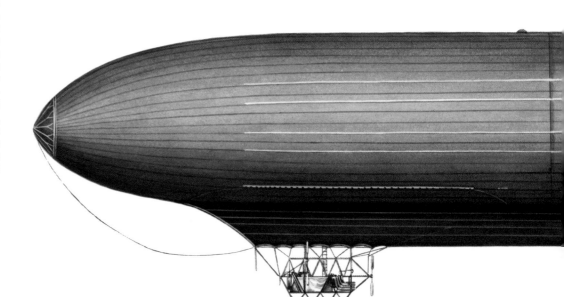

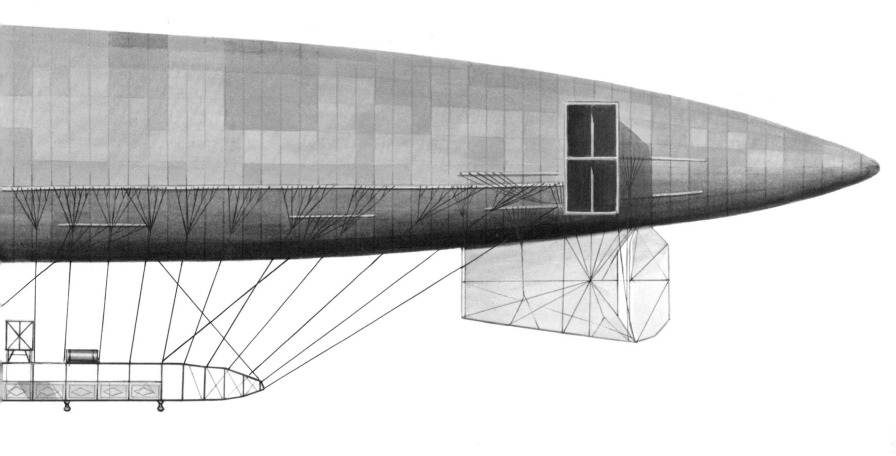

## 1911 : Siemens-Schuckert

Built for one of the branches of the German Siemens electrical complex, this aircraft was an experimental model designed for military purposes. The envelope was in the shape of a long cylinder with a blunt point for a nose and a finely tapering tail. It was 387 feet long with a maximum diameter of 43 feet, a ratio of 1:9. The envelope of 476,750 cubic feet was divided into four parts; the two largest carrying the engine nacelles. At the lower part of the hull, a tapered trapezoidal keel was the means of support for the three nacelles. The two engine nacelles, in front of and behind the central nacelle for crew and passengers, were attached to this keel by a reinforced beam, designed to distribute their weight over a greater length. Under the stern point were a horizontal stabilizing vane and two vertical vanes for steering. The envelope was also fitted with two symmetrical tail planes. This dirigible was powered by a group of four Daimler engines, each of 120 h.p., driving six airscrews positioned to the right, the left and the rear of each of the engine nacelles, and could achieve a speed approaching 45 m.p.h. The central nacelle was also fitted with two Guggenau engines of about 24 h.p. to drive the pumps for the three gas-bags inside. The Siemens-Schuckert took off on its first flight on 23 January 1911 and was bought by the German Government at the beginning of 1912. However, this type was never put into series production as Siemens began concentrating on the manufacture of combat aircraft during the war years of 1914-1918.

▽

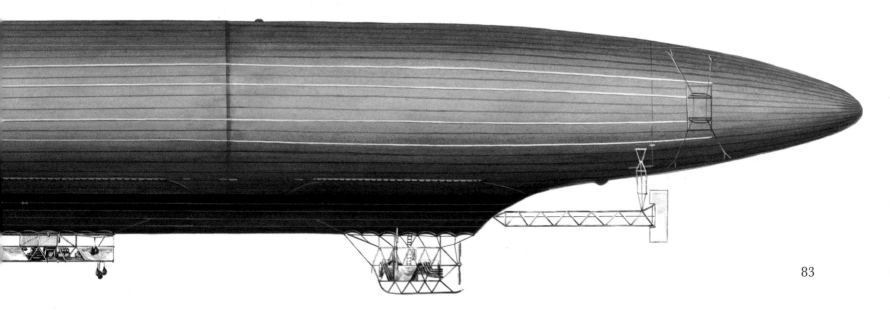

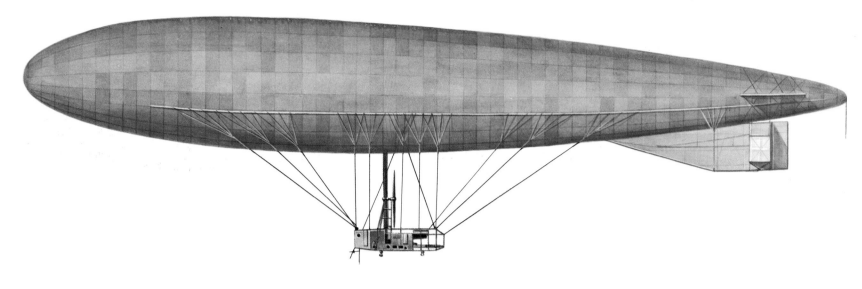

## 1912: 'Fleurus' by Chalais-Meudon

Named after a battle in which the first balloonists won renown, this dirigible was both designed and produced by the Ordnance factory at Chalais-Meudon where, some thirty years before, the famous airship *La France* had been built. *Fleurus* was 253 feet long, 40 feet in diameter at its maximum girth and had a volume of 230,000 cubic feet. It was the first French dirigible to have an envelope divided into compartments for safety reasons. A metal nacelle was slung very low under the belly and was fitted with two Clément-Bayard engines of 80 h.p. each, driving two airscrews each side, which were raised up on the ends of metal athwartships struts. Control surfaces at the stern of the envelope comprised a tail plane and, below, a vertical triangular fin to which the elevator unit was attached, the rudder being fixed on the rear extension of this fin. The first flight tests were held on 23 November 1912. In August, two years later, *Fleurus* became the first Allied airship to make a reconnaissance over enemy territory, leaving from Verdun and pushing through to Trier.

## 1912: E. T. Willows

Like the previous Willows model of 1911, this airship was built for the Royal Navy. 120 feet long, with a diameter of 40 feet, its volume was 31,800 cubic feet. The envelope was fitted with a gas-bag and had two stabilizing vanes towards the stern, one being vertical and composed of four covered parts and another horizontal vane in front of the elevator. Over the very tapering two-seater nacelle was a long pole connecting it to the hull and fitted with a suspension bolt-rope. Halfway along this pole, a 35 h.p. engine drove two lateral airscrews with swivelling shafts to help ascending or descending vertical movements. At the stern end of the pole a rudder was attached.

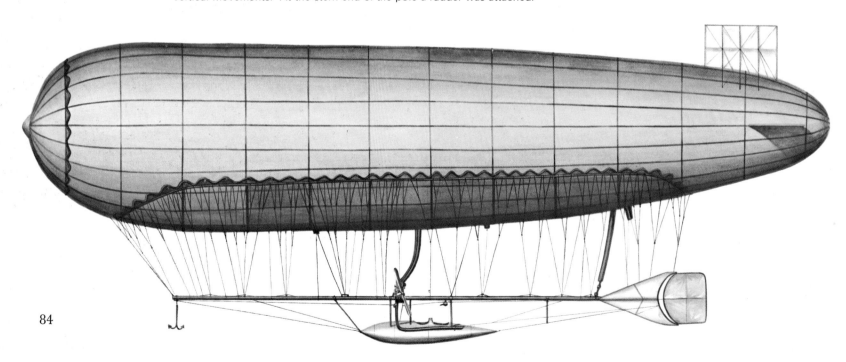

## 1913: 'Spiess'

This was the only rigid airship produced in France, and was built by the Zodiac company. The design was based on a patent registered by an engineer named Joseph Spiess in 1873, more than twenty years before the first Zeppelin patent. One noteworthy specification contained in the patent was: 'A set of balloons joined together and interconnected at their largest circumference inside a shell with which they form a single, fully integrated unit. With this system, the aircraft and the nacelle form one rigid unit, to which engines and propellers can easily be fitted.'

*Spiess* was not built until 1911 and was then presented to the French Government. It had a framework of hollow wooden beams, square in section, bound over their entire length by two bands of stout canvas. The skeleton also included a number of polygonal cross-beams with fourteen surfaces. A keel, triangular in section, acting as a reinforcing beam, was an integral part of the lower section of the hull. This beam contributed to longitudinal rigidity and distributed the load over the entire structure. The two engine nacelles were fixed to the keel and a light flooring in the keel allowed passage between them. The power units consisted of two 175-horsepower Chenu engines, driving two 13-foot airscrews placed on either side of the hull, their shafts supported by the struts built into the hull. The stern was fitted with a fixed horizontal plane, four twin-mounted vertical rudders and two twin biplane elevators. In 1913, in order to increase its lift, the dimensions were changed to give *Spiess* a length of 460 feet, a diameter of 43 feet and a volume of 579,161 cubic feet, divided up between seventeen gas bags. The first flight made after these modifications had been completed was from the aerodrome at Saint-Cyr on 30 April 1913. Although valid in design, the *Spiess* had no successors. The photograph, right, taken during assembly, shows the envelope's structure with its triangular keel.

The nacelle on *Montgolfier*, the Clément-Bayard VI scouting airship built in 1913. Made of 33-foot steel tubes, the short nacelle was fitted at each end with a kind of hollow aluminium bowsprit, firmly fastening it to the envelope. The nacelle was also equipped with two engines in tandem, each of 90 h.p., driving two airscrews at the sides and one for lift, all with adjustable pitch. Underneath the nacelle, four pneumatic legs were provided to absorb landing shocks.

Below: Astra's *Ville de Bruxelles* flying over the aerodrome at Issy-les-Moulineaux in 1910. The cruciform tail unit inflated with hydrogen is quite clearly visible. In the foreground, an Astra-Wright military biplane has two pusher airscrews driven by chains.

Opposite, right: *Colonel Renard*, another Astra dirigible is seen being pushed into its hangar at Issy-les-Moulineaux in July 1910, handled by balloon ground crew. Over the nacelle are the two biplane elevators and, at the stern end, the double rudder. The airscrew was 20 feet in diameter.

# AIRSHIPS AT WAR

## 1914-1918

At the outbreak of the First World War on 1 August 1914, Germany was better equipped with airships than either Britain, France or Russia. Her Army had nine Zeppelins, three of which were requisitioned from the airline DELAG. Their force also included one Schütte-Lanz, one Gross-Basenach and a small training ship built by Parseval. The German Navy, on the other hand, having lost both their first two units in 1913, was reduced to the Zeppelin L3 which had been commissioned in May 1914. Army airships which had been in service before the war bore the initial 'Z'; those commissioned after were coded 'LZ', 'L' meaning *Luftschiff*. Naval airships were designated by the initial 'L'.

The French Army had seven airships ready for service, three of these having been built by Clément-Bayard, two by Astra and two by the Zodiac company. It was only in 1916 that the French Navy were equipped with their own airships.

In Britain, all airships had been placed under the command of the Admiralty on 1 January 1914. On the following 1 August, out of a total of seven only four were fit for service, namely one Astra-Torres, one Parseval built under licence by the Vickers company, the old 1910 vintage *Beta* and its younger sister-ship the *Delta*.

Briefly mentioning Russia for the record, it is by no means certain that the three airships delivered before the war were still serviceable or even in existence by August 1914. The Imperial Government had received one Lebaudy and an Astra from France, and one Parseval from Germany.

Over the whole period of hostilities, the German Army had a total of thirty-four dirigibles operational on the Eastern and Western Fronts and in the South-Eastern battle areas. The German Navy had no fewer than seventy-eight in operation, a number of these having been abandoned by the Army for logistic use over the Western Front early in 1917, following severe losses caused by enemy action. This powerful fleet comprised sixty-five Zeppelins, nine Schütte-Lanz, three Parsevals and one Gross-Basenach. Of these seventy-eight units, six were used as training ships or on special missions.

In 1915, the French Army Command received five Zodiac 'cruisers' and two Astra-Torres but, in 1917, two of these units were handed over to the

**1914: The Clément-Bayard 'Mongolfier'**
The nacelle of this scout airship shows the two pusher airscrews mounted on struts, as well as the airscrew for vertical lift in the centre of its metal framework. In the foreground a part of the elevator can be seen. This photograph was taken in April 1914 while one of the transmission systems was being checked over.

Navy for the same reasons as prompted the German Army to relinquish several of theirs. By July 1918, the French Navy had a fleet of thirty-seven airships of various cubic capacities, ten being held in reserve. As for Britain, by the time the Armistice was signed, even after several had been taken out of service and some handed over to allied governments, the airship fleet had been augmented to the impressive total of 103 operational units.

It is beyond the scope of this book to describe in detail the widely differing battles fought by these lighter-than-air mastodons. Many of their crews were lost in action, shot down by enemy gunfire, in aerial combat or by anti-aircraft fire from the ground while other losses were incurred by meteorological conditions. History is an inexhaustible well of information on their exploits. This brief story concentrates on the battle rôles played by airships on both sides, whether in service with the armies or navies. The best example was the offensive against England carried out by units of the *Marineluftschiff Abteilung*, the MLSA or the Naval Airship Division.

## AIRSHIPS OPERATING OVER LAND FRONTS

From the opening of hostilities, both allied and enemy High Commands took the obvious step of putting light airships to use for the observation of enemy troop movements, artillery spotting, or strategical reconnaissance. They were also employed as offensive aerial patrols, carrying out some bombing attacks. A French dirigible was the first allied airship to cross the lines and penetrate German territory: on the night of 9 August 1914, *Fleurus* reconnoitred the enemy lines in the Sarre sector and pushed through to Trier.

Right from the outset, the Germans sent the Z6, Z7 and Z8 into action, rashly carrying out daylight raids. The Z6 was responsible for the first bombing attack of the war on the main square in Liège. Attacked by anti-aircraft fire, she was badly damaged on her return to base. The Z7 suffered the same plight after a reconnaissance flight to observe French troop movements in Alsace. On a similar mission, the Z8 was shot down by the French artillery. So began a bitter and cruel aerial war with all its losses of material and, soon, of human lives. Often accidentally attacked by their own side, airship crews could no longer venture out in daylight but crept forth after the sun had set, under cover of darkness. A classic victim of such mistaken identity was *Conté* which was attacked on sight by the French ground troops on 9 August 1914 near Lunéville and arrived back at base, its envelope riddled by hundreds of bullet holes. Thus it was during the night of 12 March 1915 that the 'Fortress of Paris' (sic) was bombed for the first time by the German LZ35 and the Z10. Paris was again raided on 29 January 1916 by the LZ79 which was irreparably damaged on its return.

Very soon afterwards, the allied air forces assumed the offensive and 7 June 1915 was a black day for the German air forces. Sub-Lieutenant Edgar John Warneford of the Royal Naval Air Service, flying a French Morane-Saulnier monoplane, bombed the LZ37 in the air, sending it down in flames near Ghent in Belgium. On the same day, two of his fellow officers, Lieutenant J.P. Wilson and Lieutenant J.S. Mills, both of the R.N.A.S. and flying Farman 'H' biplanes destroyed the LZ35 in its hangar.

The German High Command responded with the order *'Gott strafe England'* and the British Isles became the regular and unremitting objective for German airship attacks. Yarmouth, on the East Coast, had already received the sinister New Year's gift of the first Zeppelin attack in January 1915. Although family reasons had restrained Kaiser Wilhelm II, who was the grandson of Queen Victoria, from authorizing the bombing of London, the insistence of his High Command finally overcame his reluctance. So it was that on May 1915 a German Army Zeppelin, the LZ38, launched this large-scale aerial bombardment in an attempt to bring the British capital to its knees. Despite heavy losses, the bombing attacks were relentlessly pressed by airships of the MLSA which finally took over this task from the Army Airship Corps, which was disbanded on 1 August 1917.

Losses among the crews of airships servicing the French land forces were relatively low. The famous Clément-Bayard, *Adjutant Vincenot*, commanded by Capitaine Joux and Capitaine Paquignon actually made thirty-one sorties until put out of action on 1 June 1916. However, the total loss of the Astra *Pilatre de Rozier*, shot down in flames over Alsace with its nine-man crew on 25 February 1917, signalled the end of the airships' career with the French Army. Remaining units were handed over to the French Navy.

On the Eastern fronts, such as Russia and the Balkans, the hazards to German Army airships were less severe. Anti-aircraft defences were not so dense and enemy fighter aircraft less aggressive. There was thus little risk in initially employing Zeppelins and Schütte-Lanz airships, technically already out of date and with a ceiling of only just over 8,000 feet, even for daylight missions. From bases set up at Seerappen near Königsberg, at Weinaden in Kurland, Kowno in Lithuania, Pasen in Poland, Temesvar in Hungary and Jamboli in Bulgaria, these airships were sent out on regular patrols over the Baltic as well as on strategic bombing raids over Warsaw, Sebastopol, Odessa, Bucharest, as well as the oil-fields and refineries of Ploesti in Rumania. Although the Russo-German peace treaty of Brest-Litovsk on 15 December 1917 put an end to these operations on the Eastern front, hostile patrols continued over the Balkan fronts. Particularly, reconnaissance and scout patrols were mounted, and airships, acted as the eyes of the German Fleet in the Black Sea, spotting coal and oil ship convoys heading for Bulgaria and Turkey. These dirigibles also attacked Italian targets on the Adriatic Sea coast. Operating so far away from bases where they could be serviced and repaired, airships on such patrols were taken out of service on more than one occasion as a result of irreparable mechanical breakdowns or damage from emergency landings.

One of these, the LZ85, after four successive air attacks on an entrenched camp in Salonika, had to make a forced landing on 5 May 1916 in the Vardar Marshes, where its crew set fire to it. By contrast, an outstandingly successful mission was accomplished in the Balkan sector by a 'supertitan' Zeppelin of 2,418,000 cubic feet, the L59 lent by the Navy. Captained by Kapitän-Leutnant Bockholt, the L59 took off on 16 November 1917 from its aerodrome at Jamboli where an emergency hydrogen production plant had been installed, carrying a load of general supplies for the beleaguered troops under General Lettow-Vorbeck. These 'forgotten soldiers' were cut off in the Makondé area of German East Africa by British forces. The L59 made a record round flight of 4,200 miles in 95 hours flying time, nearly equalling the flight duration of 101 hours achieved by Oberleutnant Ernst Lehmann aboard the LZ120 over the Baltic from 28 to 31 July 1917. On the Western Front, over France, Belgium and Britain, German Army airships made a total of 136 bombing missions or long-range patrols, 103 on the Eastern Front and 37 on the Balkan Front. The German Army lost 25 of their 50 units in commission, 17 of these by allied action, with a casualty list of 15 officers and 37 pilots, mechanics and machine gunners killed.

For the Italians, the war started on 23 May 1915 and from that date ten airships were built, all being of the semi-rigid type favoured by Italian designers. Five of these were Forlanini airships, constructed as bombers by the Società Leonardo da Vinci in Milan. The others were built by the Government establishment Stabilimento di Costruzioni Aeronautiche on the Rome-Ciampino aerodrome under the technical direction of an engineer named Umberto Nobile. In the course of carrying out 258 bombing raids and various missions, notably naval reconnaissance flights, airships in service with the Italian Army had an operational record of 1,400 flying hours, representing 47,425 air miles.

Airships attached to the German Fleet were deployed in two ways. They intensified the bombing attacks on London which had been initiated with lesser effect by older Army units; they also carried out patrols over the sea, acting as escorts for mine-sweepers or air observation posts for the fleet which did not have sufficient ships for reconnaissance duty. The naval dirigibles were based near the North Sea coast at Ahlhorn and Nordholz, where double or revolving hangars had been built, as well as at Hage and Tondern and their activities were sufficient to spur the British into hastily mustering their counter-offensive.

A fleet of non-rigid airships of relatively small cubic capacity was already patrolling the off-shore areas, spotting mines and submarines. A defence system was also organized with fighter squadrons specially trained for night pursuit; anti-aircraft gun batteries became increasingly numerous and more active in picking off enemy bombers. By 1917, land-based aircraft were joined by twin-engined seaplanes as well as a system whereby fighter aircraft were able to take off from the decks of barges towed behind ships. These counter measures proved highly effective when considering

**Clément-Bayard IV, 'Montgolfier'**
This airship, shown during flight tests for the Army in April 1914, had an envelope volume of 229,500 cubic feet and was fitted with a very short nacelle. A double biplane stabilizer near the stern was provided with elevators for fore and aft control.

# AIRSHIPS OVER THE HIGH SEAS

*continued on page 101*

An impression of the attempt by two ships of the Imperial Austrian Navy to rescue the crew of the ill-fated *Città di Jesi* which was shot down off the coast of Istria in the Gulf of Venice.

The Italian airship *Città di Jesi*, Mark V, with a volume of 547,400 cubic feet, was powered by four Italian D I engines each developing 180 h.p. On 5 August 1915, together with two other dirigibles, it took off on a bombing mission to attack the Austrian military base at Pola on the Adriatic coast. Shot down by the Austro-Hungarian artillery, Captain Brivonesi and his crew of five were taken prisoner.

**An Italian M Type airship**

This was a semi-rigid military dirigible of 441,500 cubic feet powered by two 200-horsepower engines. From 1915 it was deployed on bombing missions striking at Austrian targets. The M II crashed into the sea and burst into flames on 8 June 1915 while returning from a raid over Fiume. The picture opposite shows the pilot's position with the altimeter on the left and the gas pressure-gauge on the right.

**'Pilâtre de Rozier'**

This Astra dirigible with a volume of 812,200 cubic feet was built in the first few months of the war. It was fitted with two separate engine nacelles. The photograph of the forward nacelle was actually taken from the rear one. During flight tests, this airship's performance proved disappointing.

## 'Adjutant Vincenot'

Based near Toul, this Clément-Bayard airship of 353,150 cubic feet had the longest war record of all army airships, from August 1914 until destroyed by enemy action on 1 June 1916. First put into service in 1911, *Adjutant Vincenot* logged a total of 231 flights.

Left: An Astra-Torres serving with the French Naval Air Arm being prepared for flight. In the background can be seen the bay, a densely woven semi-metallic network construction which formed a wind-break and provided extra protection for naval airships on entering or leaving the hangar.

## An American C Type airship

Powered by two 125-horsepower engines and carrying a ▷ crew of six, these airships were built for the American Navy during 1918. The C1 was first flown in September.

## 1916: Letourneur

Built to the specifications of Capitaine Letourneur ▷
in 1916 by the aeronautical establishment at
Chalais-Meudon, this CMT Type was put into
service with the navy. It could easily be distinguished from other units by its finely elongated
envelope and cigar-shaped nacelle in duralumin.

## Chalais-Meudon 'Fleurus'

This army airship made its first flights towards the end of 1912. During the
early days of the 1914-1918 war, *Fleurus* was the first Allied dirigible to
penetrate enemy territory, taking off from its base at Verdun and making a
reconnaissance flight as far as Trier. This aircraft was transferred to the
Naval Air Service in 1917.

The Royal Navy airships, of the 'North Sea' class,
could carry a crew of ten men, divided into two
watches. Three crewmen are seen in this photograph, taken during an anti-submarine patrol.

Photographed during trials at Issy-les-Moulineaux in 1915, the Astra *Pilâtre de Rozier* with its very long and flexible envelope proved disappointing. It was subsequently divided up into two, the parts being rebuilt into *Alsace* and a new *Pilâtre de Rozier.*

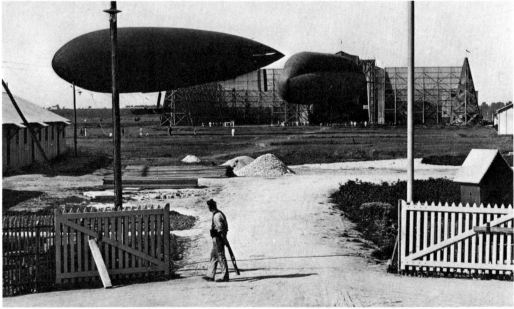

Left: A view of the French Naval Air Service base at Rochefort-sur-Mer in 1918 showing the silhouette of a Zodiac VZ4 and an Astra-Torres AT4 leaving its hangar. The wind-break structure in front of the hangar can also be seen.

that, in the three years between 1915 and 1918, only three Zeppelins were shot down by anti-aircraft batteries whereas fourteen enemy airships were destroyed by fighter airplanes or seaplanes during attacks on England.

Not only did these heavy and persistent bombing attacks boost the national pride and morale of the German people but, more important, they obliged the British chiefs-of-staff to keep a part of their air forces stationed in England. Another useful side-effect of these attacks from the German point of view was the disruption of war production by the incessant air raid warnings, during which time factories were closed down. In the eyes of the German High Command, these ends fully justified the large scale of the means thrown into these air raids throughout the crucial year of 1916 when a total of seventy-three dirigibles took part in eight large-scale bombing missions. The heaviest attack was on 2 September when a fleet of sixteen airships took off from their bases, bound for Britain.

Losses in the attacking force were heavy: twenty-three airships were brought down by allied air action, thirty were either destroyed on the ground or lost because of bad weather. On one raid alone, on 19 October 1917, only seven of the eleven Zeppelins which took part regained their bases in Germany. The four others drifted off in distress over France, the crews forced to maintain their operational ceiling of between 13,000 and 16,000 feet for hours on end without oxygen, both they and the engines suffering from the intense cold and becoming so exhausted as to be incapable of helping themselves. Although the crew of the L49 managed to land their airship safely in the Haute-Marne region, near a place called Bourbonne-les-Bains, the L45 crashed while landing near Sisteron in the Basses-Alpes and the L44 was shot down by gunfire at Chennevières in the district of La Meuse. As for the L50, this airship disappeared without trace somewhere over the Mediterranean.

Altogether, the German naval air arm's material losses amounted to 72.5 per cent of its effective strength with 389 men including some of the most experienced airship commanders such as Kapitän-Leutnant Heinrich Mathy shot down in the L31 on 1 October 1916 by Second Lieutenant W. Tempest of the Royal Flying Corps piloting a BE 2C. Another famous airship officer, Korvetten-Kapitän Peter Strasser, officer commanding the German naval air arm, was shot down in flames off the English coast by Major E. Cadbury and his observer Captain Leckie, flying a Royal Air Force DH.4 on 5 August 1918, while returning from the penultimate raid on England in the L70.

The German Navy airships made a total of 200 bombing attacks, 53 of which were raids on England. In addition, they carried out 1,145 reconnaissance or escort patrols over the sea. They played a part in the famous Battle of Jutland on 30 and 31 May 1916 when the L11, whose commander was Korvetten-Kapitän Viktor Schutze, Commodore of the North Sea Airships Division, was first to spot the British Fleet, under the command of Admiral Beatty and Admiral Jellicoe who were endeavouring to make contact with the enemy. To quote from the post-war writings of Admiral Jellicoe: '. . . The German Zeppelins, in sufficient strength, were of immense assistance to the enemy as scouts and, in favourable weather, each of them was equivalent to at least two light cruisers when thus deployed. . .'

The British Royal Naval Air Service, whose few seaplane squadrons had insufficient radius of action, quickly realized that the airship with its ability to fly long hours at low speeds and even to remain stationary was ideally suited for reconnaissance over the sea and the anti-submarine offensives against the U-boats roving in the English approaches. Indeed, only four days after the outbreak of war, on 5 August 1914, the first scouting patrol was made by a small blimp of 63,500 cubic feet, hastily put together using an old Willows airship envelope and a nacelle made from the fuselage of a BE 2 C aeroplane. Albeit rudimentary, this was actually the prototype of a whole generation of non-rigid small volume airships. They were extremely easy to fly and the crews often dropped down on any handy meadow where they camped in the shelter of a spinney, as might the crews of simple observation balloons. Some time later, bigger units were produced having a reinforced nose so that they could be moored to the airship masts provided at various bases along the coasts. Eventually, nineteen such bases were built, with twelve camps to accomodate the handling personnel.

Enemy submarine attacks in British territorial waters during the first few months of the war prompted the Admiralty to urgently order a series of these blimps in February 1915. Two private companies were the builders: Armstrong-Whitworth and Airships Ltd, producing a total of fifty units. These airships were called Sea Scout or Mark SS, carried a crew of two and had a range of over 16 hours at an average air speed of 40 m.p.h. The first, SS 1, carried out its initial patrol on 14 March 1915 and, by the end of that year, twenty Sea Scouts were already in service. In order to extend their radius of action, they were sometimes towed away from the coasts by ships of the Royal Navy. Various improved versions of Sea Scout were subsequently produced. The Mark SSP was fitted with a roomier nacelle and a pusher airscrew, the SS Zero with a volume of 70,500 cubic feet had accommodation for a three-man crew in an enclosed nacelle and the SS Twin of 98,500 cubic feet was powered by two Rolls-Royce engines of 75 or 100 h.p. and fitted out for a five-man crew. Throughout the war some 150 Sea Scouts of different design were built.

A five-man Coastal Patroller, Mark C, was put into service in 1916. The envelope was of the tri-lobed type similar to the Astra-Torres, with a volume of 176,500 cubic feet. Closely tucked up to the envelope, the nacelle was of curious construction consisting of two fuselages of the old Avro 504 biplane with the rear ends cut off and joined back-to-back. A 150 h.p. engine powered the airscrews at each end of the old fuselages making a forward traction power unit and a pusher one at the rear. An anti-aircraft gun cockpit was built on to the top of the envelope. These Coastal Patrollers had a comfortable flight duration of 24 hours and sometimes even more. Thirty of them were produced and, later on, an improved version had an even greater range with a more powerful engine and a much better silhouette: this was the C Star, one of which actually made a record patrol of 31 hours 30 minutes in April 1918.

The year 1916 also saw the appearance of the Mark NS or North Sea, also based on the Astra-Torres design but with a much better profile than the Mark C. With a volume of 356,000 cubic feet, the NS was powered by a 500 h.p. engine driving two pusher airscrews installed at the tail end of an enclosed car having accommodation for two watches of five men each. At that time, the NS was the best non-rigid airship produced in Britain. Its performance was, indeed, remarkable as patrols with a duration of 60 hours were usual in the year 1917 and, after the Armistice, one North Sea remained airborne for 101 hours, flying over 4,000 air miles. Because of their extended range, the Mark C and Mark NS airships were widely used as escorts for fleet and sea convoys.

Altogether, nearly 400 dirigibles of these different types were built between 1915 and 1918, logging 83,360 flying hours over 2,603,750 miles. And each successive year there was a significant increase in the number of hours flown: starting with 339 hours in 1915, leaping up to 7,078 in 1916, they were increased to 22,389 in 1917 and, at 53,354 hours, more than doubled in 1918. In proportion to this air activity, the losses in men and material were relatively small. Although two Coastal Patrollers were shot down in flames over the North Sea by German seaplanes operating from Zeebrugge in 1917, the total casualties in crew were only forty-eight.

It is less well-known that five rigid airships were also constructed during the war years but too late to take part in operational flying. In 1917 they were employed once or twice on escort duty but were principally used for training and as flying test-beds. Developed from the unfortunate *Mayfly* of 1911 which broke in half the second time it left its hangar, the five consisted of the R9, launched in November 1916, the R23 and R26, all manufactured by Vickers Ltd, the R24 built by William Beardmore & Co. and the R25 produced by the Armstrong-Whitworth Co. Their technical performances were completely dissimilar to those of the Zeppelins of that period. A curious historical quirk is worth mentioning, the fact that construction of the R9 which was started in 1914 was stopped in March 1915 by order of the First Lord of the Admiralty, Winston Churchill, who believed the war would soon be over. Three months later, his successor, Lord Balfour had this order revoked.

In March 1915, the French naval authorities at last decided to use small airships or blimps to seek out and attack enemy submarines as well as to locate and destroy floating mines. The first dirigibles used were two Sea Scouts and a Coastal Patroller which had been handed over by Britain. Bases were established along the Channel and Atlantic coasts. From 1916 until the end of the war the French companies Astra, Zodiac and the Chalais-Meudon ordnance works building the CM's supplied the needs of this air flotilla. Other units, handed over by the French army in March 1917, were added to the fleet whose area of operations extended to the Mediterranean and even as far as the Ionian Sea, operating from bases set up at Aubagne on the Bouches-du-Rhône, Oran in Algiers, Bizerta, and Corfu. All these units were powered by twin engines, 150 h.p. Salmsons for the Type CM, 80 to 220 h.p. Renaults for the Zodiac cruisers and the Astra-Torres. These airships were armed with one or two machine-guns while larger volume air cruisers were equipped with cannons of 47 mm. In 1918, the big Astra-Torres units with a volume of 339,000 cubic feet actually carried guns of 75 mm.

A flying school for officers and other specialized personnel was established at Rochefort-sur-Mer and continued to train airship crews a long time after the Armistice in 1918. French airships proved remarkably effective in spotting and destroying mines, in the search and attack on enemy submarines, air-sea rescue and the protection of convoys: no convoy under airship escort was ever attacked by a submarine.

In October 1917, the annual production in France was four CM's, ten to twelve Astra-Torres and the same number of small volume Zodiac units. The steep rise in flying hours from 1917 to 1918 bears witness to the increased activity of the French naval air services, the *Aéronavale française*: from 4,164 hours with 1,128 sorties in 1917, they increased to 12,133 hours with 2,201 sorties in 1918. Several dirigibles were placed at the disposal of the American Expeditionary Force at the air stations of Brest-Guipavas and Paimbœuf when the new allies landed in France.

Only four units were lost. A CMT mysteriously burst into flames off the coast of Sardinia and a Zodiac cruiser exploded after crashing into a cliff near Le Havre in fog. An Astra-Torres Type 5 and a Type 8 were put out of action by major breakdowns or by bad weather in the Mediterranean. Even so, only ten crew members lost their lives.

In May 1917, a contract was drawn up by the Chalais-Meudon company for the construction, at the Creusot workshops, of a rigid airship incorporating many of the technical refinements observed in two Zeppelins, the L45 and L49, which had crashed in France. A production programme of 1 January 1918 provided for ten other units, four to be delivered within eighteen months and six within two years. Plans had been made to establish a large air base on the Atlantic coast from which six rigid airships would operate on shipping escort patrols over the high seas. But this entire ambitious programme was cancelled at the end of 1918, its only memorial being two extraordinary hangars in reinforced concrete, 1,000 feet long and of extremely advanced design, on the aerodrome at Orly which, in the twenties, had not yet become the busy airport of today. Not one French rigid airship was ever moored there although one of the hangars sheltered a civil Zeppelin for a time after the war.

The Great War had forced the belligerents to make constant technical improvements in their efforts to increase the performance of combat dirigibles. Production programmes were speeded up, a Zeppelin being built in six weeks or sometimes less; cubic capacities were increased, enabling a greater load to be carried, radius of action extended and the operational ceiling lifted ever higher to escape counter attack whether by anti-aircraft fire or fighter aircraft. Together with all these factors, aerodynamics were influencing and improving the general design of hulls and nacelles as well as eliminating certain parasitic drag. One example of this was the widespread adoption by the Zeppelin builders of engine nacelles powering airscrews mounted in line, as opposed to the use of bevel gearing in the transmissions from engine nacelles to propellers mounted laterally. The power yield of these engine units was increased and sometimes as many as six propelled the airship. The Maybach engines used for all wartime Zeppelins were supercharged to give maximum power from 6,500 feet up to operational heights reaching 20,000 feet in the case of the MB IVa motor, which was fitted with aluminium pistons and often referred to as the 'high altitude engine'.

The evolution in the technical features of Zeppelins produced between 1915 and 1918 was particularly significant. No less than ten successive types were produced in these three years, from Type 'O' in 1915 to Type 'X' in 1918. Although the rectangular silhouette was continued for some time so as to make full use of the existing jigs for line production, the Schütte-Lanz design with its greatest diameter about a third of the envelope's length from the nose, and its better aerodynamic shape, finally convinced the engineers at Friedrichshafen of the need for change. From 1916 this form was adopted for the L 30 and subsequent units, resulting in only a momentary slow-down in production. The overall volume of these dirigibles was increasing all the time, starting in 1914 with an average of under 812,000 cubic feet, rising to 1,130,000 cubic feet in 1915, 1,942,000 in 1916, 1,970,500 in 1917 and finally reaching 2,419,000 cubic feet in 1918. Air speeds were also improved from 50 m.p.h. to 75 m.p.h. and the total motor power of 640 h.p. in two engine nacelles increased to 1,560 h.p. in five nacelles. The maximum recorded load was approximately 9,200 lbs of high explosive and incendiary bombs carried on 22 September 1916 by the L 31 of 1,949,000 cubic feet and 1,440 h.p., under the command of Kapitän-Leutnant Heinrich Mathy. The highest altitude reached was 25,500 feet on 20 October 1917 by the L 55 of 1,977,000 cubic feet and 1,200 h.p.

As for long distance aerial navigation, experience acquired by the navigators attached to all crews proved invaluable. Ground navigational aids were also developed from 1916 onwards, particularly by the Germans, using cross-bearings for positioning from direction-finding wireless stations, adopting the loop principle. Rotating radio beacons were also becoming standard equipment at certain air bases. Although the study of meteorology was making progress in such areas as cloud formation and the movements of the upper winds, forecasts were always uncertain as illustrated by the ill-fated raid on the night of 19 October 1917. Embryonic as these ground navigational aids still were, they were certainly an advance.

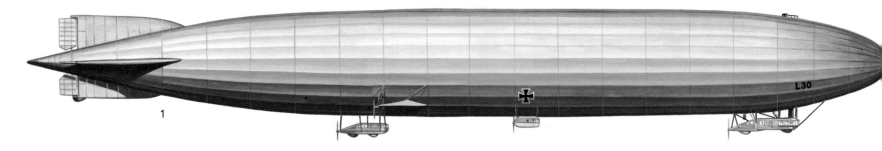

## 1 1916-1920: Zeppelin L37

This 'Super-Zeppelin' was the sixty-second built at Friedrichshafen and made its first flight on 9 November 1916: 645 feet long, with a diameter of 78 feet, it had an estimated gas volume of 1,949,400 cubic feet contained in 19 gas-bags. Six airscrews were driven by six HSLU Maybach engines, each of 240 h.p. One power unit was mounted at the stern end of the forward nacelle, a pair in small engine nacelles at each side, another pair on struts above the stern multi-engined nacelle which was also fitted with an in-line airscrew. The captain's control cabin in the nose nacelle was provided with a means of access to the inside of the hull. Air speed was approximately 70 m.p.h. Attached to the German Navy, as were all airships coded with the initial 'L', Army airships being designated 'LZ' from 1915 onwards, this Zeppelin was based on Seddin in Pomerania. Principally used for scouting patrols over the Baltic, the L37 was taken out of service in 1917. In 1920 some of its component parts were delivered to Japan in accordance with terms of the Peace Treaty.

## 2 1915-1918: Zeppelin observation nacelle

Ernst Lehmann designed this tiny, streamlined single-seater observation nacelle which was slung on the end of a 2,500 ft. cable lowered by a motor-driven winch. In overcast weather, the airship drifted along above the clouds, safely out of the enemy's sight, while the observer in clear weather below directed bombing operations by telephone. First used experimentally on 17 March 1915 during a raid on Calais, such observation nacelles only came into general use the following year.

## 3 1915: Parseval PL25

This was the first non-rigid airship used by the German military services. Its operational rôle seems to have been limited and it was the only one of its type produced. The PL25 was 373 feet long, 52 feet in diameter and had a volume of 498,000 cubic feet. With its slim, tapering shape and two 210-horsepower engines driving airscrews on each side of the nacelle, it could reach a speed of 50 m.p.h. Completely closed in, the nacelle contained the pilot's cabin, wireless equipment and engine room, and was surmounted by a short keel, accessible to the crew. A machine gun post was mounted on the top of the envelope.

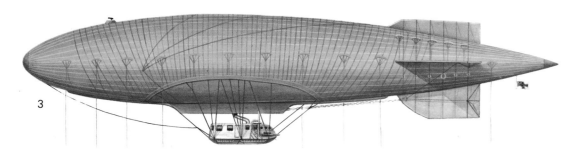

## 4 1915-1916: Schütte-Lanz SL3

This airship, which served with the army, was the third produced by Schütte-Lanz and was built to the same specifications as its predecessor of 1912, having a wooden skeleton and airscrews mounted directly on the nacelles, 513 feet long with a diameter of 65 feet and an estimated volume of 1,144,200 cubic feet. SL3 was powered by four Maybach CX 210-horsepower engines installed in two nacelles midway along each side of the envelope and in two in-line nacelles under the hull. Another nacelle under the nose was reserved solely for the flying crew. Directly above the forward nacelle a machine-gun post was mounted on the top of the envelope. The SL3 could reach a speed of approximately 55 m.p.h.

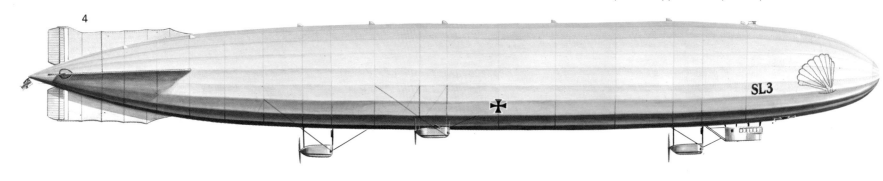

### 1917: Zodiac VZ5 cruiser

This dirigible with a volume of 106,000 cubic feet was first flight-tested at Saint-Cyr, near Paris, in 1917. The slim, pencil-shaped nacelle was fitted with two pusher airscrews at the stern, driven by Renault 80-horsepower engines. A landing wheel under the nose facilitated ground handling before take-off and after landing. Ernest Demuyter, the well-known Belgian aviator who served with the French Naval Air Service, is seen standing in the airship.

### The Vickers HMA6

In 1917, Vickers built three envelopes and two nacelles for the HMA 6 and HMA 7, based on specifications from the Parseval HMA 4.

### The British Parseval HMA4

In accordance with the programme laid down by the Admiralty, this Parseval of 353,100 cubic feet was bought from its German builder for £50,000 sterling in July 1913. Only a year later, during the night of 5 August 1914, it returned to Germany on its first bombing mission for the Royal Navy! The Parseval HMA 4 was subsequently deployed on reconnaissance and escort duties until the end of the war.

### Astra-Torres units attached to the French Naval Air Service

From 1917 until the end of hostilities, these airships were put to good service in the Mediterranean theatre on anti-submarine and convoy escort patrols. Five of them, AT2, AT3, AT6, AT7 and AT8 were sent to their bases at Alger-Baraki, Oran-La Senia and Bizerte-Sidi Ahmed from Aubagne in the South of France. Only one, the AT8, was subsequently lost off Tunis. Bottom, left, the AT6 preparing to leave its hangar in the South of France. Bottom, right, envelope and nacelle of the AT6 being transported, the airship having been unable to ride out a sudden and violent *mistral* when returning to base and its crew were obliged to deflate it. The illustration on the opposite page shows the Astra-Torres AT1 making a landing in 1917.

## Zeppelins at war

**1** Electric control panel for releasing bombs in a German military airship.

**2** Rear engine nacelle on a German naval airship of 1917.

**3** A 20 mm cannon mounted in the command nacelle of a German naval airship in 1917.

**4** Count Zeppelin wearing the uniform of a general, together with the Austrian Hauptmann Macher, aboard the naval airship L30, some months before his death on 8 March 1917.

**5** This naval Zeppelin, the L44, was one of the four airships which drifted helplessly over France while returning from a disastrous bombing raid on England between 19 and 20 October 1917. The target for a battery of 75 mm guns located near Lunéville, L44 crashed in flames at Chennevières, near Saint-Clément.

# ZEPPELIN L11

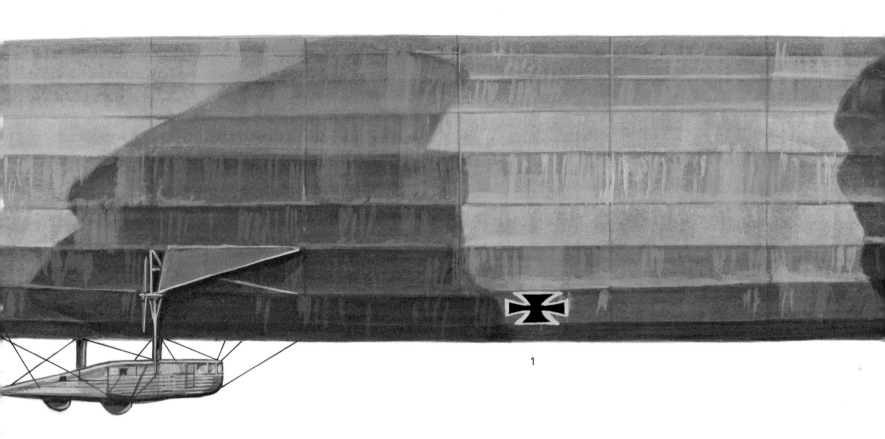

1

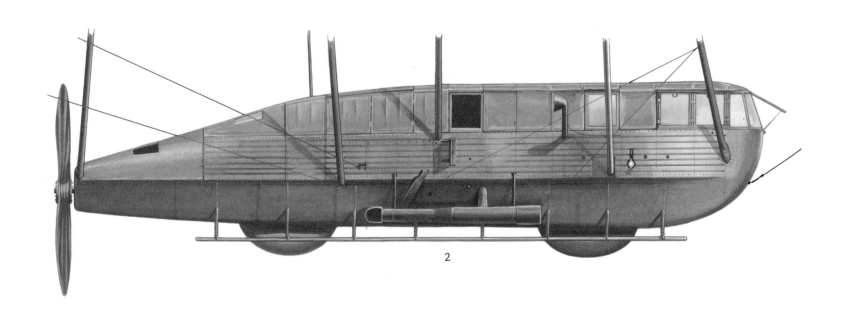

2

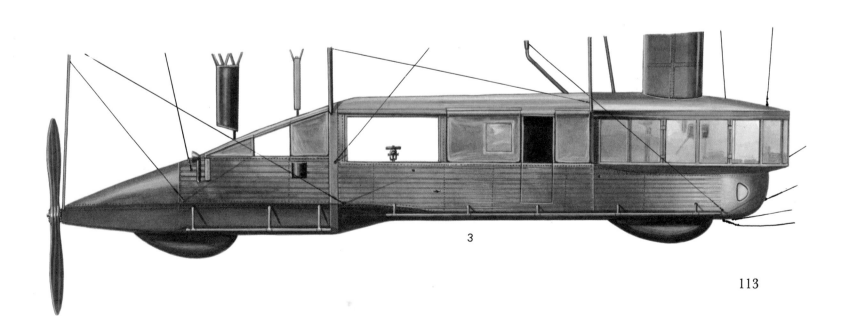

3

### Upper dorsal machine-gun post

From 1916, Zeppelins and all other German airships engaged on operational flying were equipped with 8-calibre Maxim or Parabellum machine-guns. Apart from those mounted in the command cabin and engine nacelles, there were also twin swivelling guns on the top of the envelope towards the nose, reached by a series of ladders running vertically throughout the hull. The gunners shot from behind a metal screen while farings protected them from the full force of the wind caused by the airship's forward speed. The very quick firing required to counter enemy aircraft attack, combined with the cold and the force of the wind, necessitated two gunners being always available. The objective was to prevent Royal Flying Corps pilots from firing at close range but it proved to no avail.

### Stern dorsal machine-gun post

Airship defence was completed by another gun-pit, with gunner and weapon in a hatch behind the tail fin. This arrangement was devised to minimize head resistance. However, as the bomb load was continually being increased, armament was finally reduced to light weapons carried in the nacelles.

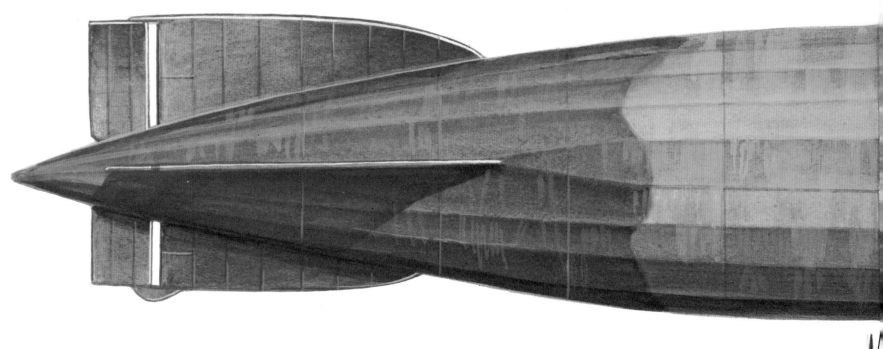

### 1 1915-1917: Zeppelin L11

A naval airship of the P type, L11 made its maiden flight on 7 June 1915: 536 feet long, 61 feet in diameter and with a volume of 1,130,000 cubic feet. It was powered by four Maybach CX engines of 210 h.p. A pair of these engines in the rear nacelle drove an in-line airscrew and two airscrews mounted above on struts. Cruising speed was about 65 m.p.h. The command nacelle, housing flying crew and forward engines, together with the rear engine nacelle, was provided with a gangway leading into the envelope, on top of which was mounted a machine-gun post. The illustration shows experiments being made with camouflage which seem to have been abandoned in favour of a uniform coating of black paint on the belly and the flanks. This was intended to foil searchlight detection while the top of the envelope was painted white to mitigate the sun's effect of expanding the hydrogen. The L11 was captained by Kapitän-Leutnant von Buttlar Treusch von Brandenfels who wrote *Zeppelins in Combat* in 1932. From August 1915 it was engaged in the bombing raids on England and in reconnaissance patrols, shadowing the British fleet, being finally scrapped on 25 April 1917.

### 2 Three-engined Zeppelin nacelle

The pressing need to increase cruising speed and maximum altitude led to certain Zeppelins being equipped with six 240-horsepower Maybach engines from 1916 onwards and, towards the end of the war, sometimes even seven. These power units, built into the nacelle, drove airscrews which were either in-line mounted on the rear of the nacelle, with two others above and to each side on struts, or from the R Type produced in 1916, mounted along the sides of the hull in small ovoid nacelles joined to the flanks of the envelope by outside ladders which, in turn, were connected to the catwalks built inside.

This drawing shows the first of the two systems, the nacelle being fitted with windows for use by the flying crew. To each side can also be seen the landing shock-absorbers, the siderail for ground handling, the exhaust pipe and, along the windowed wall, the air intake pipe for the engines with its elbow bend.

### 3 Zeppelin command nacelle

The main nacelles on Zeppelins commissioned for war service were streamlined in design, with their pusher airscrews mounted at the finely tapering stern end. A sectional view resembled the aerodynamic cross-section of an aeroplane wing.

The nacelle shown here has a cabin with large windows for the captain and flying crew, behind which was a rest area. Further back was the engine room, fitted with one, two or even three engines according to the increasingly more powerful class of Zeppelin used on operations during the war. Above the captain's cabin, a large sleeve contained a ladder leading to the inside of the envelope and sometimes also to the gunner's cockpit on the top. Two pneumatic shock-absorbers were retracted under the floor of the nacelle, to be used as required when the nacelle came in contact with the ground.

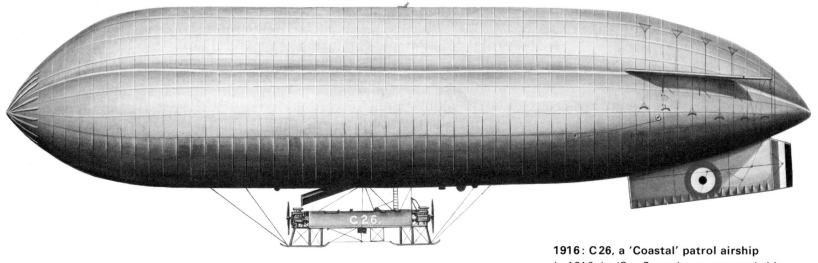

## 1916: C 26, a 'Coastal' patrol airship

In 1916 the 'Sea Scouts' were superseded by 'Coastals', airships with a three-lobed envelope similar to the Astra-Torres, with a volume of 176,500 cubic feet contained in four gas-bags. They were 193 feet long, 39 feet in diameter and powered by two 150-horsepower Sunbeam engines, one at each end of the nacelle. The 'Coastals' carried a crew of five and were equipped with a gun post on the top of the envelope. This three-lobed design allowed the nacelle to be slung close to the underside of the envelope and the resulting reduction in number and length of the suspension cables appreciably cut down head resistance. Forty 'Coastals' were produced, each being capable of carrying out anti-submarine or mine-spotting patrols of 24 hours or longer. One actually remained airborne for over 48 hours. A larger and more streamlined airship, the C Star, had an even greater operational range. Carrying its fuel tanks inside the envelope, it was 216 feet long with a diameter of 42 feet and a volume of 197,800 cubic feet.

## 1915: British 'Sea Scout'

Early in 1915, following repeated attacks on shipping off the English coasts by German submarines, the British Government ordered the building of small patrol airships. Designated SS for 'Sea Scout', these were 141 feet long, 31 feet in diameter at the largest cross-section, with a volume of 63,500 cubic feet. After the successful trials of the prototype SS1, first flown on 14 March, fifty of these small airships were ordered from two private subcontractors, Armstrong-Whitworth Ltd, and Airship Ltd from June 1915 onwards. Carrying two men, these aircraft were powered by engines of 75 to 100 h.p., giving them a speed of about 40 m.p.h. and an operational range of over sixteen hours. The nose was reinforced to take the equipment for mooring to a mast and the stern was fitted with two rectangular fins at an oblique angle to the longitudinal axis, elevator type controls being hinged to the fins for steering. The SS1 was built in a rather makeshift manner, its envelope being a spare from an old Willows airship and its nacelle the fuselage of a BE2C aeroplane, handed over to the Navy by Colonel O'Gorman of the Royal Flying Corps. Such a fuselage can be seen in this drawing of a 'Sea Scout' with its twin cockpit, landing skid and the airscrew blowing against the conduit for the two internal gas-bags.

### Above, left:

As in the case of the 'Sea Scouts', the nacelle of the 'Coastal' was initially a 'hand down' from the Royal Flying Corps. Its somewhat unorthodox design consisted of two fuselages from a very widely used flying trainer, the Avro 504 biplane, the tail sections being cut off behind the cockpit and the two nose parts joined back to back. A tractor airscrew in the nose and a pusher airscrew in the rear were each driven by a 180 h.p. Sunbeam engine. The C Star had a Berliet engine of 100 h.p. in the nose and a Fiat 260 h.p. engine in the stern. The nacelle for the 'Coastal' accommodated a crew of five, carried bombs for anti-submarine attack under the floorboards and was fitted with two Avro aircraft landing skids, one behind the other.

## 1916: 'Coastal Patroller'

Thirty-two of these airships were built, the first making its maiden flight on 9 June 1915. The three-lobed Astra-Torres envelope of 176,500 cubic feet carried a nacelle made from two Avro 504 fuselages, modified in the same way as for the 'Coastals' and equipped with the same landing skids.

## 1915: The British 'Sea Scout'

Urgent orders from the Admiralty in February 1915 following the need to protect the British coasts against German U-boat activity resulted in the production of the 'Sea Scout' series. Two characteristic features were the reinforced nose with a rod arrangement for fastening to a mooring mast and the two inclined tail-planes which made up the steering vanes. The nacelle was a BE 2 C biplane fuselage minus its tail unit. The two tubular objects suspended horizontally are the fuel tanks.

117

### The British 'North Sea' series

This airship had a three-lobed envelope of the Astra-Torres type with a volume of 353,100 cubic feet and was fitted with a long closed-in nacelle for the flying crew. Behind, a twin-engine open-work nacelle was equipped with a float, and was reached from the command nacelle by means of a rope ladder. The long cylinder seen in the picture is one of the two fuel tanks attached to each side of the hull. These airships, used for long-range escort duty, were built between 1916 and 1918.

### 1916: The end of the LZ 85 at Salonika

Based on Temesvar in Hungary, this army airship had already made two attacks on the Allied troops dug-in on the Salonika front, about 470 miles away, during February and March 1916. During a third but unlucky raid on the night of 4 May, the LZ 85 was caught by the searchlight batteries and crippled by Allied artillery, and had to make a forced landing on the marshes in the River Vardar estuary. Before being taken prisoner, Leutnant Scherzer and his crew set fire to their aircraft.

## 1916-1918: 'North Sea' NS9

The most successful of the non-rigid airship types produced for the Admiralty during the war were the 'North Seas' deployed on long range reconnaissance over the sea. Its envelope was three-lobed and similar to the 'Coastal' but had better lines: 251 feet long with a diameter of 59 feet at the largest cross-section, the volume of the envelope was approximately 353,000 cubic feet, only a third of which was occupied by six gas-bags. The 'North Sea' airships were powered by two 250-horsepower Rolls-Royce and, subsequently, Fiat engines, each driving a pusher airscrew and occupying their own nacelle which was fitted with a float. Fuel tanks were built into the envelope. In front of the engine nacelle was the elongated closed command nacelle, the two nacelles being interconnected. Carrying a crew of ten, on duty in two five-hour watches, the NS9 could maintain an average speed of about 47 m.p.h. with a range of forty hours which was frequently exceeded. In 1917, one made a flight of 61 hours 30 minutes and in 1919, after the Armistice, a record flight of 101 hours was achieved.

## 1916: The Chalais-Meudon Type T

In 1915, the aeronautical establishment at Chalais-Meudon began developing a well-designed airship with an extremely elongated envelope of approximately 197,750 cubic feet. 272 feet long and only 34 feet in diameter, the ratio was in fact 8 to 1. The short, tapering nacelle was made of duralumin, a light but strong alloy becoming more and more widely used in aircraft construction. Two Salmson-Canton-Unné 150 h.p. engines, already a well-proven design, drove the airscrews fitted to each side. The area of the tail unit, elevators and rudders were reduced to the minimum. As a result of these overall refinements in design, air speed was increased to about 62 m.p.h.

This class of aircraft was designed to escort trans-Mediterranean convoys and for submarine spotting operations. On 12 May 1916, the T1, based on Bizerta, took off on a routine flight across the Mediterranean Sea but, for an unknown reason, crashed in flames off the Sardinian coast, killing Capitaine du Génie Caussin and five other members of the crew. In 1918, another airship of the same class, the T14, equipped with a forward-firing 47 mm cannon, was named after the unfortunate commander of the ill-fated T1.

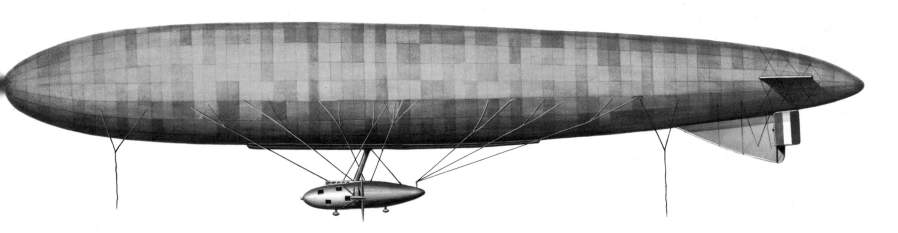

119

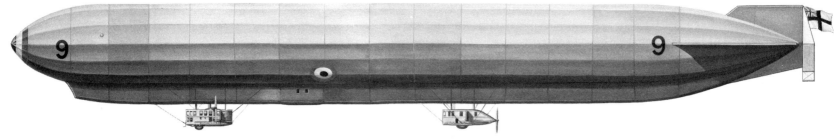

### 1916: Rigid Vickers airship R9

In 1910, impressed by the performance of the Zeppelins in service with DELAG and the military services, the British authorities commissioned the Vickers company to build a similar dirigible. In May 1911, this airship, christened *Mayfly*, made its first flight to a mooring mast fitted with a wind break and built on a pontoon. During this short trial, however, the airship broke up and was damaged beyond repair. This incident is of historical interest, being the first time an attempt was ever made to moor an airship to a mast, a practice which became customary in Britain during the war although adopted by Germany only ten years after the Armistice for *Graf Zeppelin*, built in 1928.

Vickers began construction of another rigid airship in 1914 but the outbreak of war interrupted production and work was only resumed in 1915, the HMA No. 9 being completed in 1916. The Chief Engineer for the project was Barnes Wallis, destined for even greater fame during the next war for his ingenious drifting mines, dropped by Avro Lancaster bombers of the R.A.F., which destroyed two huge dams in the Ruhr.

The R9, 'R' denoting rigid, had a volume of approximately 879,500 cubic feet, a length of 518 feet and a diameter of 52 feet. Its two nacelles were interconnected by a closed-in keel with windows down the sides. With a maximum speed of around 47 m.p.h., the R9 made its first flight in November 1916 and was subsequently used almost entirely as a training aircraft for flying crews.

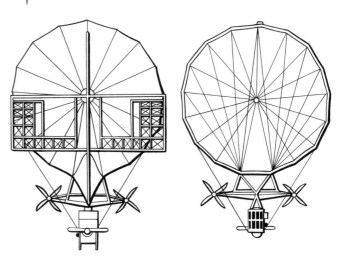

### 1916: Cross-section drawing of the Vickers R9

This airship was driven by three engines, two of 150 h.p. installed in the main nacelle driving four-bladed airscrews mounted on each side of the hull on struts. The other 250 h.p. engine in the rear nacelle drove a twin-bladed in-line airscrew. This Maybach engine had been dismantled from the Zeppelin L33, brought down near Colchester on 24 September 1916 by the British artillery, the crew being taken prisoner. The cross-section on the right is a view from the nose and shows the command nacelle, the cross-bearers supporting the airscrew shafts and its triangular keel under the envelope. The cross-section on the left shows the tail plane and control surfaces as well as the rear nacelle with its in-line airscrew.

### 1917: The Vickers rigid airship R23

The capture of the Zeppelin L33 on 24 September 1916 was turned to advantage by Vickers' design department to produce an improved version of the R9, the R23. The volume was increased to 978,200 cubic feet, its diameter of 52 feet remained the same and, at 527 feet, it was slightly longer. Like the Zeppelins of that period, its silhouette was more or less rectangular with a machine-gun post on the top of the envelope towards the nose. Underneath, a tail fin extended the back of the keel. Four 250-horsepower engines were mounted in two in-line nacelles and in two small nacelles suspended on either side of the centre of the keel. The R23 was commissioned for service in 1917 and was occasionally used to escort ship convoys but primarily for training and testing, as were its two rigid successors, the R24 and R25.

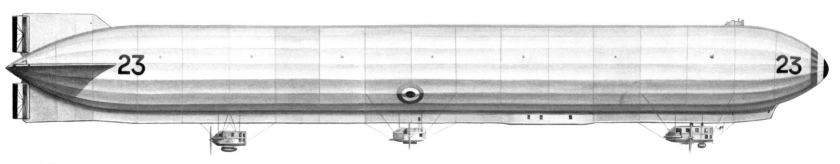

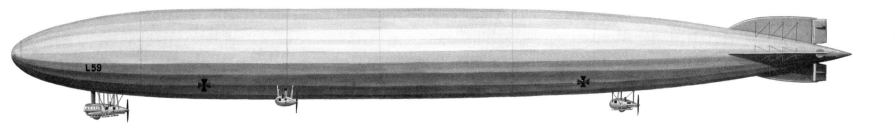

## 1917-1918: The Zeppelin L 59

The 104th Zeppelin, the naval airship L 59, was actually in the course of construction when its dimensions were modified, the length being increased by 100 feet to 741 feet, 78 feet in diameter, its volume was enlarged to 2,419,000 cubic feet, distributed between 16 gas bags. Five 240-horsepower engines were mounted in four nacelles. These changes were prompted by the need for a long range mission which, by its scope and significance, remains unique in the annals of the air war of 1914-1918.

After its first flight on 10 October 1917, Kapitän Leutnant Bockholt and his crew flew the Zeppelin to its base at Jamboli in Bulgaria. On 21 November the L 59 took off laden with nearly 50 tons of arms, equipment and medical stores for General von Lettow-Vorbeck's troops, then hard-pressed by the British forces in German East Africa. A wireless message bringing news of the beleaguered troops' surrender obliged Bockholt to turn back south of Khartoum. The L 59 therefore returned to its base with its entire cargo after a flight of 4,220 miles in 95 hours. In fact, it appears probable that the message was the work of the British Secret Service.

After this record long-distance flight, the L 59 carried out several military missions over Greece and Italy. On 7 April 1918, with Kapitän-Leutnant Bockholt and his crew aboard, the airship exploded and crashed in flames in the Otranto Straits.

This map shows the routes of the main bombing raids by Zeppelins over England in 1916, black dots indicating the actual targets.

Below: Types of nacelles fitted to different Zeppelins attached to the German Navy between 1915 and 1917. Some are solely engine nacelles, others combine the pilot's cabin in front of the engine compartment. These nacelles were installed on the following dirigibles:

1. Combined nacelle of the Z 36 or L 9; 240 h.p. engine; first flight 8 March 1915.
2. Combined nacelle of the Z 62 or L 30. A cloth-lined baffle arrangement insulated the crew in the fore part from engine noise.
3. Engine nacelle of the Z 62 or L 30.
4. Combined nacelle of the Z 62 or L 30.
5. 260 h.p. engine nacelle of the Z 93 or L 44.
6. 260 h.p. engine nacelle of the Z 94 or L 46.
7. Combined nacelle of the Z 95 or L 48; 260 h.p. engine; first flight 22 May 1917.
8. 260 h.p. engine nacelle of the Z 112 or L 70; first flight 1 July 1918.

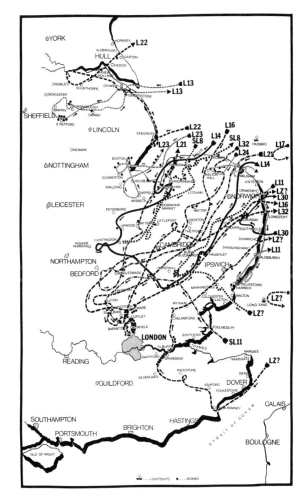

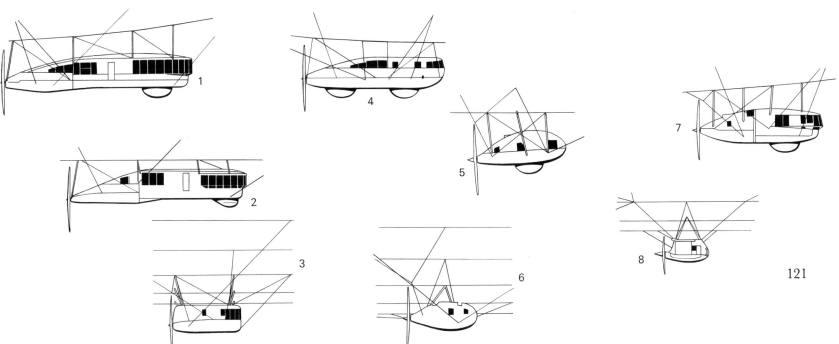

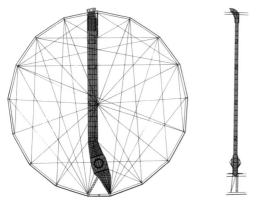

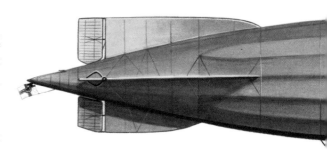

## 1918: Schütte-Lanz SL22

The SL22, the last airship bearing the Schütte-Lanz name, was built towards the end of the war and was 640 feet long with a diameter of 74 feet. Nineteen hydrogen gas-bags brought its volume up to 1,958,200 cubic feet. A total horsepower of 1,200 h.p. was developed by engines mounted in four nacelles, disposed in the same way as on the SL20. This airship made its first flight in June 1918 but took no part in military operations. Two years later, it was destroyed by the Allies.

Towards the end of hostilities, the Schütte-Lanz technicians had, rather belatedly, begun considering the use of metal longerons and tubular ribs to overcome the disadvantage of wood warping with changes in humidity.

Cross-section of the internal structure of the Schütte-Lanz SL22 showing front and side views of the shaft provided with steps leading to the top of the envelope.

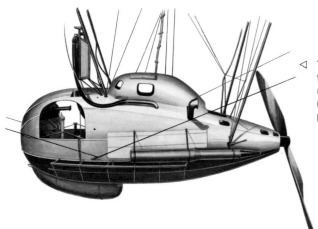

◁ The SL22 engine nacelle, its hemispherical fairings provided with portholes. Towards the nose can be seen the radiator; in the centre the rope ladder leading to the keel and, in the after part of the fairing, the carburettor air intake.

### Technical drawing of an SL22 engine nacelle

1. 240 h.p. Maybach engine
2. Radiator
3. Radiator pump
4. Reversing gear
5. Clutch
6. Carburettor air intake
7. Reversing switch
8. Oil tank
9. Silencer
10. Starter
11. Control telegraph
12. Oil and petrol gauges
13. Starting pump
14. Transmission shaft
15. Airscrew bearer plate
16. Airscrew
17. Airscrew hub
18. Window
19. Ladder
20. Handrail
21. Oil radiator
22. Clutch lever
23. Reversing lever

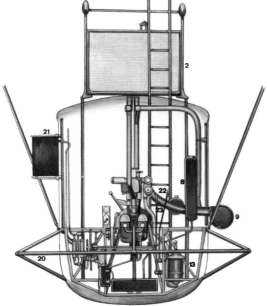

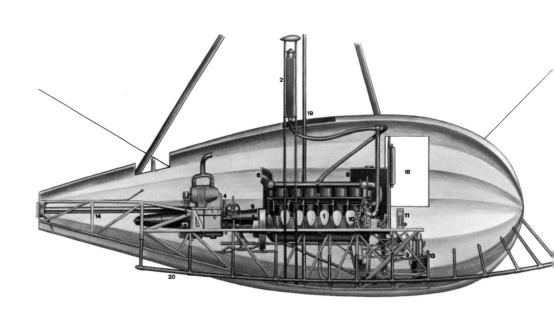

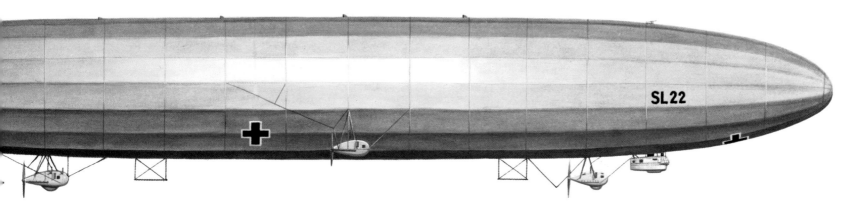

Below: SL22 command nacelle
Left, front view. Right, side view

1. Helm
2. Elevator control
3. Telegraphs
4. Ladder
5. Flood light
6. Lamp
7. Switchboard
8. Speaking-tube
9. Compass
10. Chart table
11. Signalling bells
12. Rope ladder
13. Winch cables
14. Parachutes
15. Telephone switchboard
16. Batteries
17. Lamp
18. Table
19. Aerial
20. Nose light
21. Telephone cable
22. Compass
23. Ballast

**Front and rear views of the Schütte-Lanz SL22**

The front view on the left shows how the engine nacelles were fixed to the side of the envelope by means of horizontal struts and cables. Halfway along the envelope, below and behind the pilot's nacelle, an in-line engine nacelle was stayed with cables under the airship belly.

The rear view on the right shows the cruciform tail unit assembly as well as the after engine nacelle. The long, slanting double lines on these views represent the cables used in ground-handling.

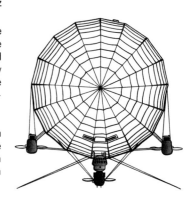

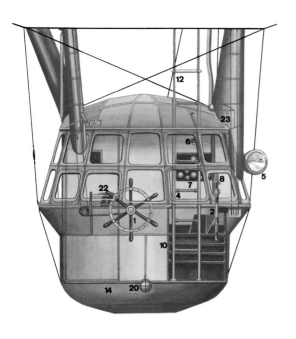

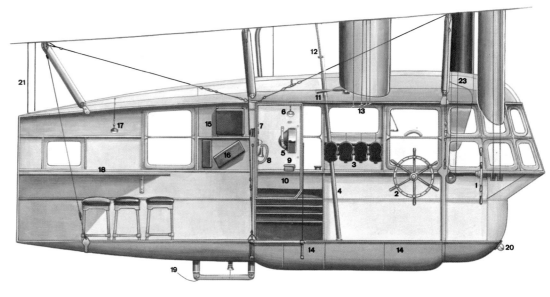

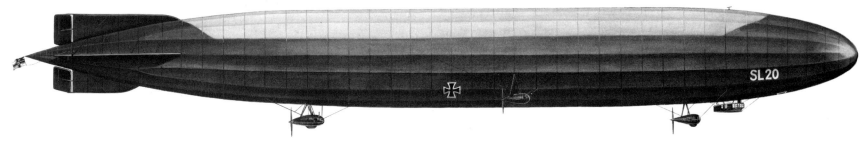

### 1917-1918: Schütte-Lanz SL 20

Completed in September 1917, the SL 20 was the first of a series of Schütte-Lanz airships built with box girders instead of the triangular sections hitherto used, but still made from wood. With a volume of 1,977,600 cubic feet, it was 650 feet long and 75 feet in diameter and powered by five 240-horsepower Maybach engines installed in four nacelles. One in-line nacelle was recessed behind the pilot's nacelle, two were fixed level with the underside of the envelope and an in-line twin-engine nacelle was mounted towards the stern. The SL 20, which had an air speed of 75 m.p.h., was based on Aalhorn in Eastern Friesland, not far from the North Sea. This large base had four huge double hangars and another two hangars were under construction at the beginning of 1918. During the night of 15 January 1918, a huge fire broke out, setting ablaze all four hangars containing the SL 20 as well as four 'super' Zeppelins attached to the German Navy, the L 46, L 47, L 51 and L 58. All five airships were destroyed in this fire, the cause of which remained a mystery, although sabotage cannot be discounted.

The illustration above shows the classic operational appointments for a night bomber as in the Zeppelin L 11.

### 1917-1920: The rigid British airship R 80

At the end of the war, the British had four rigid airships which were kept in service, further units being subsequently built on an experimental basis with a view to using them for civil aviation. The Vickers company began building the R 80 in 1917, only completing it in the second half of 1920. The R 80 was 528 feet long, 74 feet in diameter, had a volume of 1,250,100 cubic feet distributed between fifteen gas-bags and was powered by four Wolseley-Maybach 240 h.p. engines. Two engines were stepped in the after portion of the main nacelle, working singly or together to drive the pusher airscrew. Two side nacelles were each fitted with one engine driving reversible-pitch airscrews. The nose portion of the envelope was reinforced to take the gear for mooring to an airship mast, one machine-gun post was installed on the top of the envelope, another right at the point of the tail. The R 80 had a cruising speed of about 45 m.p.h. carrying a crew of twenty. Employed by the military services until 1921 it was dismantled in 1924.

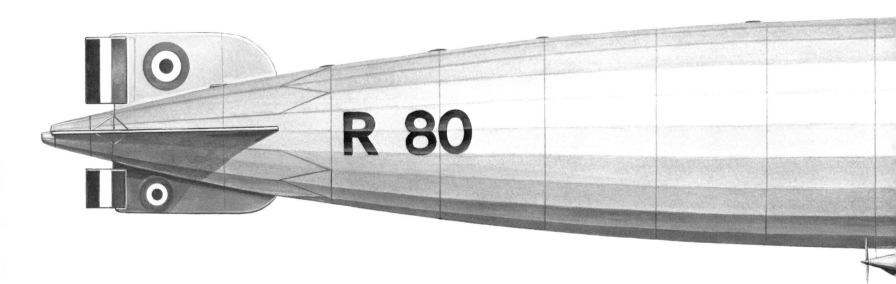

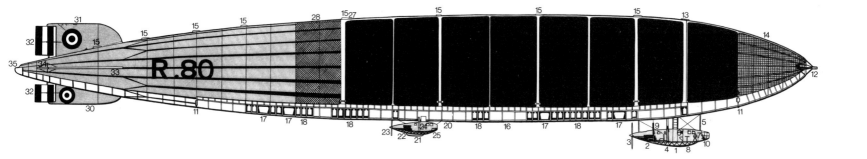

This sectional drawing of the R 80 displays some of its salient features such as the forward combined pilot's cabin and engine nacelle attached to the envelope by a flexible system of struts and a ladder leading into the envelope. The bracing cables for the special reinforcement can be seen towards the nose. A set of valves are aligned with the main circular cross ribs.

## R 80 technical drawing

1. Captain's nacelle
2. Forward nacelle engine
3. Airscrew
4. Flexible partition
5. Hollow strut
6. Wireless post
7. Elevator control
8. Landing shock-absorber
9. Radiator
10. Compass and navigational instruments
11. Water ballast discharge hole
12. Mooring system
13. Platform
14. Nose reinforcement
15. Gas valves
16. Officers' quarters
17. Water-ballast
18. Petrol tanks
19. Automatic gas valve
20. Crew's quarters
21. Rear engine nacelle
22. Engine
23. Airscrew
24. Radiator
25. Oil tank
26. Gas-bag
27. Ventilation tank
28. Steel mesh
29. Cat-walk
30. Lower tail fin
31. Upper tail fin
32. Rudders
33. Tail plane
34. Elevator
35. Observation or machine-gun post

## 1917: Sea Scout Twin (SST)

The SST of 1917 was an improved version of the 'Sea Scout' first flown in 1915, the 'T' for Twin referring to the two engines with which this type was powered. 164 feet long and with a maximum diameter of 32 feet, its volume was 60 per cent greater than the SS, totalling 100,650 cubic feet. Its two Rolls-Royce Hawk 75 h.p. engines were mounted on struts above a slim four-seater nacelle, driving two pusher airscrews and giving a maximum speed of approximately 53 m.p.h. An inclined air-shaft positioned in the slip-stream led along the belly of the envelope on each side and supplied the two ballonets. The nacelle was provided with two landing skids and slung on bolt-ropes in the form of goose-feet.

## 1915: Morane-Saulnier 'Parasol' Mark L

This 'parasol' type wing giving greater forward and down visibility and above, through a large semi-circular opening in the centre-section, was a feature adopted by the Morane-Saulnier aircraft company. Extremely manoeuvrable, the MS Mark L was 22 feet long with a wing-span of 37 feet and a wing area of 198 square feet. Powered by an 80 h.p. rotary Gnôme or Le Rhône engine, it could attain a maximum speed of about 78 m.p.h. The main wing could be banked and, like all Morane-Saulnier aircraft of this period, it had balanced elevators.

On the night of 6 June 1915, a young Flight Sub-Lieutenant of the Royal Flying Corps, R. A. J. Warneford, piloting an MS Mark L, bombed the LZ 37, returning from a raid on Calais, bringing it down in flames and thus claiming the first aerial victory over a Zeppelin.

## 1917-1918: The BE2A and BE12 fuselage nacelle

Below, left, and bottom: the Royal Aircraft Establishment at Farnborough built numerous biplanes of this type throughout the First World War, gradually improving their performance. The BE12 was the last of the series, most of which were eventually used for flying training. The initials 'BE' stood for British Experimental. The fuselages of the earlier units came in handy as makeshift nacelles for the first non-rigid 'blimps'. Originally, 'B' referred to the type and 'limp' to the non-rigid envelope but, very soon, all such small airships became generally known as *blimps*. The drawing above shows how the fuselage, less its tail unit, was adapted to form a two-seater nacelle with the under-carriage replaced by a skid. The other drawing shows an elevation of the BE12 fitted with a water-cooled engine, its four-bladed airscrew, the exhaust pipe leading out above the upper wing and the lower wing stepped back towards the tail.

The British 'North Sea' airships, put into service in 1916, were powered by two engines at each side developing 250 h.p. One of the engines can be seen in this photograph, taken during a turn, its airscrew stopped. The struts coupling the nacelle are fitted with two precarious catwalks, one for the mechanic and another lower one for the Lewis gunner.

**A rigid British aircraft-carrying dirigible**

Completed in 1919, the R33 was used experimentally in October 1925 and December 1926 to hook up and release first one, then two Royal Air Force Gloster Grebe biplane fighters, the attachment being made under the keel. Of all British airships, the R33 logged the greatest number of flying hours: approximately 800.

# HERITAGE
# OF THE GREAT WAR

## 1919-1928

What was to happen to the fifteen operational Zeppelins, for the most part built in 1917 and 1918 and each with a volume of 1,942,300 cubic feet? The signing of the Armistice on 11 November 1918 had put an end to the war. Despite severe losses, these Zeppelins still remained. Seven months after the Armistice, seven of them were destroyed by a daring sabotage operation. Seventy ships of the German fleet interned in Scapa Flow were scuttled by their crews and, forty-eight hours later, two airship crews successfully destroyed these seven Zeppelins, suspended from the beams of their hangars at Nordholz and Wittemundhaven where they had been moored, gas-bags deflated under orders from the Allied Commissions. The men, who had planned the operation in strict secrecy, suddenly cut the slings and the heavy airships crashed to the ground, smashed beyond repair. So the L14, L41, L42, L56, L63 and L65, once proud units of the German Navy, were reduced to wrecks.

Under the supervision of the Allied Commission and conforming to the clauses of the armistice terms, the other airships were handed over to the Allies. As a result, France took over the LZ113 which was dismantled so that their engineers could study the construction and the strength of the materials used. One three-engined nacelle is still conserved in the *Musée de L'Air* in France. The L72 was renamed the *Dixmude* and was able to show off its paces before its tragic end in 1923. In June 1920, Great Britain took over the L64 and L71. The L61 was handed over to Italy, component parts of the L30 were transferred to Belgium and, in the same way, the L37 finished up in the hands of the Japanese.

Although the peace treaty categorically denied the right of German aircraft constructors to build large conventional aircraft or airships intended for military use, there was no specific order to prohibit the construction of lighter-than-air craft for civil use. As a result, in 1919, the *Zeppelin Luftschiffbau* wasted little time in building two excellent dirigibles of modest volume, drawing on stocked parts for their construction. These were *Bodensee*, the LZ120 of 706,300 cubic feet and *Nordstern*, the LZ121 of 794,582 cubic feet. These were both powered by three Maybach engines developing 240 h.p., driving the airships at the remarkable cruising speed of 75 to 90 m.p.h. Their cars underneath were comfortably fitted out to carry thirty passengers. The first German airline had resumed its activity and *Bodensee* was taken over by DELAG on 24 August 1919, inaugurating a regular service between Friedrichshafen and Berlin. By the end of the year, flights of 750 miles were made, and one commercial route between Berlin and Stockholm totalled 532 flying hours carrying 2,253 passengers plus about 140 pounds of mail and other correspondence. At the beginning of 1920, just as *Nordstern* was about to join the airline, the Allies decided to put an end to even these civil operations with such large dirigibles and, in 1921, ordered *Bodensee* to be handed over to the Italian authorities. It was renamed *Esperia* and remained in service with the Italian military air services until 1925. *Nordstern* was handed over to France and renamed the *Méditerranée*, serving the French Navy for a further six years.

The old L72, *Dixmude*, taken over by France in July 1920, was captained by Lieutenant de vaisseau du Plessis de Grenédan. The French authorities had already been advised by Dr Eckener that the airship had been designed for high altitude military flying in relatively calm air. Despite this warning, after several training flights for aircrews and ground staff, *Dixmude* was used for propaganda purposes and sent out on flights of long duration. Such flights were made from France to its North African territories and the Sahara areas which risked exposing the airship to considerable air turbulence over the desert regions caused by the hot air upcurrents rising almost vertically. The first of such cruises was happily carried out between 25 and 30 September 1923 over the southern part of Algeria and Tunisia, a flight of nearly 120 hours. The second mission was to take place in December of the same year. A flight of over 2,600 miles had been planned but, on the night of 21 September, *Dixmude* crashed into the Mediterranean Sea off the Italian island of Pantellaria with a total loss of its 51-man crew. It can only be presumed that this tragic accident was due to the failure of the framework after being exposed to too much stress over too long a period of time then, encountering a hurricane force storm, the whole structure collapsed, the airship caught fire, and was lost. A few days later, fishermen from Scaicca on the Sicilian coast pulled in the body of the commander, Jean du Plessis de Grenédan, in their nets.

In 1919, the crossing of the North Atlantic by airship was being considered on both sides of the ocean. For one moment during the war years the Germans had even thought of sending the L72 on a bombing raid on New York, mostly for the propaganda effect, but much against the advice of Dr Eckener. A small American blimp, the Goodrich C5, one of several produced at the end of the war, made an unsuccessful attempt and, returning to Newfoundland in May, was caught in a squall and lost by the handling crew on the ground. But three months later it was the British effort which achieved a brilliant success when the rigid airship R34 made the first Atlantic air crossing and, surpassing this new record, the return flight as well. Major G. H. Scott was the commander to whom all honour is due for his courage and foresight. It was truly unfortunate that he was to be later killed in the terrible disaster that befell the R 101.

As for the R 38, this airship took off from East Fortune in Scotland on 2 July 1919 at 02.30 hrs. The crew consisted of six officers and twenty-one men, including three passengers, Brigadier-General A. M. Maitland, Officer Commanding the base in Britain, an American, Major J. E. M. Pritchard, and one other. This extra passenger was a stowaway, a pilot called Ballantyne, who was discovered when the airship was well under way. According to the flight plan which had been well-studied in advance, the R 38 took off with a load of 16 tons of fuel for the engines, 37,500 lbs of oil and 77,000 lbs of ballast, which left an ample safety margin equivalent to 30 additional flying hours. In fact, apart from the meteorological conditions encountered which necessitated a wide detour to avoid a storm as the airship approached Nova Scotia, when the R 34 actually made a circuit of its landing field at Mineola, 48 miles east of New York, there was still enough fuel for 40 minutes flying time. A surprising fact connected with the landing was that Major J. E. M. Pritchard actually made a parachute jump so as to land before the airship in order to direct the ground crew in handling the dirigible as the air crew brought it to the mooring. This long voyage over the sea had taken 108 hours 12 minutes continuous flying, and the navigation had been carried out with a remarkable precision using cross bearings from land-based direction finding stations and ships on the high seas. Two carrier pigeons were also carried aboard, one of them escaping on arrival, to be picked up by a steamship 800 miles from the American coast!

Four days after the R 34 had gently floated to its mooring mast, the airship took off again. It was on 10 July at 05.55 hrs that the R 34 headed out on the shorter meridional route which also took advantage of the prevailing winds. Paying great attention to orders received during the flight, Major G. H. Scott made his first European landfall on the Irish coast, then landed at Pulham in Norfolk on 13 July at 07.57 hrs after a flight of 75 hours, despite the failure of one of his five engines. Apart from this technical mishap, the rigid airship had now proved itself capable of long flights without intermediate stops.

It was, however, by sea transport that the first large airship was delivered to America. This dirigible had been ordered from the Italian designer and constructor, Usuelli, by the American Navy. It was appropriately called *Roma* and was re-assembled at Langley Field in Virginia, making its first flight on 15 November 1921. After the six Ansaldo engines had been replaced by Liberty engines to increase its speed, *Roma* made its first actual test flight on 21 February 1922, flying over a district unfortunately criss-crossed with high-tension cables. Apparently, a fault in the elevator control system sent the airship nose down, hitting the cables and exploding. Out of the forty-five members of the crew, thirty-four were killed and those who survived were seriously injured.

131

This accident happened six months after another rigid dirigible of 2,719,200 cubic feet, the R 38, again attached to the American Navy as was the ZR 2, was also wrecked. Building of the R 38 was started towards the end of 1918 at the Short Bros factory, and the design was based on the Zeppelin, but the airship was not finished until 1920. An American crew were sent over to Britain to carry out acceptance flight tests before the airship was flown over to Lakehurst, New Jersey. During tests at maximum speed, on 23 June 1921, a disquieting knocking was heard from the tail unit controls. A certain amount of work was carried out to strengthen the internal structure but it was more by rule of thumb than mathematically calculated. On its last acceptance flight test on 23 August, while making tight turns at top speed, the framework, not designed to take such stresses at low altitude, broke in half and the airship crashed into the River Humber near Hull. Only five of the forty-nine persons on board escaped death. British aviation circles deplored the loss of two of their greatest and most experienced men, Air Commodore A. M. Maitland and Major Pritchard who had been aboard the R 34 during its successful two-way crossing of the Atlantic in 1919.

During this period, the American airship constructors had not been idle. From 1919, the American Navy had commissioned the naval dockyards at Philadelphia to produce a large rigid airship of nearly three million cubic feet. The design was based on the L 49 which had crashed at Bourbonne-les-Bains in October 1917. Their work was considerably helped by engineers sent over from the Zeppelin company. Improvements were incorporated so that the airship could be moored to a mast and this dirigible, to be assembled at the Lakehurst air base and coded as the Z 31, was to use helium gas. It was actually christened *Shenandoah*, a Red Indian name which, literally translated, means 'Daughter of the Stars' and first lifted off into the skies on 4 September 1923. After successful air tests, more than 50 flights were made including one from the Atlantic to the Pacific and return, covering over 9,000 miles in 235 flying hours, from 7 to 23 October 1924. As the crew discovered, it was certainly an easily handled aircraft. On 12 January *Shenandoah* was moored as usual. About nine hours later a gale, gusting up to 60 m.p.h., tore it away from the mast. Even after having had a large gash ripped out of the nose portion, leaving some of the skeleton exposed, and with two gas-bags split open, the airship was still able to carry on like a good sailor and attach itself to the fleet, literally, by a jury mast rigged on a fuel tender. From 18 August, the Z 31 used this mast not once, but seven times in all. This sea mooring was made during the big fleet manœuvres of the time and the ship to which the *Shenandoah* moored was the *Patoka*. Lieutenant-Commander Zachary Lansdowne had not only been an airship flying-instructor in Britain during the war years but had also been one of those aboard the R 34 on its transatlantic crossing. Under the command of this officer, *Shenandoah* took off on its fifty-seventh flight on 2 September 1925 towards the Middle West. About 04.00 hrs. on the next

During one of the first French air displays after the Great War, which took place at the Buc aerodrome near Versailles in the summer of 1920, two lighter-than-air craft, an Astra-Torres airship and a Caquot 'sausage' observation balloon fly alongside a twin-engined Farman *Goliath* biplane, currently used in early days of civil aviation.

During the same air display in 1920 at Buc, a small Zodiac ST (*Sport-Tourisme*) of 35,300 cubic feet was piloted by the actress Gaby Morlay, the only woman in France holding an airship pilot's licence.

Below and on opposite page: acceptance trials being held at the Saint-Cyr aerodrome near Versailles in 1920 by the French Naval Air Service for a series of Zodiac airships of 81,200 cubic feet. These blimps were powered by two Renault 80-horsepower engines driving pusher airscrews. Carrying a crew of four, their cruising speed was about 47 m.p.h.

136

day, over Ohio, the crew were unable to avoid extremely violent air turbulence with upcurrents rising so fast that the elevators had no counter-acting effect and the airship was carried up to 6,500 feet. Release valves were opened; the airship dropped to about 3,000 feet to be carried up again another 3,500 feet. A sudden violent squall pushed the tail down. *Shenandoah* broke up into three pieces. The captain's nacelle and the tail crashed to the ground. The forward part started on an erratic flight of several miles like a free balloon out of all control. Although fourteen members of the crew with their captain lost their lives in the command nacelle, twenty of the other occupants were saved as the use of helium gas prevented the remaining part of the wreck from catching fire. The findings of the court of enquiry suggested that the accident was caused by the aerodynamic stresses on the airship, the strain undergone when tossed by the violent upcurrents, and the final blow given by the sudden squall. It may seem somewhat wise-after-the-event to comment that this accident, which had created a profound and chastening effect on the responsible authorities, could have been avoided if meteorological forecasting had been as accurate as in later years.

Some time afterwards, a Zeppelin was handed over to the United States as part of war reparations. The LZ 126 was given the American code ZR 111 and christened *Los Angeles*. This airship was to have a long, successful career in the service of the United States, a career unsullied by major incidents which, in an odd way, seemed to justify the fame achieved by the Friedrichshafen builders.

Dr Eckener was in command unofficially, although the chief pilot of the Zeppelin works, Oberleutnant Flemming was actually the designated captain. With a crew of thirty, including four American officers, *Los Angeles* took off on a delivery flight, on 12 October 1924 and, some 80 hours 52 minutes later, after crossing the Atlantic via the Azores, a flight of 6,775 miles had been accomplished when it landed on 24 October at Lakehurst. The fourteen hydrogen gas-bags were replenished with helium taken from *Shenandoah* which was then grounded for overhaul whilst extra supplies of this liquid, not so plentiful at that time, were awaited. During service with the American forces, *Los Angeles* was used as a training ship for naval crews attached to the air arm, including more than 100 officers as pupils. The airship also carried out several exercises with the fleet, and once while co-operating with the fleet at sea in 1928, the *Los Angeles* actually touched down on the deck of the aircraft carrier *Saratoga* without any special landing equipment. During the fleet manœuvres off Panama in 1931, this dirigible was used to shadow the supposed enemy fleet, an exercise carried out successfully for two hours before it was spotted. For mooring while at sea, the airship used the mast of the tanker *Patoka* anchored in the Balboa roadsteads. Successful tests were also made using this dirigible as a flying aircraft carrier. Vought VO 1 naval reconnaissance airplanes hooked up to a sort of retractable trapeze device attached to the belly of the airship in flight, dropping off again when ordered out on patrol.

The nose reinforcement of small rods is clearly visible in this photograph of the AT 16, emerging from one of the hangars at the Saint-Cyr aerodrome in 1919. After the war, this Astra-Torres unit and a Zodiac cruiser were put into service for passenger flights by the *Compagnie Générale Transaérienne* which had been set up in 1908 by that renowned patron of French aviation, Henri Deutsch de la Meurthe, founder of the famous Astra company.

In the course of a long period of activity, *Los Angeles* made a total of 331 flights, the equivalent of 4,320 flying hours, some 2,000 hours being spent at mooring masts. It was only on 30 June 1932, during the great economic 'slump' that hit America, that this old and loyal retainer was finally grounded by the air forces, never to glide majestically through the skies again.

Meanwhile, in the Old World, only two airship builders remained in France. Astra delivered the last Astra-Torres cruisers to the French Fleet Air Arm, while another was exported to Japan. The Zodiac company was to continue production somewhat longer, with two major sections, one building air-cruisers for the naval air services such as the VZ 24 in 1923 and the other making small blimps for civilian use. Most of these slight volume airships were employed on aerial publicity. Large canvas panels were hung on the flanks of the envelope to attract the curious at areonautical gatherings around Paris.

In Italy, where constructors had elected to concentrate on building semi-rigid airships, an event of the greatest importance was to take place. Colonel Umberto Nobile, well-known as a dedicated airship specialist, constructed the N 1, *Norge* which was to take the explorer Roald Amundsen on a survey flight over the Arctic ice cap.

Amundsen, who achieved fame in finding the South Pole in 1911, made one attempt to reach the top of the world in 1925 by means of two seaplanes. German Dornier Wal amphibious aircraft, built in Italy and designed to land on the sea or the polar ice fields were his choice. The expedition took off from Spitzberg on 21 May but the aircraft were forced to land 160 miles from the Pole and the expedition could not continue. After an enormous effort, a short runway on the ice was built and the only aircraft remaining in good flying state took off on the return journey. This courageous attempt to fly over the Pole had not been a complete failure as Amundsen had gathered considerable important and useful information. From then on he was absolutely convinced that the dirigible was the only suitable aircraft which could fly over these regions in relative safety.

The subsequent expedition was not so much an attempt to merely fly over the Pole but to make an aerial survey of this vast and, so far, unknown territory which stretched from the Pole to the north-west coast of America. This 'Pole of Ice' was totally inaccessible by any other means than by air and Amundsen passionately desired to discover whether this white frozen blanket covered an extension of the American archipelago or whether it was just an oceanic ice cap.

On the advice of a Norwegian officer, Lieutenant-Commander Riiser-Larsen, who had been a member of the 1925 seaplane flight, Amundsen obtained permission from the Italian government to take over the N 1, which had been successfully flight-tested after its construction in 1924. A very generous American, James W. Ellsworth, who had made a considerable financial contribution to the 1925 expedition, was patron of the new venture and the airship was purchased and baptized *Norge* on 29 March 1926. The base from which the expedition was to leave was the same as the preceding flight, and was established at Ny Aalesund in King's Bay at Spitzberg. Although the ground was frozen to a considerable depth, a complete hangar and mooring mast were built. The flight from Rome to Spitzberg, a distance of 4,750 miles, was made by *Norge* lasting 44 hours flying time, between 29 March and 6 May. The airship crossed France, made a stop at the British airship base, Pulham, then its route passed over Oslo, Stockholm, Finland, the U.S.S.R., whose government offered the use of its hangar at Gratchina near Leningrad, thence to Vadsö in the extreme northern regions of Norway where a mooring mast had also been provided. No technical misadventures were reported, the only repair being the replacement of a starboard engine cylinder-head carried out in flight.

In all, the crew consisted of sixteen men, comprising eight Norwegians, six Italians, one American and one Swedish member apart from the small fox terrier bitch, Titina, adopted as mascot since Colonel Nobile refused to be parted from his dog. Roald Amundsen and Lincoln Ellsworth, son of the patron, were leaders of the expedition, with Colonel Umberto Nobile in command of *Norge*. Lieutenant-Commander Riiser-Larsen of the Norwegian Navy carried out the duties of navigator and second-in-command. Also of the Norwegian Navy, Lieutenant-Commander Emil Hörgen was appointed officer in charge of steering controls, Captain Birger Gottwaldt was in command of wireless communications, Flight-Lieutenant Oscar Olmdal in charge of the starboard engine, Oscar Wisting was responsible for altitude controls, Fridtjof Storm Johnsen acted as assistant radio-operator, and Frederick Ramm, a journalist, completed the Norwegian nationals aboard. The Swede was Professor Finn Malmgren, a meteorologist. The Chief mechanic, Cecioni, had four Italian fitters in his charge plus Alessandrini, a trimmer and general hand.

Navigational instruments were little different to the previous seaplane flight: they comprised a solar compass, magnetic compasses, sextants and a drift indicator. Accommodation for off-duty crew was rudimentary, and even their outfits were restricted in the interests of the weight-saving. Food supplies were limited to 350 grammes per day, and these conditions were strictly enforced.

Having taken the greatest and minutest care with all their preparations, they could not have been other than surprised to see a three-engined Fokker, not far from their base, on the morning of 10 May, headed for the Pole. The *Josephine Ford* was piloted by a famous airman called Floyd Bennett with Commander Richard E. Byrd as navigator, a crew which was to make a faultless polar flight in advance of Amundsen. The Norwegian explorer, with a typical chivalrous gesture, was one of the first to congratulate the airplane crew when they returned after a flight of only sixteen hours. Although Byrd's polar flight was never doubted at the time, certain experts were to question the accuracy of the aircraft's log many years later.

While remembering that a mere flight over the Pole itself was not the main object of the Amundsen expedition, certain more explosive members of the crew were inclined to take this competitive attempt with a certain rancour.

On the next day, 11 May, at 08.55 hrs GMT, with sun shining and the air still, *Norge* took off in its turn with seven tons of fuel. There was enough fuel to supply the three engines, one of the beam engines being kept in reserve, to make the journey at the most economical cruising speed of 50 m.p.h. Byrd's Fokker with Floyd Bennett at the controls pulled into formation. The airship's rival flew alongside for a few moments, then drew away and *Norge* was left to the solitude which reigned over this immense expanse of ice desert. At 01.21 hrs, on the following morning they were over the Pole after a flight of 1,055 miles in 16 hours 30 minutes. The airship gently lost 300 feet in height and, from the main catwalk of the keel accommodation suspended underneath, the flags of the three nations represented by the mixed crew were dropped on the North Pole. The flagstaffs had specially sharpened hafts so that they would penetrate the surface and remain upright.

There were now some 750 miles of ice to cross before the farthest northern tip of Alaska, Point Barrow, could be reached. Soon, unfortunately, banks of rolling fog prevented any astronomical sighting for position fixing. Ice and frost began to form and give anxious moments to the crew; the solar compass was a frozen block. No radio was available to give valuable meteorological information; the wireless mast was covered with a thick, compact layer of snow. Now and then, pieces of ice broke off the airscrew blades; the envelope, although reinforced at such points, was holed by these flying chunks of ice, and only blocked up with difficulty.

The crew doggedly stuck to their posts as *Norge* pushed on until, during a break in the weather at 06.45 hrs GMT on 13 May, they saw the outline of the land they had ardently sought, over to port. One hour later and they were over the coast of Alaska. Now *Norge* was working along the coast in the dismal greyness, headed for the Bering Straits after 46 hours 20 minutes in the air. They had to run off to the lee of the planned course to avoid the mountains, some over 3,000 feet high. Their route was erratic; the airship was weighed down by no less than a ton of ice which coated every conceivable part of it. But the crew brought its aircraft down during a providential calm spell on to the frozen surface of a small lagoon at Teller, some 56 miles to the north of Nome on the 11 May, about 08.00 hrs GMT. This pin-point had been their destination. The first polar air crossing from Europe to America had been accomplished: it had taken 71 hours, air time.

The crew were exhausted as much by lack of rest as the glacial temperatures but, in every sense, they were warmly welcomed by Eskimos who, themselves, had come to their assistance while *Norge* was landing.

Colonel Umberto Nobile was promoted to the rank of general as a result of the success of the Amundsen expedition aboard *Norge*. Now fully confident of the ability of the dirigible to navigate over these uninviting Arctic

**1921 : The Oehmichen balloon helicopter**
On 15 January 1921, the French engineer Etienne Oehmichen, a vertical flight enthusiast, air-tested his first flying machine equipped with two lifting airscrews, 21 feet in diameter, driven by a 25 h.p. Dutheil and Chalmers engine. A balloon of 5,085 cubic feet provided stability, its lift reducing the dead weight by 154 pounds and enabling the aircraft to lift a total of 587 pounds. In this photograph, the inventor is seen using his own weight to counter-balance the engine.

1

2

### 1 1919: American Type C naval airship nacelle

Carrying a six-man crew, this nacelle, slung under a non-rigid envelope of 180,100 cubic feet, was so constructed as to be able to float. The Type C was 210 feet long with a maximum diameter of 46 feet. These airships were ordered for the U.S. naval air services towards the end of the war, their two 125 h.p. engines on each side of the nacelle giving them a maximum speed of about 62 m.p.h.

### 2 1918-1919: The French CMT dirigible nacelle

Apart from the small projection of the pilot's cabin, this enclosed nacelle built of duralumin has a remarkably streamlined form.

### 3 1919: American Type C airship nacelle

This nacelle would have been considerably more aerodynamic had it not been for the drag generated by the blunt, rectangular-fronted radiators on the two engines which were mounted on brackets.

### 4 1924: French naval air service Zodiac V6 nacelle

The large observation windows and pilot's cabin slightly overhang this enclosed nacelle which was fitted with two engines both water-cooled by a Lamblin radiator, the cylindrical shape of which minimized air resistance.

3

stretches, the Italian general had begun to dream up more elaborate plans for polar expeditions as early as the landing at Teller, and even included the idea of a transpolar route from Japan. Little did he believe then that, thirty years later, a regular transpolar air route would be an accepted reality. As it appeared that a greater range was now obtainable, plans were being drawn up for a series of geographical surveys to be three flights of 1,500 to 2,500 miles, each to be a complete exploration in itself. Plans included a voyage of exploration about the Siberian coasts and another towards the coasts of Greenland and Canada. The final triumph was to be an exploration of the polar territories, the dirigible landing on the ice to allow members of the scientific team to carry out oceanographic research.

Favourably considered by the Italian Government and with the backing of the Air Minister, the general proposition was adopted by the municipality of Milan, the city named as the point of departure. An identical copy of *Norge*, having the same volume of 653,350 cubic feet, was already under construction but subject to several modifications which were based on experience gained with its sister ship. For example, the command cabin, which also housed radio equipment and the wireless operator, was more spacious. The three engines, developing a total of 780 h.p., were insulated against the intense cold, and the envelope was reinforced with an encircling band where ice breaking off from the airscrews might penetrate the outer covering. A small inflatable car was also provided so that a member of the crew could be lowered down to the surface of the ice. Navigation and telecommunications instruments comprised five magnetic compasses, one solar compass, four sextants, one radio direction-finding loop, one transmitter, two wireless receivers, and one emergency transmitter.

Not only was much time spent on technical preparations, carried out with minute attention, but the members of the crew were also to be chosen with the greatest care. For certain propaganda reasons and as it was presumed he might take precedence over the national hero, General Umberto Nobile, Amundsen was not included. As the Norwegian explorer was fifty-three when he set out in *Norge*, he was excluded on the pretext of his age. Seven veterans of the previous exploratory flight were called on to serve, and the crew was joined by three Italian naval officers, Capitano di corvetta Adalberto Mariano and Capitano di corvetta Filippo Zappi, responsible for navigation, and Capitano di corvetta Alfredo Viglieri. Responsibility for the actual handling of the flights controls was also divided between engineers Natale Cecioni and Felice Trojani, handling the altitude vanes, and Renato Alessandrini responsible for rudder control. There were three experienced men to record the scientific findings; Professor Aldo Pontremoli and two foreigners, Franz Behounek and Finn Malmgren, who had served on *Norge*. Two Italian journalists made up the total of eighteen persons aboard the airship.

The members of the crew who were to fly *Italia*, as the airship was christened, were received in audience by Pope Pius XI on 31 March 1928.

To Nobile, the Pontiff presented a large oak cross containing a parchment in a recess hollowed out of the wood. 'As all crosses', he said, 'this, too, will be heavy to bear.' It was to be a prophetic statement. Fourteen days later, after dark, an enthusiastic crowd saw *Italia* off, on the beginning of its ferry flight to King's Bay at Spitzberg, to the hangar which had sheltered *Norge* two years before. After a flight of 1,125 miles, buffeted by violent storms, *Italia* was forced to land at Stolp in East Prussia where an old Zeppelin hangar was still in service. It was 18 April. Certain parts of the tail plane unit assembly had been damaged by the adverse weather conditions and replacement parts had to be sent from Italy with the greatest speed transport could summon at that time. Even so, they were not ready to take off again until 3 May, completing the remaining 2,180 miles by 6 May, with only one stop, hooked up to the mooring mast at Vadsö in Norway.

After a flight test of several hours, the aerial exploration started when *Italia* lifted off on 10 May. As had been planned, an aerial survey was made as far as North Land from 15 to 18 May, and produced a wealth of scientific and other information. At 01.38 hrs GMT, *Italia* took off again and headed for the North Pole. It flew along the Greenland coast for two hours then, at 17.29 hrs, approaching Cape Bridgman, the airship swung to port and on to its course for the Pole, flying on two engines in order to save fuel. A tail wind helped them along and, after the first few hours in banks of fog, the sky cleared and the visibility extended, unobstructed for hundreds of miles in every direction.

Despite the threatening distant curtain of clouds, the North Pole was reached without further ado at 00.20 hrs on 24 May, after a sun shot with a sextant had proved the position. From Cape Bridgman, their average speed over 438 miles had been 65 m.p.h. Motors idling, Nobile turned the airship in a sweeping circle round this point at the top of the world, dropped the Italian flag, then the national colours, followed by a flag of the City of Milan, a small medallion of the Virgin given to him by the inhabitants of Forli and, finally, the cross handed to him by the Pope, attached to a large streaming pennant. It was now 01.30 hrs. The sky was beginning to cloud over and the visibility was shortening so, instead of the descent to the ice by means of the inflatable nacelle, it was decided to head back to King's Bay.

The sun had disappeared, a thick fog built up as a steady blow from the south-west pushed *Italia* towards the East. Sharp snow squalls painted the envelope in white sticky crystals, then with the following heavy frost, ice began to build up. As always, the ice on the airscrews would thicken until the centrifugal force and the weight of the ice would hurl chunks off, slamming into the flanks of the hull. For eight hours the average speed fell to 30 m.p.h. Even using the third engine against the freshening wind, the speed only amounted to 40 m.p.h. On 21 May at 06.00 hrs, a wireless distress call went out. The situation was critical; the envelope was becoming heavier and heavier. Four hours later, another wireless message told the world they were fighting a westerly gale. Then there was silence.

It was 9 June before the whole story could be told. A radio message sent out by the survivors was picked up, at last, by the supply ship *Città di Milano* anchored in King's Bay. At 10.33 hrs on the morning of 25 May, now overloaded with ice that had built up on every conceivable part of the airship, *Italia* dived down on to the frozen surface below. The command nacelle was ripped off when the airship crashed. The rear engine and the mechanic looking after it was wrenched away and this unfortunate member of the crew, Vincenzo Pomella, was killed immediately. Nobile and eight of his companions were now held prisoner by the barrier ice. Less or more seriously injured, they had a few provisions between them and a wireless set. Freed from the weight of those sections which had come adrift with the crash, the envelope soared up, rapidly gaining height, with seven of the crew still somewhere in the remains of *Italia* which disappeared for ever. Although the names of those survivors wrecked on the ice cap are always mentioned when this drama of the air has been recounted, the names of those who disappeared with the wild, uncontrollable envelope were too soon and are too often forgotten. Dr Aldo Pontremoli, the four veterans of *Norge*, Chief Mechanic Renato Alessandrini and his men Ettore Arduino, Attilio Caratti, the wireless operator Ettore Pedretti, Ugo Lago and Francesco Tomaselli, the two journalists, all these disappeared practically without trace. According to the survivors with Nobile, black smoke was seen shortly after the crash and it was presumed that, completely out of control, the envelope had again smashed into the ice and burst into flames.

Much has been written and there is still a great deal to tell about those who were left, counting the long, long days, hoping to be saved. Three of them could not endure the strain of waiting and trudged off into the bitter wilderness towards what they hoped was succour and life. Professor Malmgrem died of exhaustion on the way; Mariano and Zappi were finally picked up. Such were the stories that occupied the world press. The tragedy did have its other side. A burst of solidarity brought into coordinated action Swedish, Norwegian, Russian, Italian and French flying men who went to the help of the survivors. The rescue of General Nobile by the Swedish pilot Lundberg, before Nobile's companions in distress had been themselves rescued, did not escape severe press comment.

This humanitarian international cooperation did rob science and the world of one illustrious man, Roald Amundsen. Putting aside any bitterness that he might reasonably have been expected to hold, he joined in the search. Amundsen took off in a French seaplane, piloted by Commandant Guilbaud, with his old comrade of the 1925 flight, Lieutenant Dietrichson. Somewhere between Tromso and Spitzberg, these three lives were lost. Bits of wrecked airplane recovered from the sea later on were positively identified as belonging to Amundsen's machine.

Overcome by the lasting ostracism that greeted him, General Nobile exiled himself to the USSR, the country which had rescued his companions with the Soviet ice-breaker *Krassine*.

**The R 33 moored to its mast at Pulham**
On 16 April 1925, the British rigid dirigible R 33 was torn away from this mooring mast by a squall and its nose was completely destroyed. Drifting towards Holland, it was only due to the consummate skill of the captain, Lieutenant Booth, that it was brought back to its mooring after a flight of 29 hours. In front of the rear engine nacelle on this picture can be glimpsed a biplane hooked up to the keel in preparation for the air tests made in October of that same year.

Major G.H. Scott aboard the R34 which he commanded on its double crossing of the North Atlantic in 1919. This British officer was also a member of the R100 crew which repeated this achievement in 1930. Unhappily, two months later, Major Scott was killed when the R101 crashed near Beauvais in France.

The R34 flying over St. Paul's Cathedral in London. This was the first airship to cross the North Atlantic between 2 and 6 July 1919, the return flight to Britain being made between 10 and 13 July.

Above: details of *Bodensee*, the Zeppelin LZ120 of 706,300 cubic feet. It was renamed *Esperia* when handed over to the Italian Government in 1921. Left to right: cat-walk built inside the keel, one of the ballast sacks, and the nacelle for the flying crew.

Below: This photograph, taken in a hangar at Saint-Cyr, shows the LZ121, *Nordstern*, which had a volume of 794,600 cubic feet. It was renamed *Méditerranée* after being handed over to the French Navy in 1921.

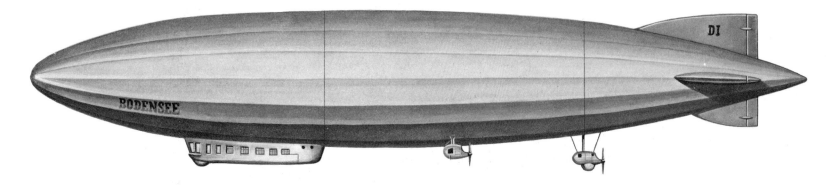

## 1919: The Zeppelin LZ120, 'Bodensee'

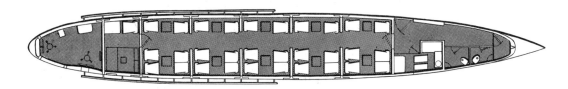

## 1920-1923: The Zeppelin L72, 'Dixmude'

Several months before the end of the war, Germany was said to be planning a retaliatory bombing raid on New York using the Zeppelin LZ114, designated L72 while in service with the Navy. Although such a mission would, in theory, have been within its range, the raid never took place and it was not until two years later, on 9 July 1920, that the L72 was flown for the first time. Shortly afterwards, under orders from the Allies, it was handed over to the French Government and renamed *Dixmude*, Lieutenant de Vaisseau Jean du Plessis de Grenédan being appointed captain. 694 feet in length and 96 feet in diameter, *Dixmude* had 15 gas-bags with a total volume of 2,406,700 cubic feet, the maximum capacity for military Zeppelins. Seven Maybach 260 h.p. engines produced a total of 1,820 h.p., two engines being installed in the after section of the commander's nacelle, four in two pairs of nacelles to port and starboard of the envelope's belly and the seventh in an in-line nacelle at the rear.

The airship was grounded for a considerable time while the hydrogen gas-bags were being replaced. During this period, a supplementary nacelle was fitted close to the underbelly of the envelope, about a quarter of its length from the nose. After the refit, *Dixmude* was put into service in August 1923. In September, it made a long cruise to Algeria and Tunisia, remaining airborne for 148 hours 41 minutes. On the night of 21 December, returning from a flight to Southern Algeria, *Dixmude* was caught in a violent storm off the southern coasts of Sicily. Already under strain from some 300 hours' flying time and intensive service for which it had never been designed, the airship broke up and crashed in flames, killing all fifty-one people aboard. This disaster marked the end of the use of rigid airships in France.

In 1919, utilizing their considerable stock of spare parts, the Zeppelin Company built a medium-range dirigible, the LZ120 which was christened *Bodensee*, the German name for Lake Constance. 396 feet in length and 61 feet in diameter, its original volume of 706,300 cubic feet distributed between 15 gas-bags was later increased to 794,600 cubic feet. Powered by four 240-horsepower Maybach engines, *Bodensee* made its maiden flight on 20 August 1919 and proved to be the fastest Zeppelin ever produced, attaining a maximum speed of 82 m.p.h. Behind the captain's nacelle was a long cabin fitted out for thirty passengers. From October 1919 until the end of that year, a regular service was run between Friedrichshafen and Berlin, 2,400 passengers as well as eight tons of mail and parcels being carried in a total of 78 flights. Flights were also made to Stockholm. By order of the Allied powers, *Bodensee* was handed over to the Italian Government on 3 July 1921, being delivered to Rome-Ciampino by Dr Eckener himself, after a direct flight of 830 miles. Renamed *Esperia*, the former LZ120 was used by the Italian air services on several missions including naval manoeuvres, being finally scrapped in 1925.

The passenger accommodation on *Bodensee* was divided into five compartments with large bay windows, interconnected by a central corridor. Each compartment had two pairs of facing chairs to port and one pair on the starboard side, with a small table between each. Behind the pilot's cabin was the wireless room and, at the back of the nacelle, toilets and a restaurant.

Maybach engines were practically standard equipment on Zeppelins during the war, the Maybach company eventually being taken over by the airship constructors. Starting with the 210 h.p. Mark CX in 1914, power was increased to 240 h.p. with the Mark HSL in 1915 and up to 260 h.p. from 1917 onwards with the Mark IVa. The illustration on the right shows the 260 h.p. six-cylinder overhead camshaft engine with a cut-away drawing of two of the cylinders.

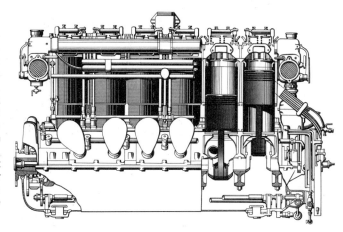

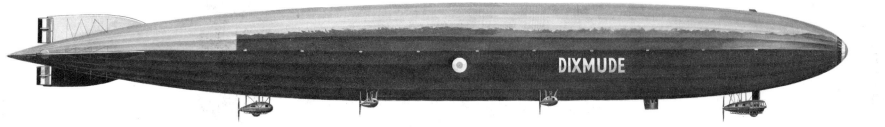

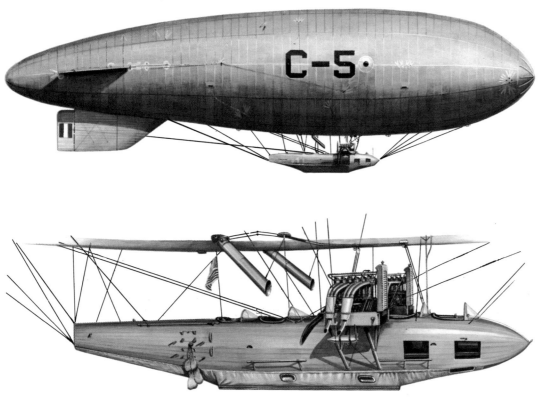

## 1919: The American C5 dirigible

In 1918, the U.S. Naval Air Service ordered thirty small, non-rigid coastal patrol Type C airships from the Goodyear and Goodrich companies but reduced the order to fifteen after the Armistice. Patterned after the British 'blimps' which had proved so successful, the Type C were 210 feet in length, 43 feet at the largest diameter and had a volume of 168,100 cubic feet. Powered by two Hispano-Suiza 150-horsepower engines they could carry a crew of six at a speed of over 60 m.p.h. In 1921, the C7 was the first airship to be filled with helium. The C5, shown here, made an attempt to cross the North Atlantic on 14 May 1919. Taking off from Long Island, it reached Newfoundland in 23 hours but, after landing, violent squalls tore it away from its moorings and the ground crew were unable to restrain it. The C5 took off on its own, crashed into the sea and disappeared.

## 1919: The C5 nacelle

Designed to minimize air resistance, this nacelle was fitted with two Hispano-Suiza engines mounted side-by-side, each driving a pusher air-screw. The two parallel supporting struts in the engine framework can be seen, as well as the engine radiators in the front and, behind, the two conduits for the ballonets. The nacelle comprised three cockpits with windscreens for the duty crew and a rest cabin with two large ports. This rest accommodation was a necessity as such airships could remain airborne for as long as 47 hours.

## 1920: Zodiac YZST

This small 'sports' airship, the letters S and T denoting *sport* and *tourisme* being proposed by the constructors for its official registration, had a volume of only 35,300 cubic feet, was 97 feet long with a maximum diameter of 26 feet, and was equipped with an enclosed two-seater streamlined nacelle with a landing skid. Powered by an air-cooled 60 h.p. radial Anzani engine, this Zodiac could maintain a cruising speed of about 37 m.p.h. Directional and altitude controls were operated by one and the same wheel mounted on a mobile column. The pilot assigned to this airship was Pierre Debroutelle.

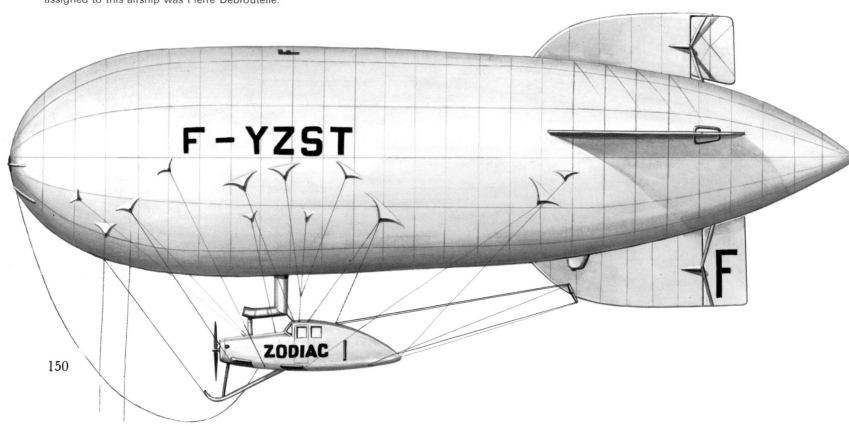

# THE BRITISH R 34 RIGID AIRSHIP

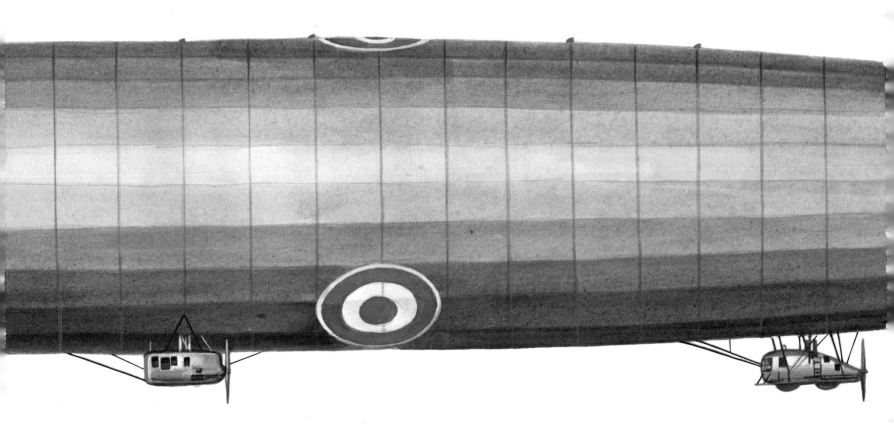

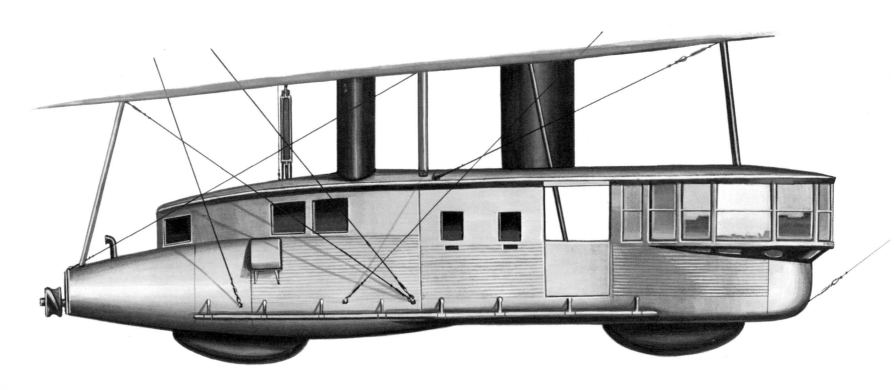

**1919: The British R 34 rigid airship**

The R 34 was built by William Beardmore & Co. during the war. Its design was based on the giant L 33 Zeppelin which had been captured with its crew when forced down in Scotland on 24 September 1916. The R 34 was 669 feet long, 77 feet in diameter and its 19 gas-bags held a total of 1,942,300 cubic feet. Powered by five Sunbeam Maori 270-horsepower engines, its maximum speed was 53 m.p.h. One engine was mounted behind the pilot's cabin, two were on opposite sides of the envelope in their own nacelles and a pair of engines drove one airscrew in a nacelle towards the tail. The R 34 made history in 1919 by being the first airship to cross the North Atlantic and make the return journey under the command of Major G. H. Scott.

According to the plan that had been carefully worked out before the Armistice, even down to the departure point and date, the R 34 lifted off from East Fortune in Scotland on 2 July 1919 and, after a masterly display of navigation in the teeth of appalling weather conditions, reached Mineola on Long Island in 108 hours 12 minutes. The return flight was made by an easier, more southern route between 10 and 13 July in 75 hours 3 minutes, landing at Pulham in Norfolk. After this transatlantic exploit, the R 34 remained in service until January 1921 when, after surviving considerable damage as a result of crashing into a Yorkshire hill in the darkness but nevertheless being brought safely back to base, it was destroyed at its mooring mast by a sudden and violent storm.

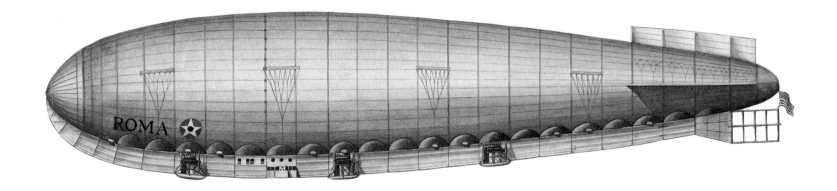

## 1921 : 'Roma'

In 1921, this airship was delivered by sea to the U.S. Army which had ordered its construction. *Roma* was a semi-rigid dirigible with a volume of 1,200,700 cubic feet in 12 gas-bags, a length of 420 feet and a maximum diameter of 75 feet. Although the original six Italian Ansaldo engines were later replaced by American Liberty engines, the name was unchanged and remained *Roma*.

## 1923-1925: The ZR1, 'Shenandoah'

This was the first rigid dirigible built in the U.S.A. as a scout aircraft for the Navy. The USS ZR1, S standing for Scout, was a technical copy of the Zeppelin L49 captured almost intact at Bourbonne-les-Bains in France on 20 October 1917. It was proudly christened *Shenandoah*, a Red Indian name meaning 'Daughter of the Stars'. Produced at the Naval Air Establishment at Lakehurst, New Jersey, with the collaboration of engineers from the Zeppelin company, *Shenandoah* had a volume of 2,825,200 cubic feet contained in twenty gas-bags. It was 33 feet longer than the L49 owing to its use of helium, which has less lifting power than hydrogen, the envelope was 676 feet in length and had a diameter of 79 feet. Six 350 h.p. Packard engines, producing a total horsepower of 2,100, were installed in six nacelles: one in-line engine in the nose nacelle, another in the rear nacelle, and two engine nacelles at each side, mounted close to the underside of the envelope. The forward nacelle for the flying crew was equipped with a ladder, enclosed in a metal sleeve, leading into the envelope. The engine that was originally fitted in this nacelle was then removed to make room for wireless communication equipment. Gear for mooring to a 134-foot mast was also provided. Maximum speed was 70 m.p.h. with a cruising speed of 46 m.p.h.

**Control nacelle of the R 34**

This nacelle had a large bay window jutting out over the forward end behind which was the helmsman's cabin, followed by those of the crewman controlling the elevators, the flying crew, the men in charge of ballast and remote control of the engines. Further back was a rest-room and, right at the after end, the engine compartment with a pusher air-screw fixed to the engine shaft. Two cat-walks were provided for access to the inside of the envelope. Also worthy of note are the vertical radiator, the long hand-rail for use by the ground crew, running along the base of the nacelle, and the two pneumatic landing shock-absorbers.

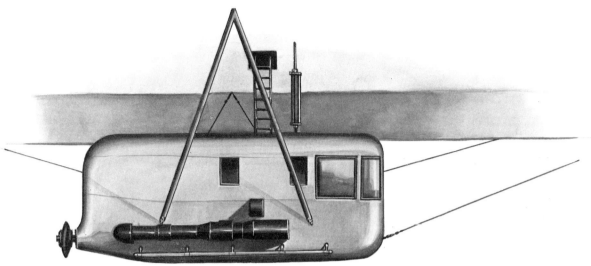

**Side engine nacelle on the R 34**

Ports were provided in the sides and the ends of this nacelle which was fitted close to the belly of the envelope and reached by a small ladder. Mounting was by means of double V-struts braced with cables. An exhaust manifold runs along the bottom of the nacelle.

**Rear engine nacelle on the R 34**

This nacelle housed two engines driving a large three-bladed airscrew, two vertical radiators grouped together, a small crew space with windows and a ladder leading into the envelope. Its lower part was equipped in a similar way to the captain's nacelle, with a hand-rail and two pneumatic landing shock absorbers.

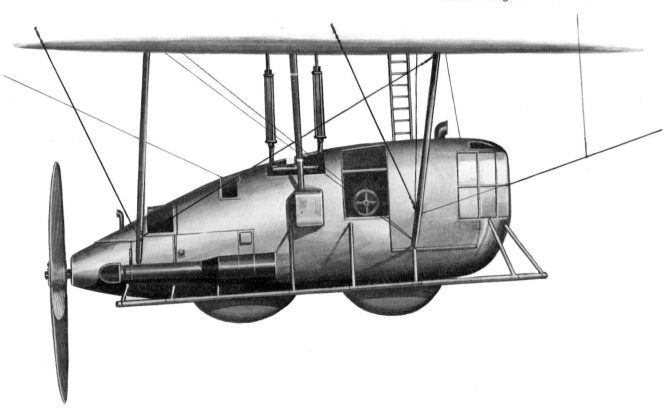

**1921 : 'Roma'**

The U.S. Army took delivery of this semi-rigid airship, built to their order in Italy, in the autumn of 1921.

Right: the over-sized triplane tail unit on *Roma*. On 22 February 1922, one of the elevators broke and the airship lost height, crashing into high-tension cables and bursting into flames. Thirty-four members of the crew were killed and nine seriously injured in this disaster.

**The ZR1 : 'Shenandoah'**

The ZR1 seen on manoeuvres with the U.S. Navy. During the summer of 1924 the rigid dirigible *Shenandoah* often moored to a jury mast rigged on the stern of a fleet tanker.

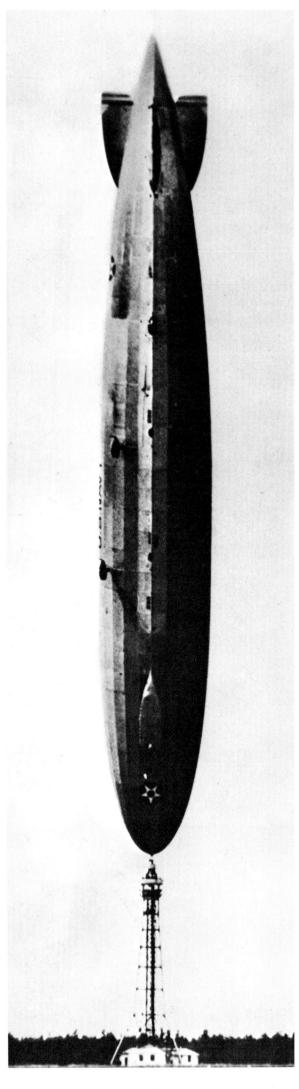

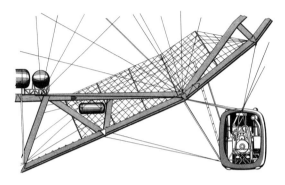

Above: Gas-cells inside the envelope of the ZR111, *Los Angeles*.
Right: Petrol tanks alongside the keel cat-walk in *Los Angeles*.

**Left: ZR111, 'Los Angeles'**

The unusual attitude of the ZR111, or ex-LZ126, in this photograph resulted from the airship being caught by a sudden shift of wind when moored to the mast at Lakehurst in August 1927 and being lifted into a vertical position.

**Above: 1924: ZR111, 'Los Angeles,' formerly the German LZ216**

Technical cross-section of an engine nacelle. This side nacelle is mounted on one of the longerons comprising the skeleton, by three struts braced with cables. This arrangement not only provided for the suspension of the nacelle but also served to transfer the airscrew thrust and engine torque to the main framework. A narrow ladder allowed the crew access to the inside of the envelope. The oblique cross-bars riveted to the longeron carry the petrol and oil tanks as well as the water supply for engine cooling. A metal network attached to the sides of the framework evenly distributes the pressure from the gas-bags.

1930: The ZR111, *Los Angeles*, acting as an aircraft carrier. A Vought UO1 Navy reconnaissance biplane is seen here, preparing to hook-up to the trapeze arrangement lowered by the airship crew, by means of a special device fixed to the centre section of the wing.

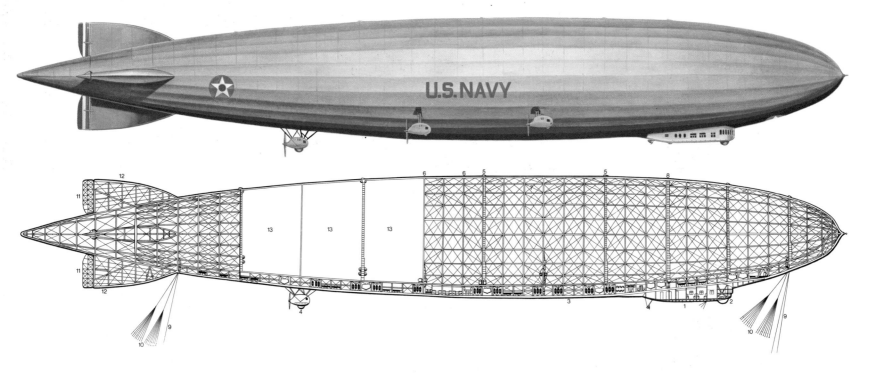

**Above: Longitudinal cross-section of the ZR111, 'Los Angeles'**

1. Passengers' nacelle
2. Command and pilot's nacelle
3. Keel cat-walk
4. Rear engine nacelle
5. Main ribs
6. Secondary ribs
7. Bracing
8. Observation platform
9. Ground mooring cables
10. Ground arresting cables
11. Rudder
12. Tail fin
13. Gas-bags

### 1924: ZR111, the ex-LZ126 renamed 'Los Angeles'

After the skeleton of the British R38, a rigid dirigible destined for delivery to the U.S.A., broke up near Hull on 23 August 1921, it was decided to build a large rigid airship in Germany under the provisions for reparations contained in the peace treaty. This Zeppelin, the 126th to leave the factory at Friedrichshafen, was baptised *Los Angeles* and bore the American code number ZR3. 656 feet long and 90 feet in diameter, this airship had a volume of 2,472,000 cubic feet, almost 353,000 more than the last combat Zeppelins. Five reversible 440-horsepower Maybach engines were fitted in five nacelles, two on each side of the envelope and one in-line nacelle towards the tail. Under the nose, a long, spacious nacelle was equipped for the flying crew and captain. Test flown on 27 August 1924, the dirigible was delivered under the command of Dr Eckener, making the flight from Friedrichshafen to Lakehurst in 81 hours, between 12 and 15 October, at an average speed of 62 m.p.h. In America, the gas-bags were inflated with helium and *Los Angeles* was put into service with the U.S. Navy, being used for flying training, as well as taking part in fleet manoeuvres, mooring to jury masts rigged on ships and even landing on aircraft carriers without any special equipment. In 1929, the same airship gave a successful demonstration of hooking-up and releasing Navy fighter and reconnaissance aircraft. It was not until 1932 that *Los Angeles* was finally taken out of service after an exceptionally long and distinguished career, having achieved the record number of 4,320 flying hours.

**Right: Fittings in the main nacelle of the ZR111, 'Los Angeles'**

1. Barograph
2. Device measuring the traction force of mooring cables
3. Outside air thermometer
4. Variometer
5. Inclinometer and barometer
6. Inclinometer panel light
7. Gas pressure gauge
8. Helm position indicator
9. Elevator control
10. Gyroscope
11. Water ballast control panel
12. Gas control panel
13. Hand lamp
14. Gas thermometer
15. Magnetic compass
16. Turn indicator
17. Panel Lamp
18. Helm Position indicator
19. Helm
20. Navigator's table lamp
21. Mooring cable release
22. Navigation table
23. Ground handling cable release
24. Morse signalling lamp
25. Signalling bell
26. Telegraph
25. Loud-speaker and channel switch
28. Telephone switchboard
29. Air speed indicator
30. Floodlight switch
31. Nacelle lighting

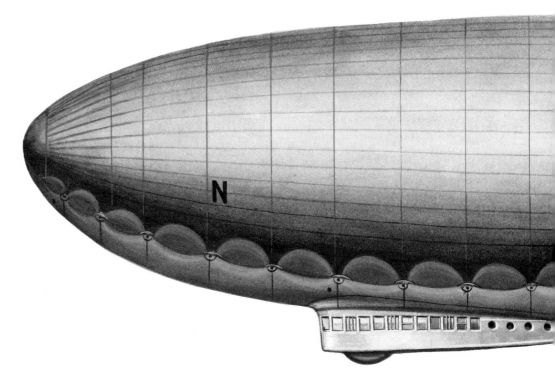

## 1925: The Goodyear 'Pilgrim'

*Pilgrim*, with its volume of 55,000 cubic feet, was the prototype of a long series of non-rigid airships built by the Goodyear-Zeppelin Corporation, later to become the Goodyear Aircraft Corporation. *Pilgrim* was powered by an air-cooled radial engine driving a pusher airscrew at the tail end of an enclosed nacelle and producing a maximum airspeed of about 50 m.p.h. The airscrew's slipstream was used to feed an internal ballonet by means of a short duct.

The smallest unit produced by the Goodyear Corporation, *Pilgrim* was also the first American non-rigid airship to have an enclosed cabin nacelle, resulting in its being called 'the first American air yacht'. This nacelle was attached to the underside of the envelope by means of a short keel. The nose was later braced to take the necessary fixing for mooring to a mast.

## 1922: Nobile Mark N

An Italian engineer, Umberto Nobile, designed this semi-rigid airship which was carefully studied by the *Stabilimento di Costruzioni Aeronautiche* of Rome. Its volume was calculated at 607,400 cubic feet and its overall length at 348 feet, these being the maximum dimensions which would allow the airship to use the principal hangars in service in Italy. The keel had a maximum height of ten feet and was triangular in section except directly above the combined captain's nacelle and passenger cabin where it was rectangular. This keel was slung under the envelope by a 'bridge' system, a feature of this type of dirigible, consisting of about twenty semi-elliptical reinforcements spaced at regular intervals over its entire length. Three 260-horsepower Maybach engines were housed in one in-line and two lateral nacelles attached to the keel by steel cables. Estimated maximum speed was about 62 m.p.h. and the ceiling 13,000 feet, accommodation being provided for a normal crew of seven and twenty passengers. Although this project as such never materialized, it did form the basis of the N1, built in 1924 and subsequently christened *Norge*, in which Amundsen, Ellsworth and Nobile made their famous transpolar expedition.

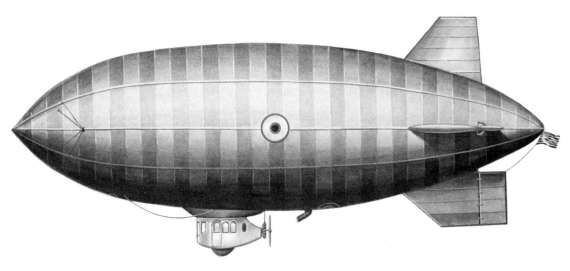

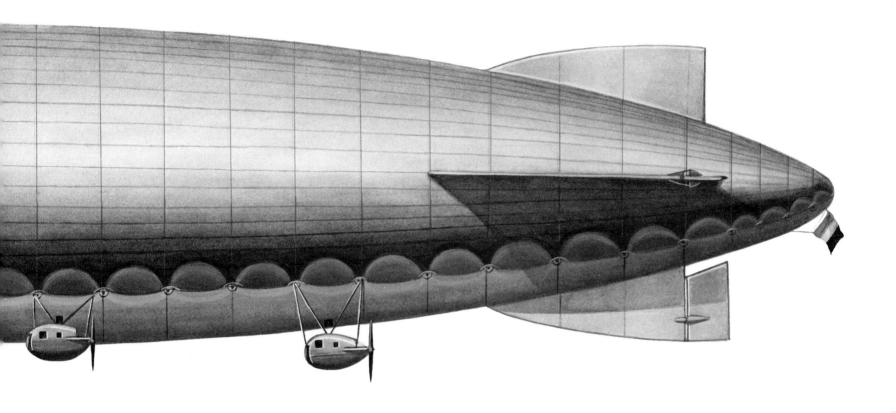

## 1923: Zodiac VZ24 naval airship

Ordered for the French Naval Air Service, these scouting airships were 191 feet long with a maximum diameter of 39 feet and a volume of 141,250 cubic feet, 47,700 cubic feet being occupied by the gas-bag. Two Hispano-Suiza 150-horsepower engines, restricted to developing only 130 h.p., were fitted to each side of the nacelle giving the VZ24 a maximum speed of 53 m.p.h., cruising speed 47 m.p.h. with a four-man crew. An auxiliary Anzani 6-horsepower engine was provided to power the gas supply system in the case of main engine breakdown. Normally, the airscrews directed the air flow into a double, angled sleeve, the input end of which could be moved behind one or other of the airscrews, the other end leading to a shaft bent up at right angles extending from the enclosed nacelle. The nacelle, a beamlike framework of tubular steel, was slung under the envelope by a series of bolt-ropes made into goose-feet and fitted with two sprung landing skids. Two machine-guns could be mounted on the nacelle.

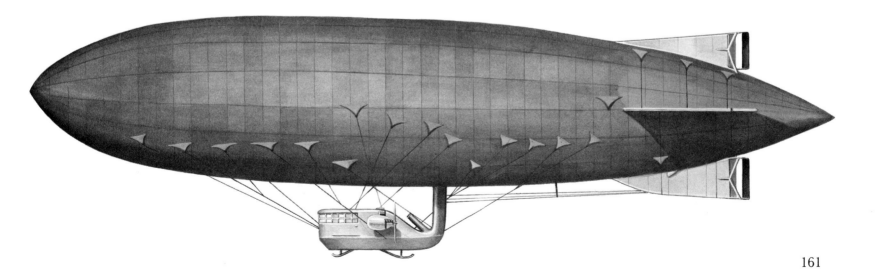

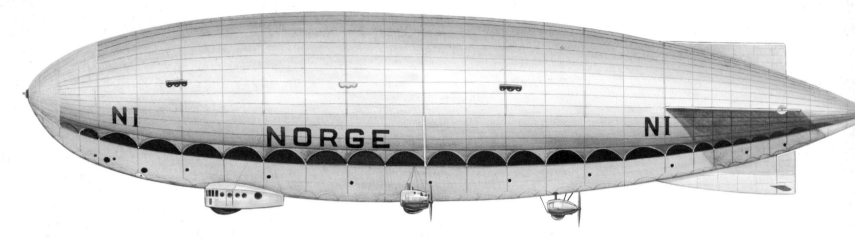

### 1926: Nobile N1, 'Norge'

The Norwegian explorer, Roald Amundsen, financed by his American patron, James W. Ellsworth, ordered the building of this semi-rigid dirigible for an expedition to the North Pole and the Arctic icecap. Based on the airship designed by the Italian Colonel Umberto Nobile, *Norge* had a triangular keel closely following the belly contour of the envelope; 262 feet long, the N1 had a volume of 678,000 cubic feet and was powered by three 260-horsepower Maybach engines, two of these being fitted in a pair of nacelles halfway along either side of the envelope and the third in an in-line nacelle near the stern. A long command nacelle was fitted towards the nose and a small observation nacelle could be lowered from the airship by means of a winch. The 16-man crew had access to the keel over its entire length. Colonel Nobile was in command of the aircraft and Norwegian members of the crew were in charge of elevator and rudder controls.

First flown in April 1924, *Norge* took off from Rome on 10 April 1926, arriving at its Arctic base in King's Bay, Spitzbergen, on 7 May. On 11 May, the airship headed for the Pole which it reached the next day. Following the flight schedule despite the fog, the frost and the ice with which *Norge* was heavily laden, the airship landed at Teller in Alaska only a mile or two from Nome, their scheduled landing point, thus completing a remarkable flight of 3,437 miles in 68 hours 30 minutes.

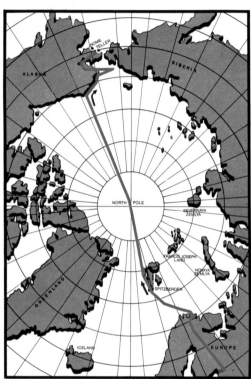

Map showing the transpolar route taken by *Norge* and the Amundsen-Ellsworth-Nobile expedition from King's Bay in Spitzbergen to Teller in Alaska in May 1926.

### 1928: Nobile N4, 'Italia'

Fourth dirigible in the series designed by Umberto Nobile, *Italia* had the same dimensions, volume and horsepower as the N1, *Norge*. As a result of the experience gained aboard *Norge* during its transpolar flight, the envelope was reinforced to withstand the impact of the ice flung off the airscrew blades.

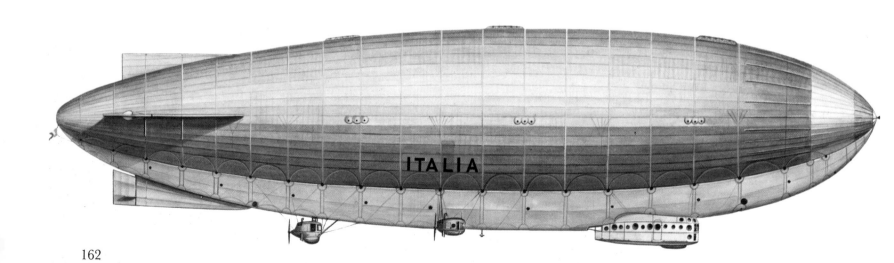

*Norge* during its flight to the arctic base in Spitzbergen.

*Norge* at the British aerodrome at Pulham on its way to the North.

# THE ADVENTURE OF THE FORGOTTEN GIANTS

## 1928-1958

Three months to the day after the loss of Roald Amundsen and his companions, an airship rose up from the German banks of Lake Constance. The spectre of *Italia* flitted across the minds of many people in aviation when *Graf Zeppelin* appeared. Named after that stubborn pioneer of rigid dirigibles for either peaceful or warlike pursuits, this new airship was to open up a new era in civil aviation. Its unprecedentedly long service was to confound all those who had doubted the future of the piloted airship.

It was 18 September 1928, two years after Germany had been granted permission to build large volume dirigibles once again, when *Graf Zeppelin* took off on her first flight. For over one year, public subscriptions had provided the funds and reflected public confidence. 'Graf' as it was familiarly called, was a veritable ocean-going liner of the air. The captain's nacelle or 'bridge' housing navigation and radio equipment as well as the flying crew on duty, was built on to a dining saloon fitted with bay windows which could be opened. Adjoining this section were ten cabins, each with sleeping accommodation for two persons, two large washrooms, one toilet. The whole car was completed with an electrically equipped kitchen. A crew of thirty-seven was housed in the keel where they rested between watches or ate their meals. October of the same year saw the beginning of the regular commercial air service. With eighteen passengers aboard, the first North Atlantic voyage of 5,178 miles was flown between Friedrichshafen and Lakehurst. A part of the tail plane was slightly damaged as a result of controls being clumsily handled and, although the mishap was put in order during flight, *Graf* was late on her estimated time of arrival. Overall, the flight had taken five days, from 11 to 15 October. The return journey, free from accidents, was made between 29 October and 1 November.

Cruises to Palestine and Algeria were undertaken early in 1929, shortly followed by a remarkable round-the-world cruise from 1 August until 4 September. Dr Eckener was in command while Kapitän Ernst Lehmann, Kapitän Flemming, Kapitän Hans von Schiller, and Kapitän Max Prüss were responsible for navigation and flight controls. *Graf Zeppelin* covered the

A rear view of the British dirigible R 100 at its mooring mast at Cardington, from where it took off on its memorable crossing of the North Atlantic in 1930.

165

31,000 miles in various stages. The flight from Friedrichshafen to Lakehurst, a distance of 5,215 miles was made at an average speed of 55 m.p.h., the return journey of 4,418 miles at 80 m.p.h. mean flying speed. From Friedrichshafen to Tokio, 7,030 miles were flown at an average speed of 69 m.p.h., thence to Los Angeles, another 6,033 miles at 76 m.p.h., from this Pacific Coast city to Lakehurst 3,013 miles were covered at 58 m.p.h., and from Lakehurst back to its base on the shores of Lake Constance, a flight of an average speed of 78 m.p.h. was logged over a distance of 5,299 miles. This astonishing world flight had taken 21 days, 7 hours and 22 minutes with 3,000 hours 16 minutes flying time.

The end to this glorious year for *Graf* was celebrated with a flight of 2,973 miles over the Balkans. However, that year was not without its dramatic moments. While airborne on another trip to the United States, four of its engines which had been modified against Dr Eckener's advice, suddenly failed while the dirigible was over the French part of the Rhône valley, swept by a strong *mistral*. Very nearly wrecked, the airship made an emergency landing at the Naval Air base of Cuers-Pierrefeu near Toulon, helped by the ground crews. There, *Graf* was safely parked in a hangar, no equal to the cathedral-like structures at Orly, which was too far to be reached without overwhelming risks. After engines had been changed, the huge airship regained its home base at Friedrichshafen to prepare for the world flight. Dr Eckener was not at all reticent in his public gratitude for the assistance given by the French authorities; a flicker of friendship between ex-enemy neighbours and, however fleeting, a sign of that underlying camaraderie among flying men.

In 1930, among other successes, the first flight to Latin America ended successfully at Rio de Janeiro, after one stop for stores and fuel, at Pernambuco. The return journey was made via the United States and the North Atlantic. The following year, the old project first dreamed up by Count Ferdinand von Zeppelin, a long exploratory reconnaissance of the Arctic cap, became a reality during 'Polar Year'. Over 8,312 miles were logged between the 28 and 30 July over Leningrad, Franz Josef Land, the Barentz Sea, Nicholas Land and the Island of Nova Zembla. The airship also came down to sea level in one of the Hooker Island coastal bays to exchange mailbags with the Soviet ice-breaker *Malyquin*.

From 1931, *Graf Zeppelin* made regular commercial flights to Brazil, sometimes making the return trip by the United States and the North Atlantic. During one of these flights in 1935, while approaching Pernambuco, the crew was informed that a revolution had broken out on the ground. They patiently cruised about near Recife until the political heat had cooled off. When the airship landed, an unintentional flight record of 118 hours 40 minutes flying time had been established.

The year before, the Deutsche Zeppelin Reederei, the carrier responsible for the transatlantic air services had celebrated the millionth kilometer flown by this airship, which then had 9,845 flying hours to its credit. *Graf*

*Zeppelin* was withdrawn from the airline on 18 June 1937 after eight years and nine months of unbroken service. During this time, the airship had made 144 transatlantic crossings, flown 1,059,545 miles in 17,177 hours, carried 13,110 paying passengers and 34,000 non-paying persons including crews, and had shipped 95,040 lbs of freight and 116,790 lbs of mail.

Over in the United States of America, the *Shenandoah* catastrophe had not diminished the Navy's faith in the viability of the rigid dirigible. Actually, only a few months after this airship's tragic end in September 1925, the Aeronautics Bureau made a recommendation to the Navy Department to put into effect a large production schedule for building airships of the same class, to be carried out over a period of five years. The plan also included the building of two powerful rigid airships as well as an airship base on the Pacific Coast. The recommendation was accepted and a law passed by the Senate in June 1926. At the beginning of 1927 tenders were invited. As a result, the Goodyear Zeppelin Corporation, licensed to apply Zeppelin patents at that time, and based on Akron, Ohio, were appointed as constructors to the U.S. Government.

A very advanced technological approach had been worked out and the airships were to be coded ZRS4 and ZRS5, the initials RS standing for 'Rigid Scout'. Overall sizes were more or less identical, each having a cubic volume of 6,427,100 cubic feet with engines developing 4,480 h.p. Because of the use of helium gas as a lifting medium, the eight Maybach engines were built into the keel which facilitated maintenance during flight. The keel was also large enough to have a built-in hangar for fighter or reconnaissance aircraft. Enough fuel was carried aboard to allow a radius of action extending more than 10,600 miles. There were other innovations. Reversible pitch airscrews were designed, which could also be turned upwards. Water vapour from the exhaust gases could also be recovered.

The building of *Akron* commenced on 2 November 1929 by Vice-Admiral William A. Moffett, Chief of the Aeronautics Bureau, when he sealed a gold rivet into one of the transversal ring ribs of the skeleton. The maiden flight was made on 23 September 1931. One month later, *Akron* passed naval acceptance tests and was commissioned under the command of Lieutenant-Commander Charles E. Rosedahl. The first service flight was made on 3 November the same year when *Akron* was airborne for ten hours with 207 persons aboard. After Naval acceptance, the airship was employed on manoeuvres with the fleet.

All went well until 3 April 1933. On a routine flight to cross-check naval radio direction stations off the New Jersey coasts the dirigible ran into a violent storm. As static electrical charges forced the crew to pull in the wireless aerials, all meteorological information was cut off. For this same reason it was impossible to set the altimeter to local barometric pressure and a thick haze covered the area. The sudden change in barometric pressure at such a low altitude was fatal and the crew could do little to avoid impending disaster. *Akron* pitched nose down. Ballast was dropped in an attempt to prevent the airship diving but she crashed into the sea by the tail and the waves quickly saw to the end of *Akron*. Only three out of the sixty-seven man crew survived. Among the missing was Vice-Admiral Moffett. Only one month before, his wife had christened the ZRS5 with the name of *Macon* when it was towed out of its hangar. *Akron* had flown a total of 400 hours during its naval service. On 21 April 1933, ZRS5 took to the air for the first time. This airship had the remarkable air speed of 110 m.p.h. *Macon* was commissioned into full service, and attached to the new airship base at Sunnyvale, California, during June.

Despite the events which led up to the loss of *Akron*, the same flight schedules were ordered for *Macon* which duly left the base in 1934 to carry out exercises with a fleet review off the Californian coast. During the return flight turbulent conditions were encountered necessitating harsh and sudden movements for the flight controls to hold the airship on course. At Sunnyvale, temporary repairs were made to individual damaged parts without, apparently, having the whole tail unit and control surfaces overhauled or even examined. On the next flight, *Macon* again ran into turbulent weather which exerted more strain on the repaired parts. It was 12 February 1935. The whole top section of the steering vanes ripped away, the broken debris puncturing the three stern gas-bags. Out of control, *Macon* crashed into the sea off the Californian coast and slowly sank. The airship went down so slowly that, apart from two members, the crew had time to clear the wreck and were saved. In two years of service with the Navy, *Macon* had flown 1,798 hours.

As a result of the two crashes, the U.S. Navy had no rigid dirigibles operational. Naval, governmental and civilian courts of enquiry were set up to study the safety and practicability of such lighter-than-air craft. In 1938, the construction of a new airship, 2,966,000 cubic feet in volume, was approved but, owing to lack of funds, the design never left the drawing board stage. The era of rigid airships in the U.S. Navy came to an end.

While the LZ127, *Graf Zeppelin*, continued its successful career in civilian service, yet another country, Great Britain, had not dropped the idea of using rigid airships. One of these dirigibles, the R33, had been torn from her mooring mast at Pulham in 1925 by a sudden, violent squall. After a precarious flight of twenty-nine hours with her nose badly damaged, she was able to return safely to her base. Completely repaired and back in operational flying order, the R33 was used as an experimental aircraft carrier with a device for launching and retrieving a De Havilland or Gloster Grebe biplane.

In 1924, the Imperial Defence Committee decided to embark on a considerable construction programme and the two large airships, the R100 and R101, were commissioned, one from Vickers, and the other by the Government Royal Airship Works. Their profile was more elongated than previous dirigibles and, as a result, they were built with a more aerodynamic form. In conjunction with the airship production, mooring masts were

The back of a souvenir postcard addressed to the author by the well-known aviator Charles Dollfus, commemorating his air voyage to South America aboard the *Graf Zeppelin* in October 1932. Philatelic examples of this kind are highly sought after.

ordered to be erected near Montreal, at Ismalia in Egypt, and a large hangar was built at Karachi, India. The R 100 was built by the Aircraft Guarantee Company, a subsidiary of Vickers, at Howden, north of the River Humber. It was designed by an engineer who was to attain even greater fame during the Second World War, Barnes N. Wallis. His ability had already been proved during the construction of the R 9 and R 80 between 1917 and 1921. The R 100 was 709 feet long, 133 feet in diameter and had a volume of 5,649,000 cubic feet. Power was supplied by six Rolls-Royce petrol Condor aero engines developing 700 h.p. each, and currently in use with conventional aircraft. Fourteen hydrogen gas-bags were fitted inside the duralumin framework covered with cotton and several layers of goldbeaters' skin of German origin. Major G. H. Scott was the test pilot and the airship made seven proving flights totalling 150 hours air time, then made a further flight of 54 hours with 56 persons aboard in January 1930. Based on Cardington, the R 100 took off on 29 July to cross the Atlantic to Canada with a complement of 42 crew and 13 passengers. The airship was commanded by Captain R.S. Booth, with Major Scott and Wing-Commander R.B. Colmore under him, and Squadron Leader E.L. Johnston as navigating officer. Although the R 100 ran into a storm during the flight, it was moored at St Hubert, the airport for Montreal after 78 hours 31 minutes flying time. The R 100 had covered approximately 2,310 miles at an average speed of some 46 m.p.h. After a fortnight tied up to her mooring mast, the R 100 took off again for the return crossing on 13 August, with the same load. Prevailing winds considerably helped the ground speed and the R 100 moored to the mast at Cardington in Britain three days later, after a flight of 56 hours 30 minutes. But after this successful flight, for political reasons, this airship never took to the air again.

On the other hand, the R101 made its first flight on 14 October 1929. Built by the Royal Airship Works, a Government controlled organisation at Cardington, its maiden flight was only possible after considerable modifications resulting from teething troubles. Most of these derived from power-weight ratio questions relating to the Beardmore diesel Tornado engines being as much as double the calculated values. Therefore, in order to successfully complete the Empire Route to India via Egypt with a useful pay-load, the whole construction was modified to include an extra central section with an additional hydrogen gas-bag, thereby increasing the volume from 4,981,318 to 5,438,300 cubic feet and the pay-load from 25 to nearly 50 tons. But the margin of flight safety did not increase in proportion. Major G.H. Scott tartly remarked that a resoled shoe is never as sound as the original, and his words were soon to be tragically vindicated.

After three months of hard work, by 1930, the flight tests were still inconclusive, particularly as the hydrogen gas-bags were leaking. While all this was going on, the Imperial Conference was held at London in the autumn of that year. The Dominion delegates were stressing the distance over which communications had to travel and the long time between sending and receiving. As a direct result of these complaints, Lord Thompson of Cardington, Secretary of State for Air, then decided to demonstrate that communications could be speeded up. The R101 was ordered to take off for India on 4 October. He also stated that, apart from the million to one chance, this airship was as safe as a house.

A proving flight was made on 1 October. An engine breakdown prevented the airship being tested at full speed. Finally, it was decided to make this final test during the flight with all passengers aboard. So the dead-line was observed and on the evening of 4 October the R101 with a temporary Certificate of Airworthiness, took off from Cardington under the command of Flight Lieutenant H. Carmichael Irwin. Fifty-four persons were aboard including the best-known names in aviation. At about 600 feet over the Channel, R101 pitched and rolled through rainstorms, buffeted by winds of up to 40 and 50 knots, somewhere off the north-west coast of France. According to an eye-witness the airship was only about 300 feet above ground as it passed over land near Abbeville. At 02.05 hrs on the 5 October, the R101 started to go down by the nose. The officer handling the elevator controls struggled to keep the ship on an even keel, water was poured out but all attempts were futile. Three minutes later the airship dived into a slight rise near Beauvais at Allonnes. In a few seconds, over five million cubic feet of hydrogen became an inferno, no doubt after contact with the hot engines and red hot exhaust pipes.

There were only four survivors: these crew members were miraculously saved when the ballast tanks split open and the water doused the flames around them. All other officers, crew men and passengers perished. Apart from the great loss of private lives, this somewhat reckless and half-prepared venture had obliterated some of the most famous names in airship development, men such as Lord Thomas of Cardington, Air Vice-Marshal Sir Sefton Brancker, the Minister of Civil Aviation, and Major G.H. Scott. Again, hydrogen gas was a killer and it was to claim even more victims.

Following this disaster, mourned by aviation circles both in Britain and France, the British authorities decided to break up the R 100. The remains were sold as scrap metal for the ridiculous sum of £450 sterling.

Those responsible for the direction of aviation policy in Great Britain decided, once and for all, to discontinue the development of rigid airships.

On the other hand, *Graf Zeppelin* continued to ply between the Continent and the Americas. Flights were made with an extraordinary punctuality and only the finest equipment as well as comfort for the passengers was the order of the day. In order to avoid being discommoded by the weather, the *Graf*, an airborne luxury liner, altered course according to meteorological forecasting and weather observations. Such was the success of this carrier of passengers and freight, another rigid airship was ordered, to be especially fitted out for a regular air service between Germany and the United States of America.

Towards the end of 1934, the Friedrichshafen works started to build their 119th Zeppelin, the LZ 129. In honour of the President of Germany who had died that year, this Zeppelin was christened *Hindenburg*. The Deutsche Zeppelin Reederei impatiently awaited delivery of the new airship whose design incorporated new and improved features. This dirigible had much improved aerodynamic lines; four diesel engines, which developed a total of 4,200 h.p., were designed to propel this huge dirigible at an estimated speed of 80 m.p.h. Of the greatest volume yet built, 6,709,810 cubic feet, this sky liner offered future passengers more living space, a phrase which was becoming a popular slogan in Germany even then. Accommodation was much more extensive than in *Graf Zeppelin* and comprised twenty-five double cabins, initially, on two decks in the hull, each with hot and cold running water but without windows looking outwards. This layout was later changed to thirty-five double cabins and two single cabins. The entire passenger accommodation was as luxurious as any transport of the period. A library was installed, a reading and writing room, a bar and smoking saloon, sealed off from the rest of the airship and the saloon was even fitted out with a grand piano built from aluminium.

For reasons of safety, *Hindenburg* was originally designed for the use of helium as a lifting gas but was finally obliged to use hydrogen. The United States had a practical world monopoly of helium and the U.S. Government refused to waive the law forbidding the export. For several years, American airships had used this domestically produced gas but the main reasons for the refusal to the German request were political as well as commercial competition by United States carriers. At that time, American airlines were planning transatlantic flights with four-engined Boeing 314 flying boats to be put in service with Pan-American Airways. These had the same number of seats for fare-paying passengers as *Hindenburg*, namely, seventy-two.

Gas-bags filled with hydrogen, the LZ129 lifted off on 4 March 1936, decorated with huge swastikas on her tail unit. More internationally minded than most at that time, Dr Eckener had opposed such markings on *Graf Zeppelin*. After domestic propaganda flights during Germany's elections, *Hindenburg* took off on her first ocean crossing on course for Rio de Janiero before beginning the regular North Atlantic service. By the end of that year, this huge rigid dirigible had already carried 1,002 paying passengers, flown 1,915,625 miles in 2,744 hours flying time.

The new and completely modernized airport at Frankfurt-am-Main had become the base for the old *Graf Zeppelin* and, now, the new *Hindenburg*. Here, the perhaps justifiably optimistic Deutsche Zeppelin Reederei set up new offices with a view to developing their air services. However, according to reliable sources, the company had received several letters openly threatening the airship with sabotage by political extremists if *Hindenburg* ever landed at Lakehurst. Some of these were even handed over to the Washington Administration by the German Embassy, which did not, it seemed, take them lightly, but the carriers imperturbably carried on.

On 6 May 1937, the anniversary of the first flight from Germany to the United States, *Hindenburg* had made its seventy-third crossing under the command of Kapitän Max Prüss with Kapitän Ernst Lehmann as observer. Thirty-six passengers were aboard. About 15.30 hours local time, the airship was on the point of flying over the Empire State Building as usual, to give the passengers a view of Manhattan Island. In radio touch with Admiral Rosendahl, commanding the Lakehurst base, Kapitän Prüss was warned of a storm blowing up in that area and stood off, cruising over New Jersey while awaiting a break in the weather. By 18.00 hours, the weather had cleared sufficiently for a landing and, one hour later, the captain made his final approach to the mooring mast, 200 feet high. The first handling cables had just been dropped when a flame suddenly appeared towards the stern of the hull near the root fixing for the upper rudder fin. In a flash, the whole airship was alight and such was the heat from this blazing torch that it actually rose several feet, gaining an appreciable height, before it slumped and crashed to the ground. Water ballast had been let go in vain. Nothing was left but a huge wreck glowing red in a pall of thick black smoke. Despite his serious burns Kapitän Lehmann attempted to save some of the victims. He died during that night. Both officers and men stationed at the Lakehurst base made heroic efforts to penetrate this huge brazier. One of them lost his life, too. This terrible accident cost the lives of twenty-two crew members and twelve passengers. Survivors totalled sixty-two persons, two thirds of those who had embarked on the last voyage of this giant airship. Some of the passengers who escaped were entirely unscathed.

A considerable controversy remained as to the cause of the accident to *Hindenburg*. After an enquiry which lasted several months, Dr Eckener, who happened to be travelling in Austria at the time of the crash, Kapitän Prüss who was momentarily blinded during the catastrophe, and other surviving officers did come to a summary conclusion. It was presumed that an explosive mixture of air and hydrogen formed at the stern of the hull, the hydrogen escaping from a gas-bag punctured by the rupture of a bracing wire stay during a turn on to the final approach. This explosive mixture could then have been set off by an electrostatic spark generated by the difference in potential between certain points on the outside of the envelope and the envelope itself. It was also suggested that this could probably have occurred because of ambient conditions, the envelope being soaked during the recent rain, the subsequent build-up of electricity and the sudden discharge, similar to lightning, earthing through the mooring cable when it touched the ground. However reasonable this theory might have been on technical grounds, in view of the threats mentioned above, the idea cannot be dismissed that this might have been sabotage by an anti-Nazi militant among the many exiles who had escaped the Hitler regime by emigrating to the United States. It is possible that a delayed action bomb could have been placed aboard or, for that matter, a silenced gun firing an explosive or an incendiary bullet could have been camouflaged as a camera and used near the landing site. However, there can only be conjecture as the mystery has never yet been solved.

This disaster sounded the knell of the commercial use of large rigid dirigibles in that short period of peace between the wars. Zeppelin Luftschiff-bau had started building the LZ130 with traction instead of pusher airscrews, designed for hydrogen gas-bags and it was named *Graf Zeppelin II*. After the maiden flight on the 14 September 1938, thirty other flights were made, for testing and inland tourism. Work on the subsequent airship, the LZ131 was brought to an end by the outbreak of the 1939-1945 war.

This Second World War finally brought the glorious years to a practical and unromantic end when Marshal Herman Göring ordered the airships to be scrapped to provide metal for the production of conventional heavier-than-air craft for the Luftwaffe in March 1940. More or less preserved as a museum piece in one of the hangars at Friedrichshafen, *Graf Zeppelin*, which might have merited better treatment, was also lost in the melting pot for the insatiable Luftwaffe squadrons: *sic transit gloria mundi*.

Although the Americans had not achieved much success with their ventures in the world of rigid dirigibles and since *Graf Zeppelin* had proved its commercial worth and led the field, there were still other constructors with faith in the rigid airship and their own designs, in France, the Soviet Union and, even, in the United States. These airships were smaller than the Zeppelin giants but were equally worthy of note.

The Zodiac company in France were still building Class V or cruisers of 1,200,690 cubic feet, and delivering them to the French Naval Air Service but they had a very limited radius of action. They also produced airships for escort duty. These were called Class E, of 353,150 cubic feet and which were the result of the last scheduled production of the First World War. Among other types produced were the V10 and V11, a bi-lobed semi-rigid airship and a non-rigid tri-lobed unit respectively, carrying four persons and powered by two Salmson engines, each developing 120 h.p., and fixed to out-riggers at right angles to the longitudinal axis of the hull. The semi-rigid bi-lobed escort Class E7 could accomodate seven persons and was fitted with two Hispano-Suiza engines of 350 h.p. In 1938, a twin-engined sister ship was built, the E8, to be the last of her class. In this time of peace the French naval authorities seemed to favour the production of the smaller cruisers or *vedettes*.

From 1934 and until the outbreak of the war, Zodiac was also to produce a complete series of *motoballons* for the French Army. Underneath these motorized balloons which were based on a standard deflatable sausage-shaped type, an elongated pencil-shaped two-seater nacelle was fixed in such a way as to be readily detachable as desired. This nacelle also carried the engine, was of monocoque wood construction with elevators for controlling vertical movement in the nose and a rudder astern. Equipped with a 60-horsepower Salmson engine, these *motoballons* could fly at 31 m.p.h. with a range of two hours. Small air-dinghies, as they could have been called, they could be assembled or dismantled in less than ten minutes. By 1937, a new model appeared which was mounted with rigid fins for flight stability instead of the flexible fabric pockets on the envelope of classic design used as stabilizing vanes on static balloons. This modification increased the speed to about 45 m.p.h.

The Zodiac company appeared less conservative in their design approach as they contributed to the production of a somewhat curious heavier-than-air flying machine called the Devil's Helistat. Devil was actually the pseudonym derived from the name of a manufacturer of orthopedic appliances. A small dirigible of 21,188 cubic feet was fitted with a two-seater ultra-light nacelle of magnesium steel alloy equipped with two Salmson engines. A 60-horsepower engine drove a traction airscrew and a 12-horsepower engine drove a four-bladed rotor with reversible pitch, mounted on a vertical shaft, which actually had the effect of decreasing the weight of this blimp by as much as 154 lbs. This odd aircraft was flown in a similar manner to a conventional aeroplane. Taking off from its base on the aerodrome of Toussus-le-Noble near Versailles, it proved itself extremely manoeuverable. The advantages gained from this original system were to be again demonstrated by the small Goodyear blimps which appeared in America after the war.

In this field of 'gyro-aviation' a knowledgeable pioneer called Etienne Œhmichen was the first man to fly one officially recorded kilometer from take-off to landing, in a primitive helicopter of his own design at Valentigney in the Doubs region. To certain of his experimental aircraft he had attached an elongated or a spherical balloon so as to achieve an additional stabilizing effect. These lifting gas-bags were either manufactured by Zodiac or by the aeronautical equipment manufacturers Claude and Hatton, whose materials were used for the *Hélicostat* of 1932.

The fourth vertical flight machine designed by the French engineer Etienne Oehmichen in 1931 was called *Hélicostat*. Here it is seen flying at Orly on 21 October of that year. A single 40 h.p. Salmson engine drove two rotors with inclined shafts and two traction airscrews which were reversible and had variable pitch blades. A streamlined envelope of 19,400 cubic feet with fins acted as an auxiliary stabilizing device. *Hélicostat* flew more than two hundred hours in all weathers and responded to all manoeuvres devised by its inventor and builder. In the background can be seen the top of one of the huge concrete hangars on Orly aerodrome.

In the U.S.S.R., the Government had been extremely impressed by the arctic flights of *Graf Zeppelin* and, at the beginning of the thirties, laid down a programme for the construction of seven dirigibles. General Nobile was still living in the Soviet Union after being rescued by the crew of a Russian ship following his disastrous flight over the Arctic. As a result, the authorities were able to draw on his technical know-how and experience. The first, *Klim Voroshiloff*, with a volume of 777,000 cubic feet was a semi-rigid dirigible. Ready in November 1933, it had been prepared for the sixteenth anniversary of the October Revolution, and was capable of carrying sixteen passengers and crew.

Early in 1934, a team of technical specialists were working on plans for a dirigible with a chrome-nickel steel envelope, with a volume of 282,550 cubic feet, powered by two engines each developing 600 h.p. Although the plans were passed by the *Dirigiblestroi*, the Technical Committee for the Construction of Dirigibles, little more was heard of this venture. Two years later, under the auspices of the same committee, a semi-rigid airship of about 882,860 cubic feet was specially designed for future Arctic flights. The DP9 was to be fitted out with eight double cabins for passengers, a reading room, a smoking room, and an electrically equipped kitchen. The following year the Soviet Government announced that the V6, another semi-rigid airship had made a flight of 130 hours 27 minutes, piloted by Igor W. Pankow. According to the Russian claims, the record established and held by *Graf Zeppelin* in 1935 had now been beaten. On 5 January 1938 the V6 was destroyed. The last published information on developments in the Soviet Union before the outbreak of the Second World War, claimed that a V8 had been designed for regular commercial flights between Moscow and Leningrad. In the same year the V6 was destroyed, flight tests were being made for the V10 at Moscow airport during the month of May.

Besides the construction of large rigid airships for the U.S. Navy during the thirties, and the non-rigid blimps for the Army which used them until 1936, an interesting experimental dirigible was built in 1929. Designated as the ZMC or Zeppelin Metal Clad, this airship proved itself to have quite remarkable features as an experimental aircraft tested over several years. The ZMC had been so christened because of its metal envelope which consisted of a laminated sandwich with a layer of duralumin $1/32$ in as a filling protected from corrosion on both sides by layers of very thin aluminium, the product being called 'alclad'. Designed by a well-known pioneer aviator, Ralph H. Upson, to have a volume of 100,160 cubic feet, the basic work started in 1921 with the helpful cooperation of Carl B. Fritsche, and the airship was eventually constructed by the Aircraft Development Corporation of Detroit. Bands of alclad were applied in a spiral fashion round a framework of twenty-four longerons and twelve transversal circular ribs. Among other innovations, the metal-skinned envelope was fastened to the frame and the bands joined together by a powered riveter, 'stitching' at the rate of 135 rivets per minute, in 3 rows. No less than a total of over

3 ½ million rivets were used. Rivets were stitched in so as to produce two vertical halves of the dirigible which were then swung together to produce the entire hull. This metal envelope was pumped full of helium at a slightly higher pressure than the ambient atmosphere and two gas-bags were also included to be used as pressure compensators. The ZMC was familiarly known as the *Tin Bubble*, having a length less than three times the diameter. The tail unit had eight radial control surfaces placed symmetrically and accurately so as to take full advantage of the airflow. The nacelle was attached directly to the underside of the hull and was fitted with two Wright Whirlwind engines each producing 220 h.p. The ZMC2 was taken from Detroit and delivered to the Naval Air Services base at Lakehurst in 1929 where the crews were to receive training. After acceptance trials, the ZMC2 had an enviable length of service with the Navy, more than twelve years which is a record, particularly for an airship of such unique construction.

Building went on with classic equipment for the Army and Navy after the war years, the Goodyear Zeppelin Corporation acting as principal government sub-contractor. From the autumn of 1939, however, the company was renamed the Goodyear Aircraft Corporation, severing connections with the Zeppelin Luftschiffbau. Today, it is known as the Goodyear Aerospace Corporation. During those pre-war years this firm specialized in building small non-rigid airships filled with helium, mostly for service with the U.S. Army which, between 1923 and 1935, were supplied with fourteen twin-engines Class TC dirigibles from 197,700 to 317,850 cubic feet in volume. Some of these were also fitted with a small 'cloud car', a streamlined nacelle on a cable which could be dropped below cloud level into areas of greater visibility. This device was very similar to that used by the Zeppelins during the First World War while operating over London unseen by the anti-aircraft gunners.

During 1937, no doubt because of the rapid progress in airplane technological matters, the U.S. Army handed over its last six units to the U.S. Marine Corps which maintained its own flotilla of blimps up until 1962.

Throughout the Second World War, these small airships rendered considerable service to the U.S. Navy. The American Marine had only ten of them when Pearl Harbour was attacked on 7 December 1941. By the end of hostilities, no less than 168 were in service, most of them built by Goodyear. The squadrons had 134 Class K units of 423,775 cubic feet which, with four Class M airships of 635,700 cubic feet, were used for coastal patrol. Twenty-two Class G of 194,250 cubic feet served as training aircraft for crew and servicing or ground handling personnel. All in all, this was an extremely efficient service and some of their operations were quite remarkable. Fifteen squadrons operated from fifty bases. The blimps were sent out on anti-submarine and convoy patrols off the Pacific and Atlantic coasts even as far as Rio de Janeiro. After the American forces landed in North Africa these navy blimps were even operating over Mediterranean waters. During hostilities, 55,900 missions were completed with 550,000 hours flown, the squadrons having escorted 89,000 ships which, under this aerial protection, suffered no losses from enemy surface action.

Six Class K blimps of 14 Squadron crossed the Atlantic in pairs to serve in the Mediterranean theatre of operations. The first two, K 123 and K 130 left South Weymouth in Massachusetts on 29 May 1944 to make a flight of 3,100 miles via Newfoundland and the Azores in about 50 hours flying time, arriving in Morocco at Port Lyautey, now called Kenitra, on 1 June 1944. Next year, two Class K blimps made the crossing by way of Bermuda and the Azores from Weeksville in North Carolina, a flight of 62 hours and a distance of 3,500 miles. In the Mediterranean theatre, these Navy blimps were able to carry out a great variety of missions owing to the flexibility of their operation. Apart from anti-submarine patrols which included attack by depth-charge when enemy underwater presence was suspected, these naval air units combined with ships of the fleet for navigation purposes, reconnaissance and surface searches, air-sea rescue, mine spotting, acting as air observation posts, on aerial photographic missions and, *inter alia*, the calibration of special equipment.

After the war ended, the naval airships' activity was severely limited. At this time, the development of electronic equipment was in full stride and the dirigibles attached to the Navy were used as flying laboratories for testing instruments and, at the same time, to find means to improve their own performance. On 2 November 1946, the XM 1, which was actually an old M 1 with its volume increased to 716,900 cubic feet, established a flight record of 170 hours 17 minutes without refuelling. In 1953, the ZPG 2, the first of Class N, with a volume of nearly 1,000,000 cubic feet was commissioned. Plans for this class of airship had been drawn up towards the end of the Second World War and now the ZPG 2 was used to perfect inboard installations, particularly early warning radar equipment. From this dirigible, the ZPG 2W was developed and these units were formed into a squadron in July 1957.

Only four months previously, a ZPG 2 had beaten the existing flight record by patrolling 9,500 miles over the Atlantic and the Carribean Sea, an impressive 264 hours 14 minutes in the air without refuelling, revictualling or receiving any outside assistance. Thus the feasibility of constant round-the-clock patrols was definitely proved. By 21 July 1958, the first unit of type ZPG 3W took off. With a volume of 1,438,221 cubic feet this was the largest non-rigid airship ever produced. On the top of the envelope the ZPG 3W carried a huge rotating radar aerial, an effective early-warning installation. Accommodation was provided for twenty-five, and this airship was equipped with the most advanced equipment available at the time. But the end of the U.S. Navy's airship programme was in sight. Delivery of its fourth and last ZPG 3W was taken in 1960. The U.S. Navy ended such aerial activity in 1962 when U.S. Air Force units took over the establishment of early-warning and immediate-warning systems. A chain of stations were set up, linked to heavier-than-air craft on constant patrol.

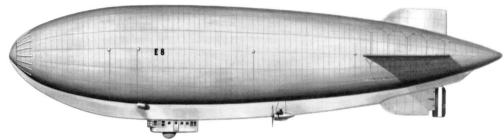

## The British airship R100

The R100 was built by the Airship Guarantee Co., a subsidiary of Vickers, and based on the design of the well-known engineer, Barnes N. Wallis. With a volume of 5,650,375 cubic feet, its length was 709 feet and maximum diameter 133 feet. Powered by six Rolls-Royce Condor engines, totalling 4,200 h.p., the R100 successfully crossed the North Atlantic to Canada and made the return flight between 29 July and 16 August 1930 after being moored for several days to its mast at Saint-Hubert, Montreal.

### 1931: Zodiac E8 scout airship

A navy dirigible used for scouting purposes, the E8 was the first semi-rigid built by Zodiac. The envelope, formed in two lobes, was 262 feet long with a maximum diameter of 56 feet and a volume of 353,150 cubic feet. A long keel, accessible to the crew and triangular in section, ran along the belly of the envelope from the nose practically to the tail. The nacelle for captain and flying crew was slung under the keel and an engine nacelle, equipped with a 350 h.p. Hispano-Suiza engine, was fitted about halfway along each side. With an eight-man crew the Zodiac E8 could attain a maximum speed of 70 m.p.h.

### 1929: The British rigid dirigible R101

Despite the accident in August 1921 which befell the rigid R38, destined for America, the British Government nevertheless ordered two large rigid airships to be built for commercial use. The R100 was constructed by a Vickers' subsidiary and the R101 by the government-owned Royal Airship Works at Cardington. The skeleton of the R101 had ten polygonal unbraced ribs joined together with 30 tubular steel longerons.

Originally 732 feet in length with a diameter of 131 feet, the R101 was found to have insufficient lift when flight tested, owing to its weight being considerably greater than at first calculated. An extra 44-foot section was therefore inserted in the centre of the envelope, thus almost doubling its payload and increasing its volume to nearly 5,500,000 cubic feet distributed between 16 gas-bags. Five Beardmore Tornado 650 h.p. diesel engines were mounted in one in-line nacelle, one in-line twin-engine nacelle and one nacelle on each side. Behind the first engine nacelle was a short command cabin and, lower down under the envelope, two large galleries were fitted out for passenger accommodation which included a restaurant and a smoking room.

Although a series of flight tests had been scheduled for the R101 following the modifications to its structure, only one flight of 16 hours was made before the airship took off for India via Egypt on a mission undertaken as a result of the Imperial Commonwealth Conference then being held in London. On 1 October 1930, despite unfavourable weather conditions, the airship lifted off and headed for France. Flying at low altitude, buffeted by squalls and impeded by low cloud and unrelenting rain, the R101 soon found itself in difficulties that proved too much for its already precarious inherent stability. It is thought that the outer covering split, which in turn contributed to the rupture of the gas-bags. During the night, near Beauvais, its tail crashed into a low hill, the airship burst into flames, killing fifty of its occupants although four members of the crew were saved in the inferno, doused with water from the ruptured ballast tanks. With this disaster the era of British rigid dirigibles came to an end.

Cross-section of the ribs of the British rigid dirigible R101 built by the Royal Airship Works, Cardington. These polygonal rings were made from unbraced steel tubes.

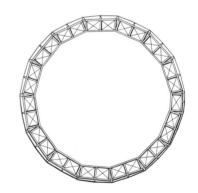

The R101 lifts off from its base at Cardington on a test flight in 1929. The large amount of water-ballast being dropped from the nose was to ensure the longitudinal trim of the airship.

Today, only the small Goodyear civilian blimps are to be seen in the skies over the United States of America. A striking total of 300 had been produced since 1917, only 56 of which had been used for commercial or experimental purposes. Between 1928 and 1932 small airships called *Puritan*, *Volunteer*, *Mayflower I*, *Vigilant*, *Defender*, *Reliance* and *Resolute* followed one after the other. The three 'musketeers of the air' and, as in the novel by Alexandre Dumas there were actually four, if the *Europa* destined for export to the Old World can be included. They were all considered by their builders as 'air yachts' and carried the names of the national winners of the America Cup. The doyen of them all is *Mayflower II* based on Miami, Florida, which made its first flight in 1968. Based on Los Angeles, California, *Columbia* was first flown in 1969 as was *America*, based on Houston in Texas. Apart from *Mayflower* with a volume of 145,900 cubic feet and powered by two 175-horsepower engines, all these small units are slightly over 200,000 cubic feet and powered by two 210-horsepower Continental engines. Envelopes are made from synthetic materials, usually Dacron impregnated with Neoprene, maximum air speed being 50 m.p.h. with a carrying capacity of six passengers when they are not fitted up for use by television production companies or equipped for other work, such as aerial photography. Take-off is very similar to a conventional aircraft in that a short run on the wheel in the base of the nacelle precedes flight but as most of the overall weight is supported by the helium gas with which these blimps are filled, only a small amount of the total engine power is required to fly at the usual slow speeds, so that the passengers can have a good view as the aircraft leisurely drifts over areas of interest.

The American public, accustomed to spectacular visual manifestations, enjoy seeing these small airships floating at about 1,000 feet above the ground after dark, the sides lit up with electrical displays, called *Skytaculars* by the Goodyear company. Each side of the envelope is fitted with two frames about 100 feet long and 25 feet high, carrying 3,750 small coloured electric lamps connected by a maze of approximately 72 miles of wire. Fed by magnetic tape, an electronic reader programmes the lighting effects to compose animated drawings based on an incredible number of themes from sports to the merely fantastic, publicity for various consumer products, or messages drawing attention to social services and various charitable organizations, so proving that technical progress can lead from the utilitarian to the enjoyable.

Paul Renard and Arthur Krebs could never have permitted themselves to indulge in such wild imaginings nor dared to look so far into the future when they floated in the sky over Chalais-Meudon in their primitive pilotable flying machine. No one could have even dreamed of such a sight as these multi-coloured air signs, anchored in the starry sky over Florida from where, today, men take off in their space ships to familiarize themselves with that other floating space station, the moon.

Opposite: With one of the two huge reinforced concrete hangars at Orly aerodrome in the background, a semi-rigid, tri-lobed Zodiac scouting airship is seen preparing to take off with the assistance of a ground crew from the French Naval Air service.

182

1

2

**1928: The German dirigible LZ127, 'Graf Zeppelin'**

**1** Keel cat-walk.

**2** Inside framework showing the longitudinal beams, ribs and a ballast bag.

**3** Pilot's cabin, showing the elevator control and, to the right, the helm.

**4-5** On the left, a double passenger cabin arranged for daytime use and, on the right, the same cabin transformed into sleeping accommodation. During flight, passengers enjoyed aerial views from the large bay windows.

**6** The dining saloon.

4

5

# GRAF ZEPPELIN LZ127

| | | |
|---|---|---|
| – – – – | 11-15.10.1928 | Friedrichshafen to Lakehurst |
| – – – – | 29.10.1928 | Lakehurst to Friedrichshafen |
| = + = + =· | 23-25.4.1929 | Friedrichshafen, Bordeaux, Lisbon, Tangiers, Marseilles and Friedrichshafen |
| ·············· | 1.8.1929 | Friedrichshafen to Lakehurst |
| ·············· | 8.8.1929 | Lakehurst to Friedrichshafen |
| –·–·–·· | 15.8-4.9.1929 | Friedrichshafen, Yakoutsk, Port Ayan, Tokio, Los Angeles, Chicago, Lakehurst and Friedrichshafen |
| ·– – – – | 18.5-5.6.1930 | Friedrichshafen, Seville, Recife, Rio de Janeiro, Recife, Lakehurst, Seville, Friedrichshafen |
| =o==o=( | 9.10-11.10.1930 | Friedrichshafen, Nuremberg, Frankfurt-on-Oder, Kaliningrad, Moscow, Nuremberg and Friedrichshafen |
| = = = = | 9-13.4.1931 | Friedrichshafen, Marseilles, Cairo, Helouan, Cairo, Jerusalem, Cairo, Spalato, Vienna and Friedrichshafen |
| –o——o— | 30.6-6.7.1931 | Friedrichshafen, Yarmouth, Reykjavik, Berlin and Friedrichshafen |
| + + + +- | 24-30.7.1931 | Friedrichshafen, Leningrad, Franz Josef Land, Leningrad, Berlin and Friedrichshafen |
| ======= | 18.8.1931 | Friedrichshafen, Troyes, Eastbourne, Brighton, Norfolk, London, Cornwall and Friedrichshafen |

The following aerial voyages were made by *Graf Zeppelin* between October 1928 and August 1931 before it was assigned to regular transatlantic flights which continued until June 1937.

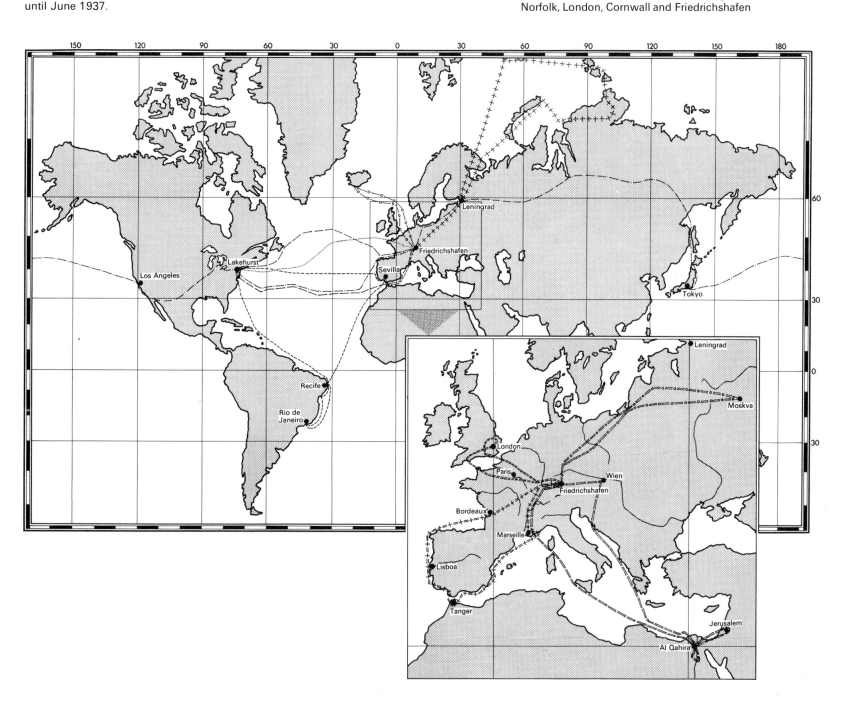

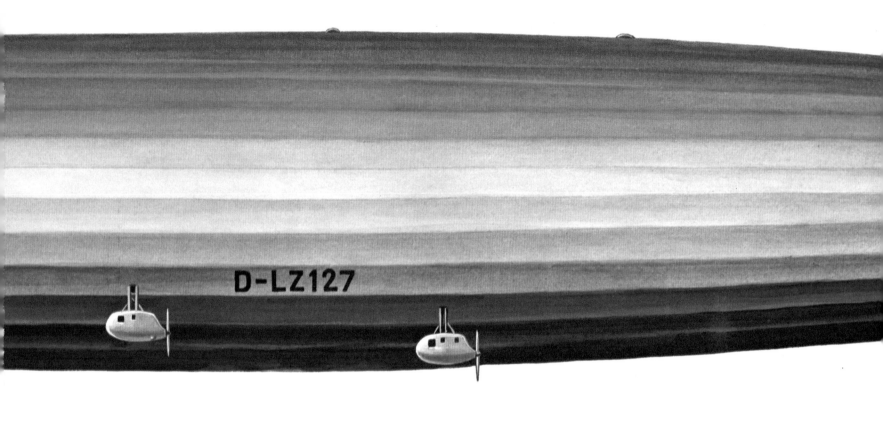

D-LZ127

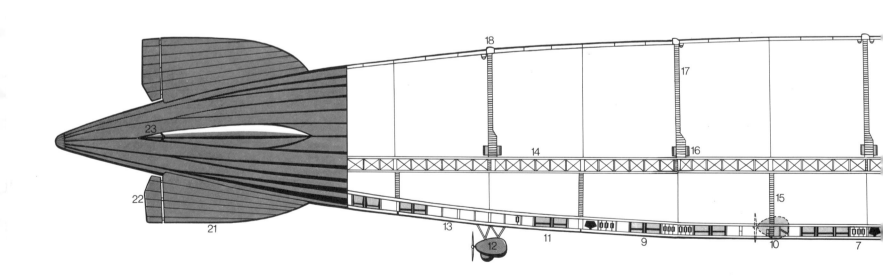

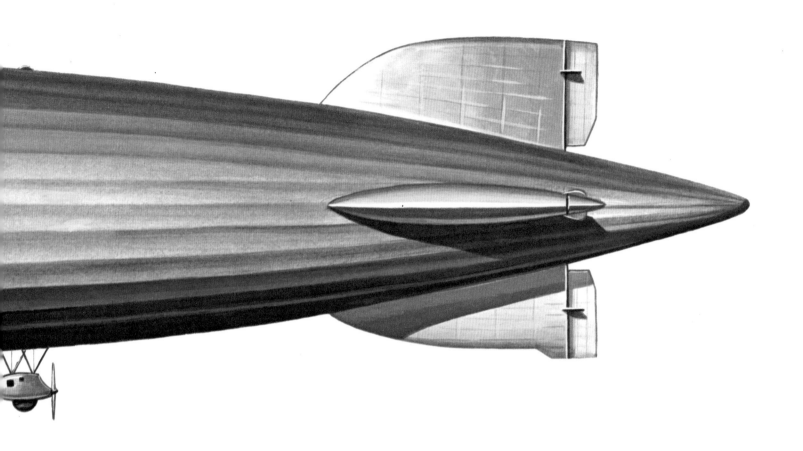

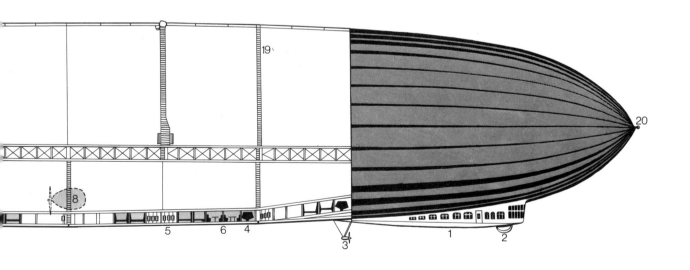

## 1928: The LZ127, 'Graf Zeppelin'

Sectional and plan views of the main 98-foot command nacelle showing the flying crew stations with the helm in the centre and the elevator control at the side. Aft of this group were navigation and radio cabins, the electrically equipped kitchen and a 16-foot square dining room and saloon, fitted with sixteen armchairs and large, partially-opening bay windows. Behind this was a corridor leading to ten double sleeping cabins with outward-facing ports. At the very back of the nacelle were toilets and large, separate washrooms for men and women. Evidently no effort had been spared to make a flight in the great *Graf Zeppelin* a comfortable experience.

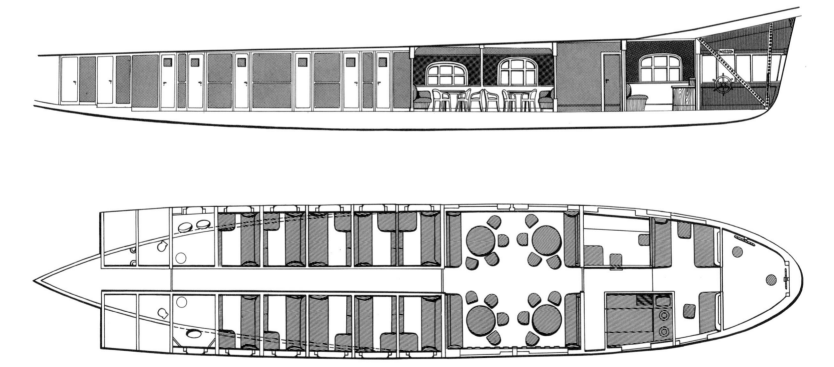

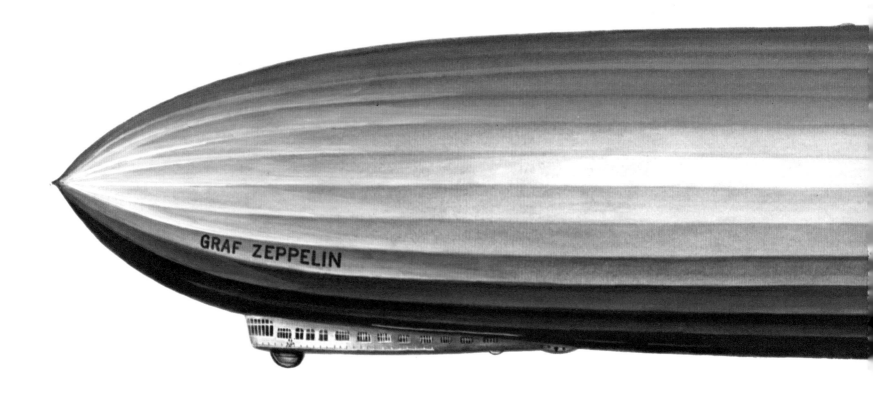

## 1928: The LZ127, 'Graf Zeppelin'

The LZ127, in fact the 118th Zeppelin built, formed the prototype for all future commercial airships. 776 feet long and 100 feet in diameter, its 17 gas-bags had a total volume of 3,708,000 cubic feet. Four 530 h.p. Maybach engines were installed in two pairs of nacelles on each side of the envelope and a fifth identical engine in the stern in-line nacelle was also equipped with a reverse gear. The forward nacelle for the captain and flying crew contained accommodation for twenty passengers. Rest quarters for the forty-four man crew were provided in the keel under the envelope reached by a ladder inside a round tubular passageway running from the forward nacelle. An observation post was built into the top of the envelope and the nose was fitted with the necessary equipment for mooring to a mast. The LZ127 had a speed of approximately 70 m.p.h. and a range of some 6,250 miles.

A very unusual feature of this airship was that, except for take-off and landing manoeuvres requiring fast acceleration, the engines used a compound of hydrocarbon and methane, named *blau-gaz* after its inventor. Stored in 12 gas-bags, this mixture had the same specific weight as air, thus simplifying static balance while cruising.

*Graf Zeppelin* made its initial flight on 18 September 1928. On 11 October the giant airship made its first transatlantic crossing to the U.S.A. During its long career, the LZ127 made 144 crossings of both the North and South Atlantic, as well as a remarkable round-the-world flight of 31,000 miles in 12 days, 12 hours, 20 minutes between 1 August and 4 September 1929. In 1931 an aerial survey of the Arctic with several maritime stop-overs was also carried out. Only taken out of service on 18 June 1937, *Graf Zeppelin* was proudly preserved in a hangar at Friedrichshafen until March 1940 when it was destroyed on the orders of Marshal Göring.

### 'Graf Zeppelin'

1. Control nacelle and passenger accommodation
2. Pneumatic shock-absorber
3. Electric heating motor
4. Ballast
5. Oil tanks
6. Crew's rest room
7. Fuel tanks
8. Forward side engine nacelle
9. Freight compartment
10. Stern side engine nacelle
11. Crew's sleeping quarters
12. Stern engine nacelle
13. Lower cat-walk
14. Central cat-walk
15. Ventilating flue
16. Release valve in case of over-pressure
17. Gas evacuation flue
18. Air intake
19. Ladder to observation platform
20. Mooring gear
21. Tail fin
22. Rudder
23. Elevator

## 1929: The U.S. dirigible ZMC 2

In the late twenties, the Aircraft Development Corporation of Detroit, Michigan, under the directives of the engineer and aviator Ralph H. Upson, began building a rigid airship of a very unusual kind that was to be a more successful 'repeat' of a similar dirigible built in 1897, the ill-fated German *Schwarz*. This was the ZMC 2, the initials M and C denoting metal-clad. The view from the nose, on the right, shows the concentric strips of 'alclad' forming the outer skin as well as the ends of the eight fins with control surfaces, symmetrically arranged and projecting from the circumference of the envelope. The closed-in nacelle, fastened to the centre of the envelope and braced with cables, is fitted with triangulated struts supporting two radial engines driving twin-bladed airscrews. Under the nacelle, a small triangular keel acted as a landing skid.

The envelope, above, of 203,900 cubic feet, was 149 feet long and 53 feet at its greatest diameter, representing a ratio of only 2.83:1. Its outer skin was constructed from sheets of 'alclad', duralumin sheets sandwiched between two very fine sheets of pure aluminium. The entire 'sandwich', only one tenth of an inch in thickness, covered twenty-four longitudinal formers and twelve ring frames. The entire airship was also covered with alclad foil, varying in thickness from 12 to 17 hundredths of a millimetre and the whole unit joined together with three and a half million countersunk rivets. Apart from two ballonets to regulate pressure, occupying about a quarter of the total volume, the envelope was filled directly with helium. Towards the tail, eight stabilizing vanes and control surfaces were spaced at 45° intervals round the envelope. The closed nacelle, attached to the underside of the envelope, was equipped with two Wright Whirl-wind J5 air-cooled engines of 220 h.p., giving an air speed of about 48 m.p.h.

On 19 August 1929, the ZMC 2 took to the air for the first time and, shortly afterwards, was put into service with the Navy as a flying training aircraft based on the Naval Air Station at Lakehurst. For over twelve years, the ZMC 2 had an unblemished record, being finally scrapped in 1942. About 1930, its constructors were planning to build a larger airship with a volume of 3,778,700 cubic feet, to be powered by eight engines totalling 5,000 horsepower but the unexpected onset of the economic depression prevented this.

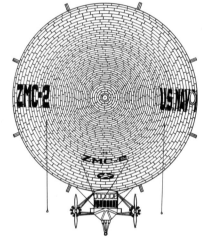

Below: this plan view shows the internal system of longitudinal formers and the cables staying the nose and tail of the nacelle. Behind, the two power units can be seen. Five of the eight stabilizing vanes visible are fitted with control surfaces used for steering and as elevators.

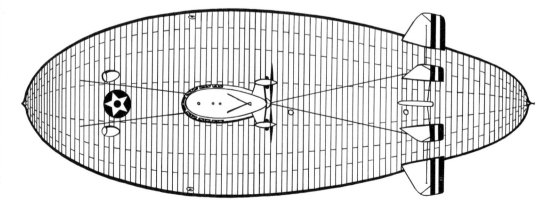

The U.S. Navy's metal-skinned ZMC2 in flight during the thirties. The eight fins with their small control surfaces can be seen symmetrically arranged round the circumference of the envelope and the triangular skid under the nacelle is also visible.

At the beginning of the twenties, a certain Claude C. Slate of Glendale, California, designed a similar metal-skinned dirigible with accommodation for thirty passengers. Completed in 1929, this was never tested because of financial difficulties arising from the economic slump. However, Claude Slate & Co., a company registered at the end of the Second World War, now has a similar design on the drawing boards, the SMD100 air cargo carrier, powered by turbo-jet engines in the nose. This is just one of the many present-day attempts to resuscitate the great ships of the air.

**The U.S. Navy's ZPG 3W, a non-rigid airship**

With a volume of 1,483,200 cubic feet, this was the largest non-rigid airship ever produced. The ZPG 3W made its maiden flight with a crew of 25 men on 21 July 1958. Equipped with a radar dome on the top of the envelope, it was designed as a flying unit in the Early Warning System. A small auxiliary observation nacelle, which can be seen protruding slightly under the envelope, was fitted in front of the main nacelle. The ZPG 3W was the last type of airship employed by the American Naval Air Service. In 1962, all lighter-than-air craft were finally taken out of service.

## The American TC13

On 30 June 1937, the U.S. Army abandoned its airship programme and handed over four Type TC units to the Navy. One of these was the TC13 which had been built by Goodyear in 1933. With a length of 230 feet and a diameter of 37 feet, it had a volume of 353,100 cubic feet and was powered by two Pratt & Whitney Wasp Junior engines of 235 h.p. One of its crew of eight could be lowered in a small observation nacelle, the 'cloud car', on the end of a 1,000-foot steel cable. The TC13 took part in wartime operations and remained in service until 1943.

## The American K2

The Goodyear Company started building Type K airships in 1937 under the directives of the U.S. Navy which had decided to put scouting blimps into service. The K2, which was first flown in December 1938, had a volume of 399,100 cubic feet and was powered by two Pratt & Whitney Wasp engines of 550 h.p. driving tractor airscrews. Several of these units were used in the Mediterranean theatre of operations during the last war and four of them made the Atlantic crossing to their war base at Port-Lyautey in Morocco, a flight of some 3,125 miles.

## 1954: The non-rigid U.S. Navy ZPG2W

Derived from the Type N series built in 1951, the ZPG2W was conspicuous for its slanting fins and control surfaces, as well as the radar dome on top of the 988,800 cubic foot envelope. This airship was deployed as an aerial radar station in the U.S. Early Warning defence system. As proof of its ability to maintain the long watches required by such a system, the ZPG2W was airborne for 11 days during a flight in 1957 when it took off from Weymouth in Massachusetts, flew to Africa and returned to Key West in Florida, a distance of nearly 10,000 miles.

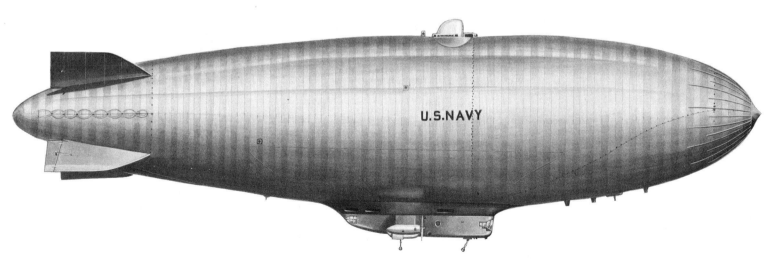

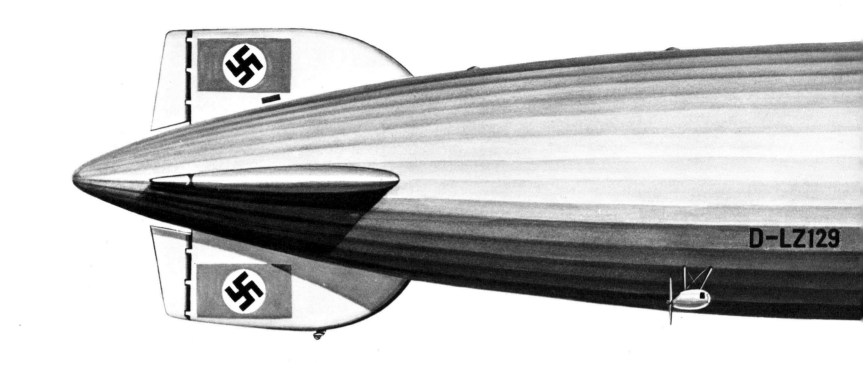

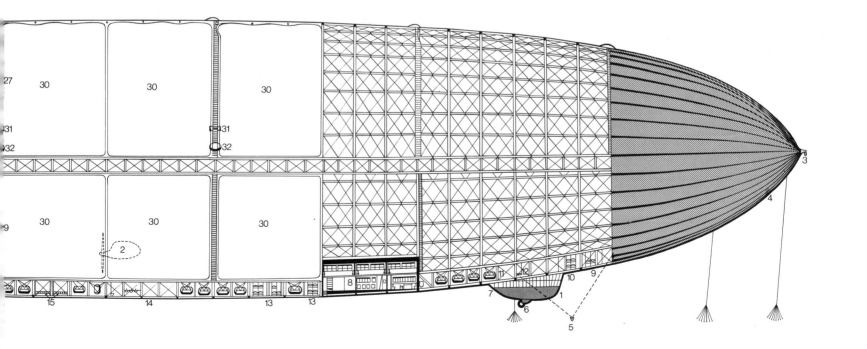

**1929: 'Hindenburg'**

Younger sister ship of *Graf Zeppelin* which flew the Germany to Brazil route, the LZ129 was built for regular North Atlantic crossings and had a less elongated but more aerodynamically shaped envelope than the older dirigible, its length-diameter ratio being 6:1 as opposed to 8.7:1 for the LZ127: 804 feet long and 135 feet in diameter, *Hindenburg* had an unprecedented volume of 6,709,800 cubic feet, distributed over 16 gas-bags. Four Daimler-Diesel 1,050 h.p. engines, installed in two pairs of nacelles at each side of the envelope, drove airscrews with reversible blades, giving a maximum speed of 81 m.p.h. and a cruising speed of 70 m.p.h. The small command nacelle was placed forward under the nose and accommodation for fifty-five passengers, subsequently increased for seventy-two, was inside the envelope where, apart from individual cabins, a large lounge with inclined windows, a dining room and a saloon with an aluminium grand piano were placed at their disposal. A smoking-room and bar, completely sealed off from the rest of the airship, was installed lower down in the keel.

*Hindenburg* had been designed to use helium but, for diplomatic and commercial reasons, the American Government refused to lift its ban on the export of this non-inflammable gas, of which America was then the sole producer. Thus, there was no alternative but to use hydrogen.

The LZ127 made its maiden flight on 4 March 1936. On 6 May 1937, after its 63rd Atlantic crossing, as the crew were preparing to tie up to the mooring mast at Lakehurst, fire suddenly broke out at the tail and on the top of the envelope. Minutes later, the whole blazing mass crashed to the ground. Of the ninety-seven persons aboard, sixty-two survived. As far as German aviation was concerned, the greatest loss among the twenty-two crew members killed was the famous airship captain, Ernst August Lehmann.

As the fire started at the top of one of the tail gas-bags near the leading edge of the upper tail fin, the not unreasonable hypothesis has since been advanced that the disaster might have been politically motivated, either by the explosion of a delayed-action bomb or, more plausibly, by an incendiary bullet fired from the ground at that immense target, its tail unit emblazoned with huge swastikas.

**Longitudinal cross-section**

1. Command nacelle
2. Engine nacelles
3. Mooring gear
4. Ground mooring cables
5. Apparatus for dropping moorings
6. Landing gear
7. Wireless cabin
8. Passengers' saloon
9. Captain's cabin
10. Crew's quarters
11. Post room
12. Luggage room
13. Crew's rest room
14. Electrical generating installation
15. Luggage rooms
16. Ground mooring cables

17. Apparatus for dropping moorings
18. Stern mooring gear
19. Rear fixing cable for shock-absorber
20. Stabilizing vane
21. Elevator
22. Rudder
23. Tail fin
24. Main ring rib
25. Auxiliary ring rib
26. Longitudinal cross-bracing
27. Gas exhaust flue
28. Air intake
29. Staircase
30. Gas-bag
31. Blow-valve
32. Over-pressure safety valve.

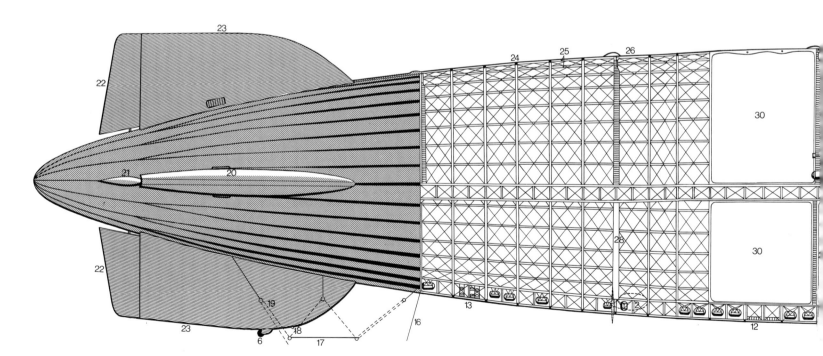

## 1936-1937: The LZ129, 'Hindenburg'

**1** Aboard *Hindenburg* in May 1936, the helmsman Schoenherr is on duty in the front of the command nacelle. Next to him stands Flugkapitän Prüss.

**2** A photograph taken in May 1936 showing Flugkapitän Prüss near the elevator controls, looking out of one of the wireless cabin windows.

**3** Partial view of the internal framework of the LZ129 showing a rib ring in the foreground with the intricate system of bracing which interlocked it with the longitudinal former.

**4** The saloon on the starboard side with the passage leading to it. The famous aluminium grand piano can be seen in the background.

**5** Max Schmelling, who had just become world boxing champion after his victory in the United States, looks out of one of the bay windows in the promenade deck during his return flight to Germany.

**6** The sealed smoking-room in the lowest part of the keel. Even here, the use of matches or cigarette-lighters was strictly forbidden.

**7** The final tragic appearance of *Hindenburg* as it approached its mooring mast at Lakehurst, New Jersey, on 6 May 1937.

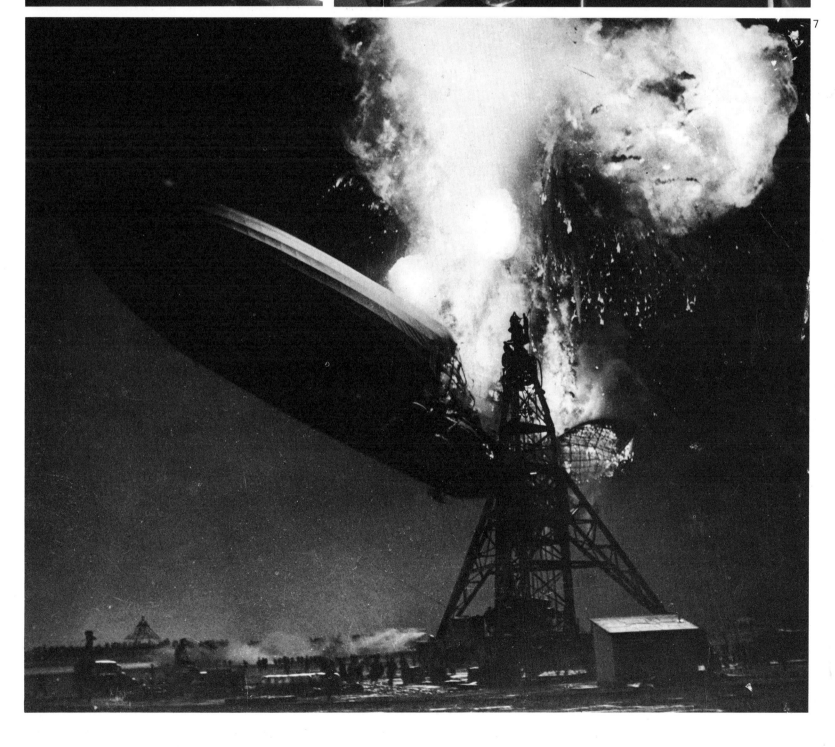

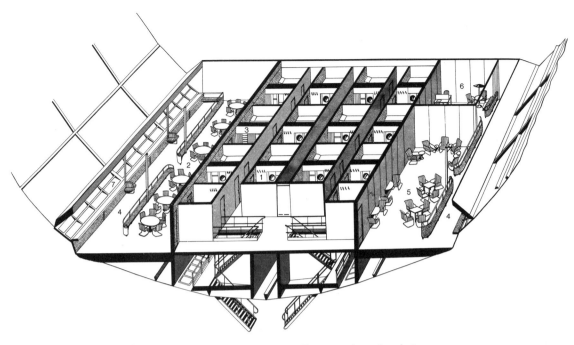

## Plan of the interior fittings

a-g: Oil tanks
h-i: Drinking water tanks
 j: Used water tanks
k-m: Water-ballast tanks
 n: Cooling-water tanks
 o: Baggage-room
 p: Spare parts store
q, r: Food reserves
 s: Engineers' cabin
 t: Ventilators
 u: Sanitary fittings
 v: Workshops
 w: Corridor leading to engine nacelles
 x: Stairway
 y: Passageway to the water-ballast

1. Command nacelle
2. Passenger accommodation
3. Wireless cabin
4. Post room
5. Store-room
6. Crew's quarters
7. Main store-room
8. Store-room
9. Electricity generating installation
10. Store-room

## Perspective view of passenger installations

1. Cabins
2. Dining room
3. Office
4. Covered walk
5. Lounge
6. Reading and writing room
7. Windows

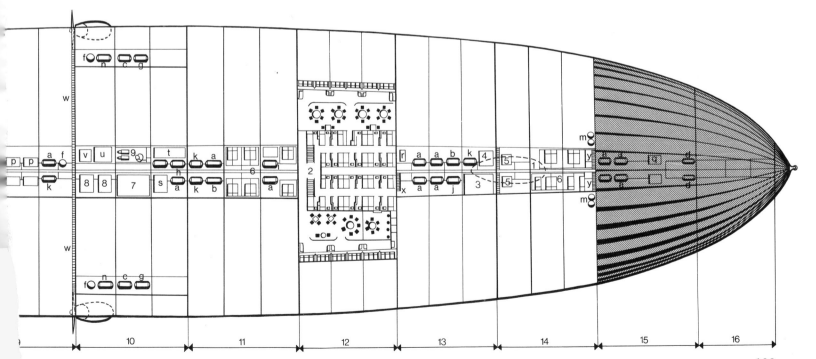

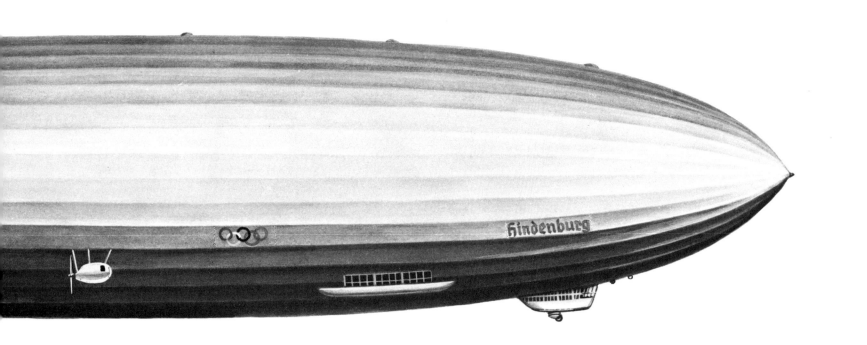

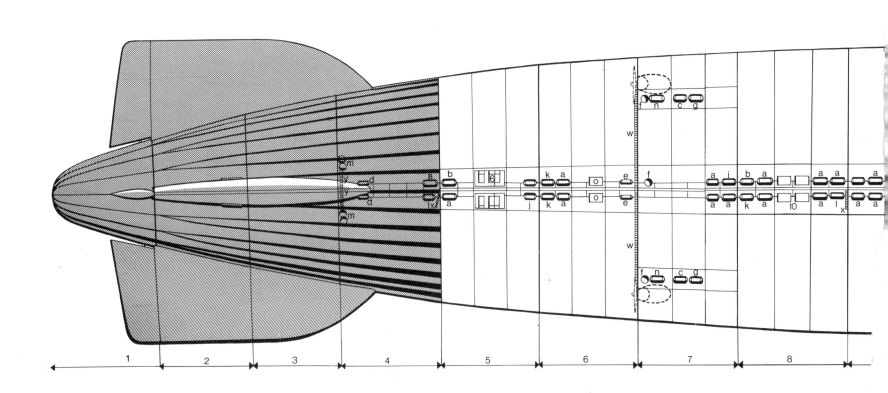

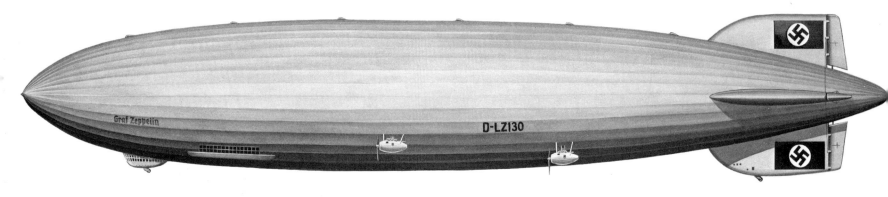

## 1938 : The German LZ130

Despite the tragic accident to *Hindenburg*, the Zeppelin Luftschiffbau continued work on the LZ130, a replica of the ill-fated LZ129. The new airship, again bearing the name *Graf Zeppelin*, had identically the same dimensions, volume and engine installation as *Hindenburg*, the only difference being in the passenger accommodation, cabins being built athwartships instead of longitudinally and with one bunk over another.

The LZ130 made its first flight on 14 September 1938. Because it was again impossible to obtain helium from the U.S.A., hydrogen had to be used, with the result that the dirigible was never put into regular airline service and made only some thirty test flights and aerial tours within the German frontiers. Under orders from Marshal Göring, both the new and the old *Graf Zeppelin* were scrapped in March 1940, the light metal in their skeletons being used to build combat aircraft.

## 1931 : Zodiac VII naval scouting airship

Based on the Astra-Torres design and carrying a crew of four, this airship was 148 feet long, 43 feet at its maximum diameter and its three-lobed envelope had a volume of 120,000 cubic feet, the nose being reinforced for mooring to a mast. At each side of the fully enclosed nacelle, attached to the belly of the envelope, was an air-cooled Salmson 9 Ac 120 h.p. engine, giving the Zodiac VII a maximum speed of 62 m.p.h. and a cruising speed of 47 m.p.h. Two curved air-shafts on either side of the top of the nacelle supplied the ballonets and a small skid fitted under each motor cowling protected the airscrews from contact with the ground.

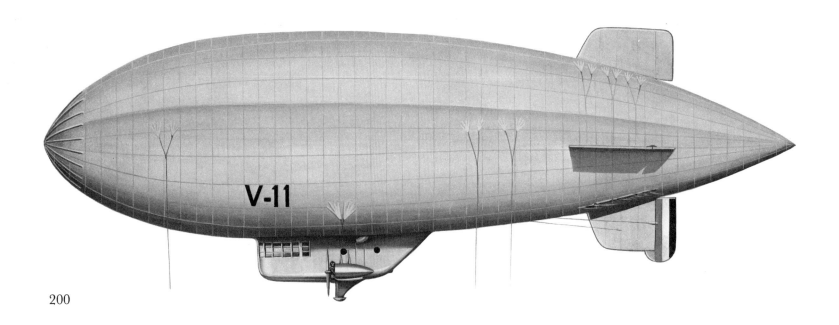

**The German LZ127**
The LZ127, the first *Graf Zeppelin*, flies over a four-engined Dornier *Super Wal*, taking off from Lake Constance while another Dornier, a twin-engined *Wal*, makes an approach above.

**Worm's eye view of the Goodyear blimp 'America'**
This original view of *America* clearly shows the structural reinforcing of the nose and the short, tapering nacelle with its two symmetrically placed engines. The sides of the envelope are covered with a galaxy of different coloured electric bulbs, the switching being programmed to enable a wide variety of illuminated words and animated figures to be formed into advertising messages when the blimp was flown after dark. Goodyear named this 'Skytacular' while, on the larger airship *America*, it was called 'Super Skytacular'.

202

**The Goodyear blimps
'Mayflower' and 'America'**

*Mayflower* was the 297th airship produced by Goodyear and the 53rd used for commercial purposes. Based on Miami, Florida, it was first air-tested in 1968. With a length of 157 feet and 50 feet in diameter, its volume is 145,850 cubic feet and with its two 175-horsepower Continental engines, a pilot and six passengers can be carried at a maximum speed of 50 m.p.h., a cruising speed of 35 m.p.h., with a ceiling of nearly 10,000 feet and a range of 500 miles. The envelope is equipped for Skytacular displays consisting, in this case, of 3,080 red, green, blue and yellow miniature electric bulbs fitted on panels 103 feet long and 14 feet wide on each side of the envelope and connected up by over 25 miles of wire.

*America*, the younger but larger sister-ship, was produced in 1969 and is based on Houston in Texas. This Goodyear blimp with a volume of 200,400 cubic feet, a length of 190 feet and a diameter of 49 feet is powered by two Continental engines of 210 h.p. each, giving *America* a maximum speed of 50 m.p.h., a cruising speed of 35 m.p.h. with a ceiling of 8,400 feet and a maximum range of 500 miles, carrying a pilot and six passengers. Its Super Skytacular equipment consists of 7,650 bulbs on panels 103 feet long and 24 feet wide, necessitating 80 miles of electric wiring.

# 1931 : USS 'Akron'

In 1924, having acquired the licence to build airships in the United States using the Zeppelin patents, the Goodyear Tire and Rubber Co. of Akron formed a subsidiary, the Goodyear-Zeppelin Corporation. In the summer of 1927, it received orders from the U.S. Navy for the construction of two giant rigid airships, the ZRS 4 and ZRS 5, christened respectively *Akron* and *Macon*. Unfortunately, both were destined for tragic ends. The ZRS 4, built at the naval air service base at Akron, was 771 feet long, 131 feet in diameter and had the greatest volume of any airship yet produced, containing 6,427,300 cubic feet of helium. Eight Maybach engines of 560 h.p. were installed inside the envelope. These engines were equipped with reverse gear and a remote drive to the airscrews which could be turned to any angle. In the vertical position, these airscrews provided extra lift during take-off and when heavy landings were foreseen. Fitted to the outside of the envelope, above the engine nacelles, were eight sets of five panels made of aluminium tubing which, by condensing the water vapour contained in the exhaust gas, helped to trim the airship in normal flight. Apart from the command nacelle and the eight engine nacelles, a small emergency nacelle, 15 feet long and 3 feet in diameter, with its own controls was built into the lower section of the tail fin. The armament consisted of seven machine-gun posts and the maximum speed was in the region of 85 m.p.h.

*Akron* was a veritable flying aircraft carrier with a built-in hangar under the envelope for five fighter airplanes which extended the crew's range of observation and served as eyes for the fleet, inboard radar systems not yet being in use. A retractable, electrically powered trapeze device could drop the aircraft clear of the airship and hook them up again during flight. One of these aircraft is shown releasing the trapeze in this illustration.

*Akron* first took to the air on 23 September 1931 and subsequently made a long series of flights under the very able captaincy of Lieutenant Commander Rosendahl, logging 1,700 flying hours before disaster struck. On the night of 3 April 1933, the airship was caught in a hurricane force storm off the coast of New Jersey, violent currents forcing it down into the sea. Out of a crew of seventy-six, there were only three survivors and among those who lost their lives was Admiral William A. Moffett, commanding the U.S. Naval Air Service.

## Aircraft suspension equipment

The Curtiss F-9C2 was a two-seater biplane fighter 19 feet long, with a wing span of 29 feet. Powered by an air-cooled 400 h.p. engine, its maximum speed was about 180 m.p.h. Here it is shown suspended by its cross-shaped hook from the retractable trapeze consisting of two folding lattice girders. A small weighted flag was used as a signal for the different manoeuvres.

1. The F-9C2
2. The aircraft's overhead hook
3. Platform supporting the trapeze equipment
4. Open trap
5. Closed trap
6. Winch
7. Stress beams
8. Monorail
9. Trapeze in retracted position
10. Trapeze axle
11. Bracing trapeze
12. Trapeze in lowered position
13. Counterbalance weight
14. Operating cable
15. Observation nacelle (cloud car)
16. Fork centering device
17. Extinguisher

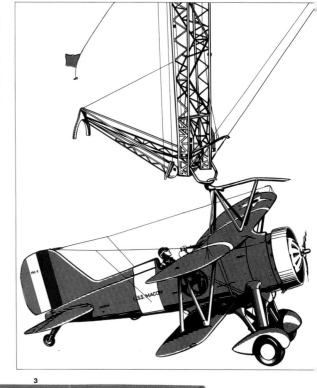

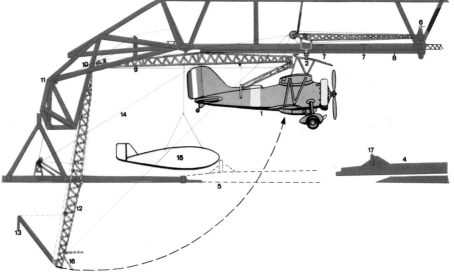

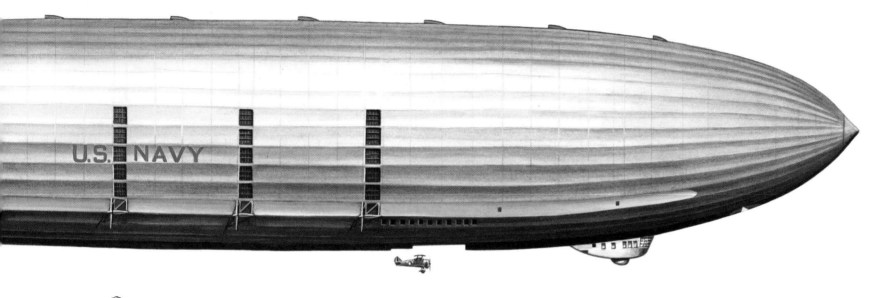

## Power unit

This Maybach V-12 cylinder engine, mounted inside the envelope, used a reduction gearbox and bevel gears to drive a twin-bladed wooden airscrew which was attached by struts to the side of the envelope and which could be turned upwards, downwards, towards the nose or the tail. Fuel, oil and water tanks were mounted on cross-beams inside the envelope. The large elbowed pipe conducted the exhaust gas into the external water vapour condensers. The figure of a crew member gives an idea of the size of the installation.

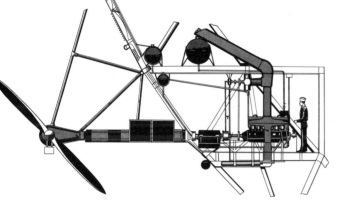

## Forward nacelle

Fixed to the underside of the envelope, this nacelle housed the captain, pilot, navigator and wireless operator who could communicate by telephone with the engine nacelles and the small emergency nacelle. Large windows were fitted over the whole length, and included in the pointed tail. A retractable flight of steps with a hand-rail provided access to the ground and swivelling floodlights were fitted directly below one of the windows. The illustration also shows the hand-rails for use by the ground crew and the pneumatic shock-absorber.

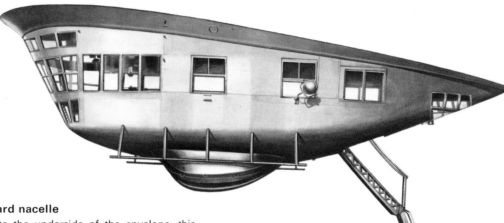

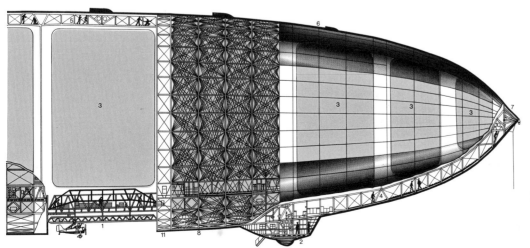

### Technical forward cross-section of 'Akron'

1. Hangar and crew's quarters
2. Command nacelle
3. Helium gas-bags
4. Lower cat-walk
5. Upper cat-walk
6. Gun post
7. Observation platform
8. Intermediary ribs
9. Gas-bag and cross-stays
10. Winch platform
11. Main rib

### German aerial advertising units

During peace-time, German promoters enthusiastically employed small, non-rigid airships as publicity media for commercial and even industrial promotion. As early as 1910, the Parseval PL 6 carried publicity for a chocolate manufacturer. Between the two World Wars, the Parseval-Naatz PN 28 and PN 29, as well as the semi-rigid units built by the Raab-Katzenstein aircraft company of Krefeld were also used for tourist flights and for advertising campaigns. These promotional ideas were revived in 1957 with the construction of an airship of 154,000 cubic feet. This was a joint venture in which Metallwerk Friedrichshafen GmbH, which had taken over the Zeppelin Company, provided the metal parts and the Ballonfabrik of Augsburg built the envelope. This was the first airship in Europe to be filled with helium and, during 1970, it made a long publicity tour through France.

On 13 August 1972, *Flying Musketeer* made its first flight and, shortly afterwards, on 30 October, a second similar airship appeared. Called *Flying Japan*, this was built for and delivered to the Land of the Rising Sun. Both had been built at Mülheim for a company called Westdeutsche Luftwerbung in Essen-Mülheim specializing in aerial publicity. The lower tail fin of *Flying Musketeer* carried a beer advertisement and the polyester envelope was fitted with 10,000 lamp bulbs over an area of 131 feet by 26 feet.

Both airships, coded the WDL1 and WDL2, have a volume of 211,900 cubic feet, a length of 197 feet and a maximum diameter of 47 feet, the nacelle being 24 feet long. Both are powered with two Rolls-Royce Continental engines of 180 h.p. driving tractor airscrews. Carrying a two-man crew and eight passengers, they have a maximum speed of 62 m.p.h. and a range of 250 miles. Two further airships, one of 706,300 cubic feet and another of 2,260,150 cubic feet are now under consideration.

**1942: A U.S. Navy Type K airship undergoing two routine hangar operations**

Above, the almost deflated envelope spread out on a protective floor covering. In the background the nacelle can be seen on trestles. Below, the envelope during one of its periodic inflations to prevent the inside surfaces from sticking together when not in use. The interior bracing cords attached to serrated material strips can also be seen. The two men give an idea of the envelope size.

## Inside the Goodyear hangar at Akron, Ohio

Above, the lamp bulbs are being fitted into the illuminated Skytacular panels.

Below, an envelope on its protective floor covering is in the early stages of inflation and the gas forms a dome. Five weights to hold the envelope down are seen in the foreground. To the left, several inflated envelopes can be seen, held down by their weights.

On the opposite page, the Goodyear *Europa* with the American registration on its tail unit and fitted with illuminating Skytacular panels is destined for a wide variety of aerial demonstrations over Western Europe. Re-assembled in Great Britain at the Royal Aircraft Establishment in Cardington, *Europa* made its first flight from there on 8 March 1972. Its dimensions and general characteristics are identical to those of *America* which has been previously described.

**A Russian Soviet design for an airship powered by atomic energy, published in the German magazine 'Der Flieger', July 1972**

1. Command cabin
2. Helium gas-bags
3. Upper passenger deck
4. Heliport for arrivals and departures
5. Tail plane and elevators
6. Nuclear reactor for a turbo-prop unit
7. Tail fin and rudder
8. Anchoring device
9. Inboard aircraft hangar
10. Lift
11. Passenger cabins
12. Freight storage
13. Pilot's cockpit

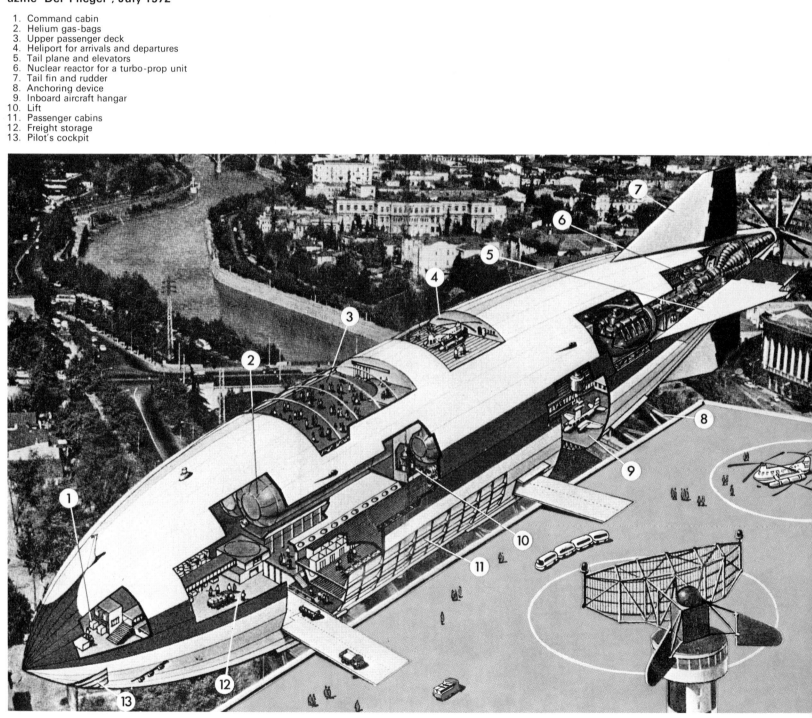

# POSTSCRIPT

## TOMORROW...

Man will always be tempted to speculate that, before the end of this century, these giant ships of the air may once again sail the skies. There is no evidence at present to confirm or deny such a prediction and, in fact, important meetings took place in Paris and London in 1974 to discuss and review progress. The use of atomic power to propel submarines has set active minds in several countries to consider the practicability of employing this force to drive huge dirigibles. Technological progress and man's endeavour to discover more about the universe wherein his small planet revolves, leaves little more for science-fiction addicts to invent in their fantasies. Already, fertile minds are imagining these mammoths with passenger cabins like blocks of flats, served by lifts, crew quarters with workshops for maintenance and repairs during flight, built into the keel on several decks. They have even imagined hangars in the keel for communications aircraft, heliports on the top surface of the envelope for use by air-taxis plying a door-to-door passenger service, not to mention all the other amenities demanded by air-travellers on today's transatlantic air flights in airplanes.

For technical dreaming to give way to reality, no other motive force than atomic power is possible, even if such an installation would necessitate construction on a gigantic scale. A nuclear reactor in a conventional aircraft is unthinkable if only because protection against harmful radiation would need a very thick and heavy lead wall between the crew and passenger accomodation and the energy source. Sufficient engine power to propel such a weight plus payload is technically possible in an airship with a hull of some 1,000 feet in length. Thousands of horsepower could be developed by turbo-engines, powered by nuclear reactors built into the stern to drive these aerial mastodons, calculated as having between 9 and 20 million cubic

**The Goodyear Aerospace Corporation's concept of inter-city travel through congested areas**

These five artist's impressions demonstrate the potentialities of a dirigible called *Dynastat* combining, as its name suggests, both static and aerodynamic lift. The multi-lobed envelope has two engines mounted on each side which could be pivoted from the horizontal to the vertical so as to make accurate, controlled landings on the roof of a terminal building. Radar-controlled flights over a pre-determined ground track would permit regular day-and-night services at a height of between 500 and 3,000 feet, considerably lower than the altitude used by commercial aircraft. According to the Goodyear Aerospace Corporation, the *Dynastat* would be particularly valuable in relieving traffic congestion in such notorious areas as the North-East Corridor linking Boston, New York and Washington.

feet of lifting gas and capable of transporting some 300 to 500 passengers.

Feasibility studies have been made on broad lines in the United States, West Germany and in the U.S.S.R. for several years. Among the obvious advantages of such airships is the practically unlimited radius of action, the protection of the environment against noise and pollution, and the economic yield per unit in fare-paying passengers and freight. It has been estimated that the fuel consumption of Uranium 235 for a dirigible constructed to accomodate 1,000 passengers in making a complete circuit of the world, would be only 17.6 ozs.

Passengers would have transport available at a speed somewhere between that of the old ocean-going liner and the new supersonic aircraft. It does not seem possible that the speed of a liner, as we know it today, can be increased much more than the present 28 to 32 knots. There would be no question of sea-sickness or travel ailments as the huge bulk of the airship would easily ride any air turbulence, and inertia would be reduced to an imperceptible level. This means of transport would be the answer for the long air voyage.

As for freight, these enormous dirigibles could take on the ferrying of single shipments in the order of 250 tons, and would be ideal for loads which are unable to be divided up such as elements for civil engineering projects, bases for space projectiles, the ponderous on-site installations necessary for the development of natural resources, just to quote a few examples. Compared with maritime cargo transported at a surface speed of between 10 and 20 knots, it has been calculated that these immense dirigibles driven by turbo-engines powered by nuclear reactors could attain an air speed of 80 to 100 knots, or even more. Whether or not these dreams may come true cannot be determined today or yet tomorrow but the accelerating progress of space and aeronautical technology has taught us to be wary of prejudging events and that technical miracles sometimes come to pass.

# COMPARATIVE INDEX
## OF AIRSHIPS

## 1852-1972

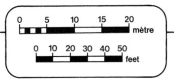

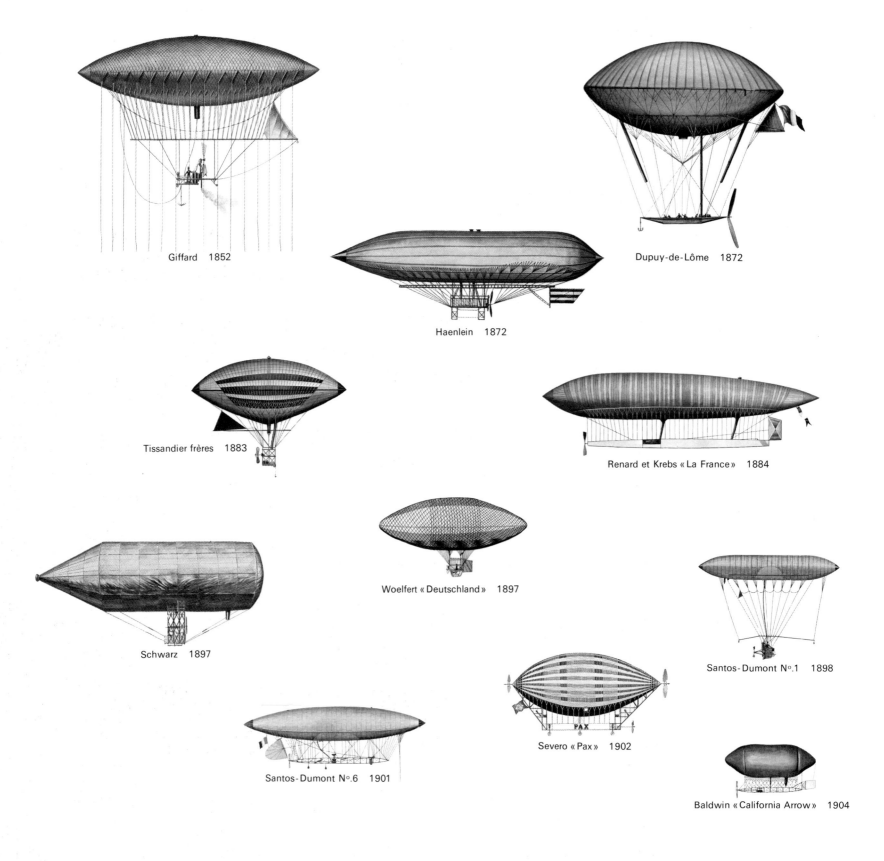

Giffard 1852

Dupuy-de-Lôme 1872

Haenlein 1872

Tissandier frères 1883

Renard et Krebs «La France» 1884

Woelfert «Deutschland» 1897

Schwarz 1897

Santos-Dumont N°.1 1898

Santos-Dumont N°.6 1901

Severo «Pax» 1902

Baldwin «California Arrow» 1904

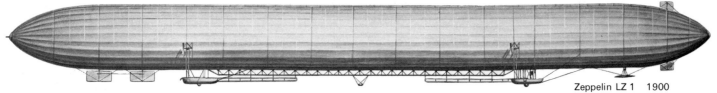

Zeppelin LZ 1 1900

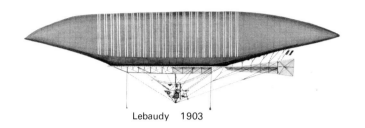

Lebaudy 1903

Santos-Dumont N°.9
« La Baladeuse » 1903

Zodiac I 1908

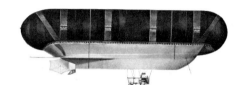

« Nulli Secundus » II 1908

Surcouf-Deutsch-de-la-Meurthe « Ville de Paris » 1906

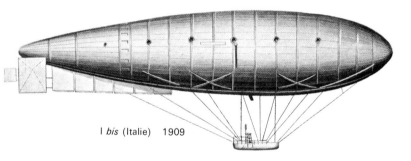

Baldwin 1908

Lebaudy « Liberty » 1909

Forlanini « Leonardo da Vinci » 1909

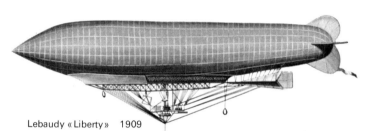

I bis (Italie) 1909

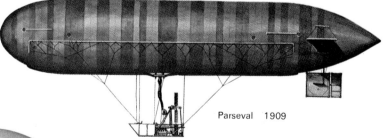

Parseval 1909

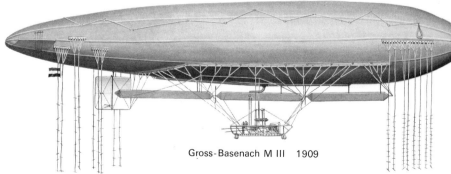

Gross-Basenach M III 1909

0    5    10    15    20
mètre

0  10  20  30  40  50
feet

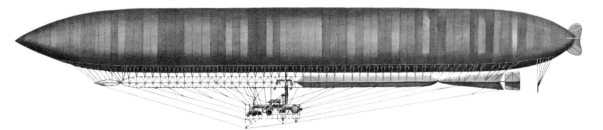

Lebaudy «Morning Post»   1910

Willows «City of Cardiff»   1910

Zeppelin LZ 10 «Schwaben»   1910

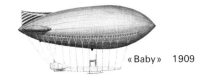

«Baby»   1909

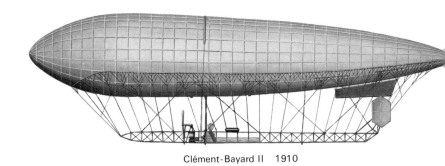

Clément-Bayard II   1910

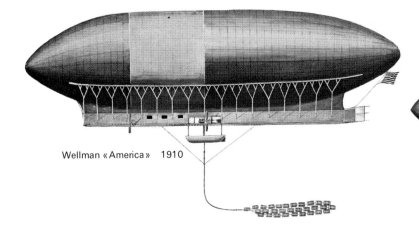

Wellman «America»   1910

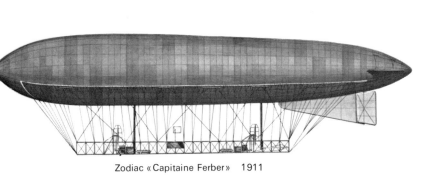

Zodiac «Capitaine Ferber»   1911

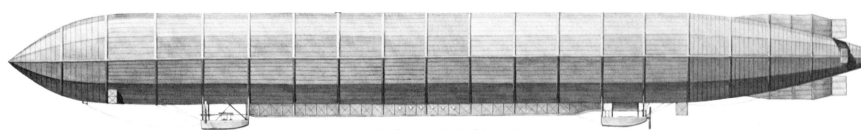

Vickers Sons and Maxim R 1   1911

« Beta » 1910-1912

Chalais-Meudon « Fleurus » 1912

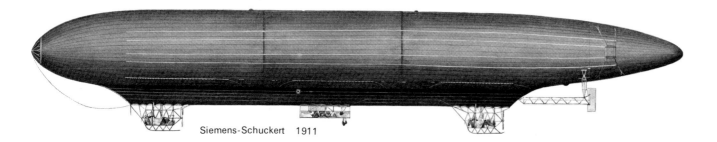
Siemens-Schuckert 1911

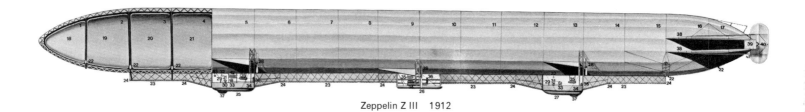
Zeppelin Z III 1912

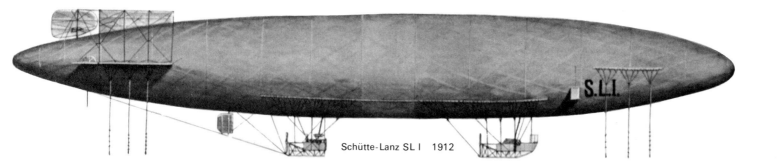
Schütte-Lanz SL I 1912

Zeppelin LZ II « Viktoria Luise » 1912

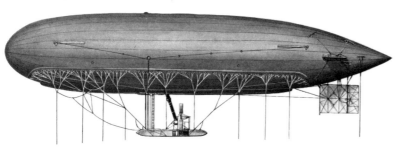
Parseval PL VII 1912

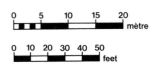

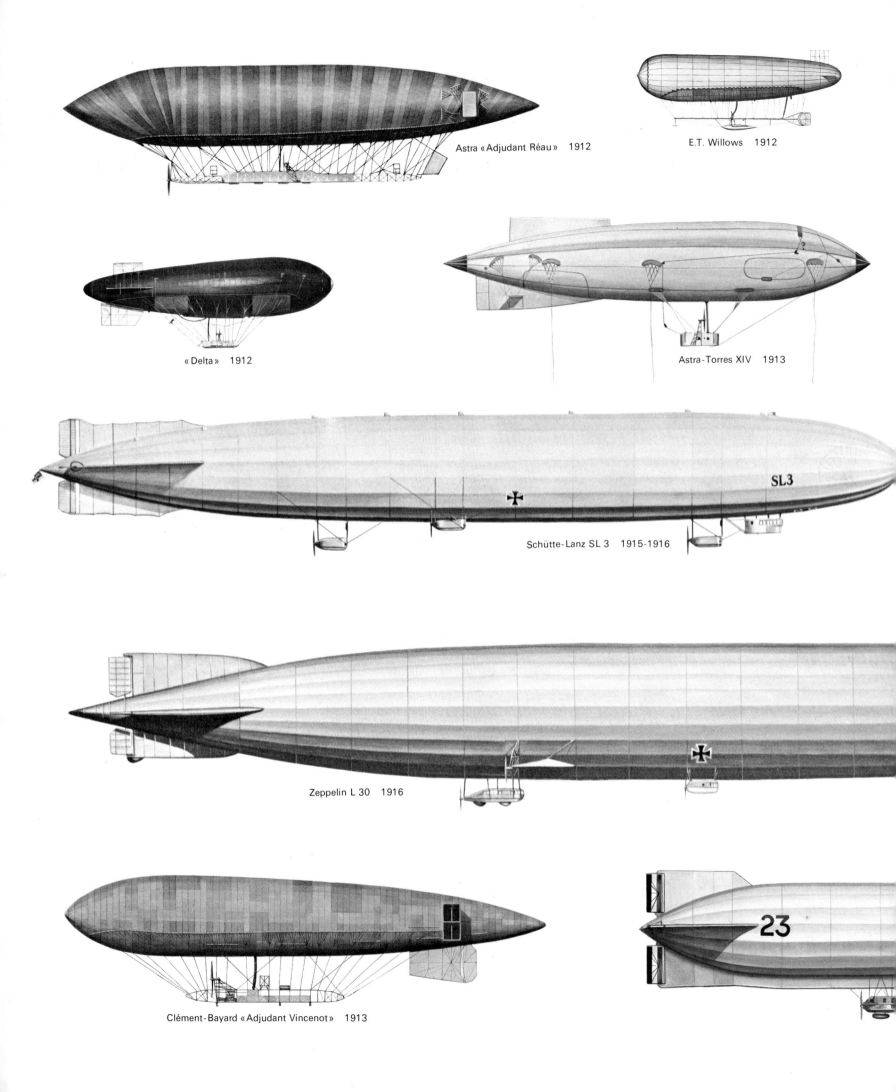

Astra «Adjudant Réau»   1912

E.T. Willows   1912

«Delta»   1912

Astra-Torres XIV   1913

Schütte-Lanz SL 3   1915-1916

Zeppelin L 30   1916

Clément-Bayard «Adjudant Vincenot»   1913

23

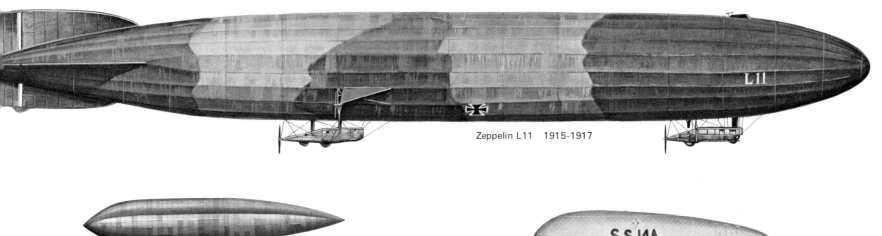

Zeppelin L 11    1915-1917

Astra-Torres I    1912

«Sea Scout»    1915

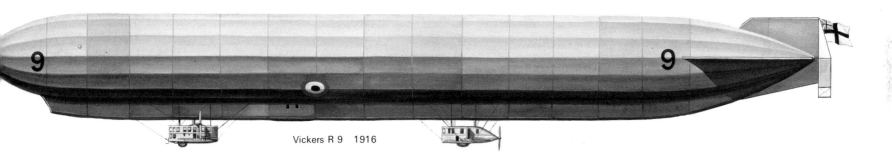

Vickers R 9    1916

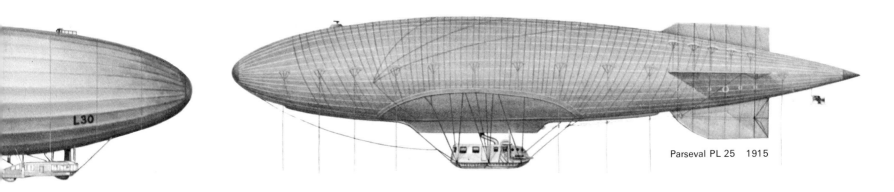

L 30

Parseval PL 25    1915

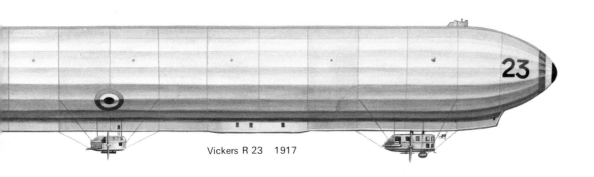

Vickers R 23    1917

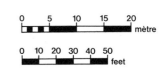

```
0    5    10   15   20
▮▮▮▮▮▮▮▮▮▮▮▮▮▮▮▮ mètre

0  10  20  30  40 50
▮▮▮▮▮▮▮▮▮▮▮▮▮▮▮▮ feet
```

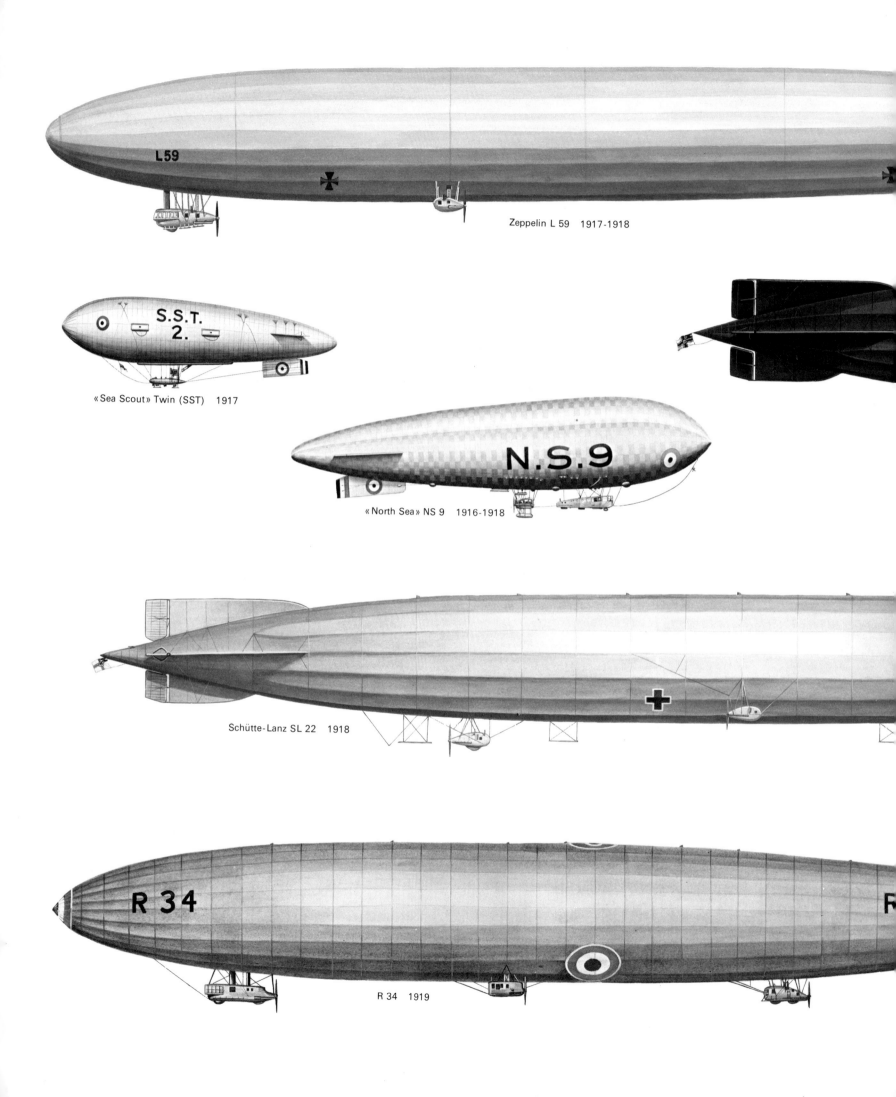

Zeppelin L 59   1917-1918

«Sea Scout» Twin (SST)   1917

«North Sea» NS 9   1916-1918

Schütte-Lanz SL 22   1918

R 34   1919

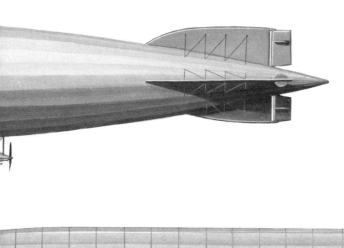

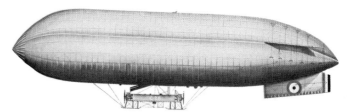

Coastal C 26   1916

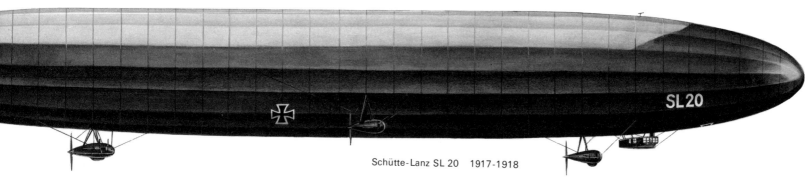

Schütte-Lanz SL 20   1917-1918

Chalais-Meudon type T   1916

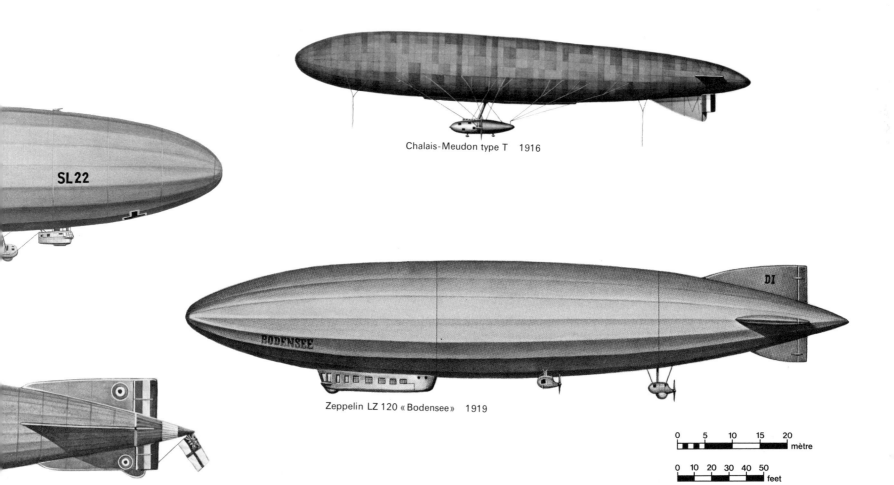

SL 22

Zeppelin LZ 120 « Bodensee »   1919

| 0 | 5 | 10 | 15 | 20 |
|---|---|---|---|---|
mètre

| 0 | 10 | 20 | 30 | 40 | 50 |
|---|---|---|---|---|---|
feet

223

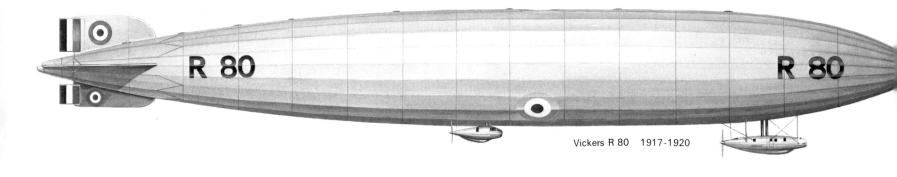

R 80

R 80

Vickers R 80   1917-1920

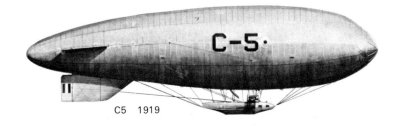

C-5·

C5   1919

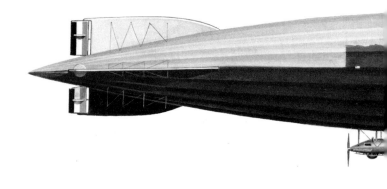

F-YZST

Zodiac YZST   1920

ZR-1

U.S. NAVY

ZR 1 «Shenandoah»   1923-1925

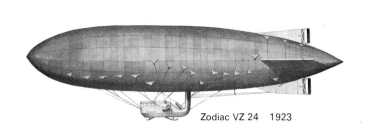

Zodiac VZ 24   1923

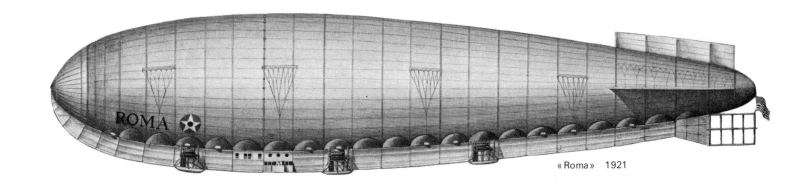

« Roma »   1921

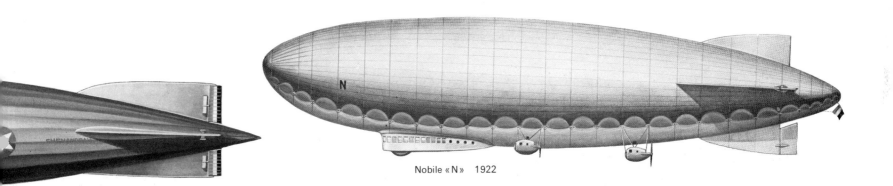

Zeppelin L 72 « Dixmude »   1920-1923

Nobile « N »   1922

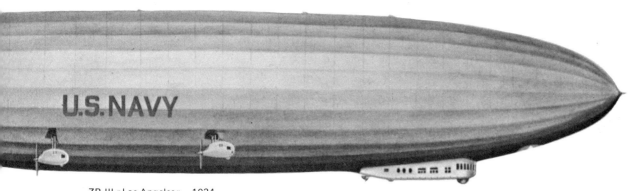

ZR III « Los Angeles »   1924

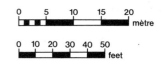

0   5   10   15   20
mètre

0   10   20   30   40   50
feet

225

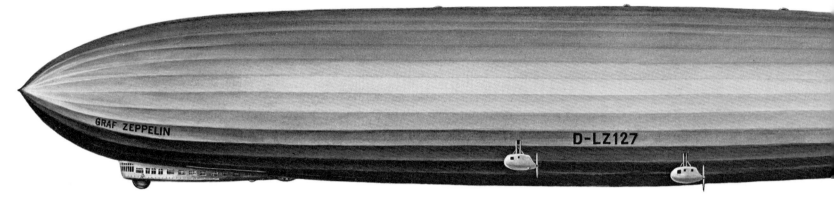

Zeppelin LZ 127 « Graf Zeppelin »   1928

Nobile N4 « Italia »   1928

ZMC 2   1929

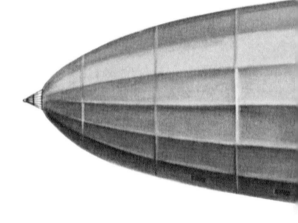

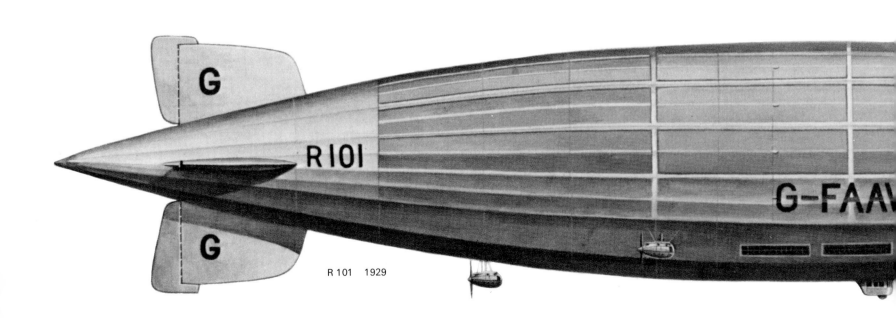

R 101   1929

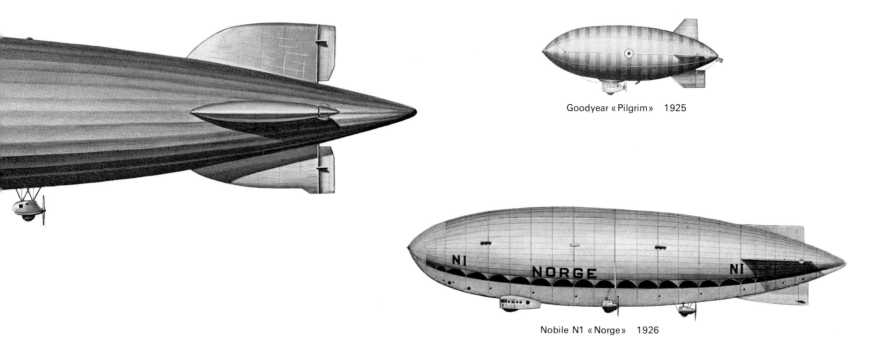

Goodyear « Pilgrim »   1925

Nobile N1 « Norge »   1926

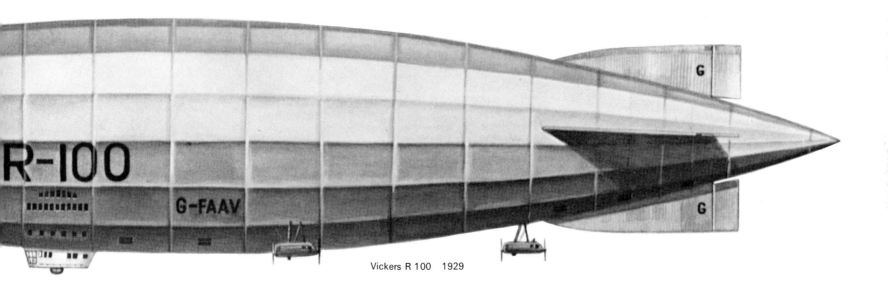

R-100

G-FAAV

Vickers R 100   1929

R 101

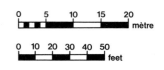

0    5    10    15    20
mètre

0   10  20  30  40  50
feet

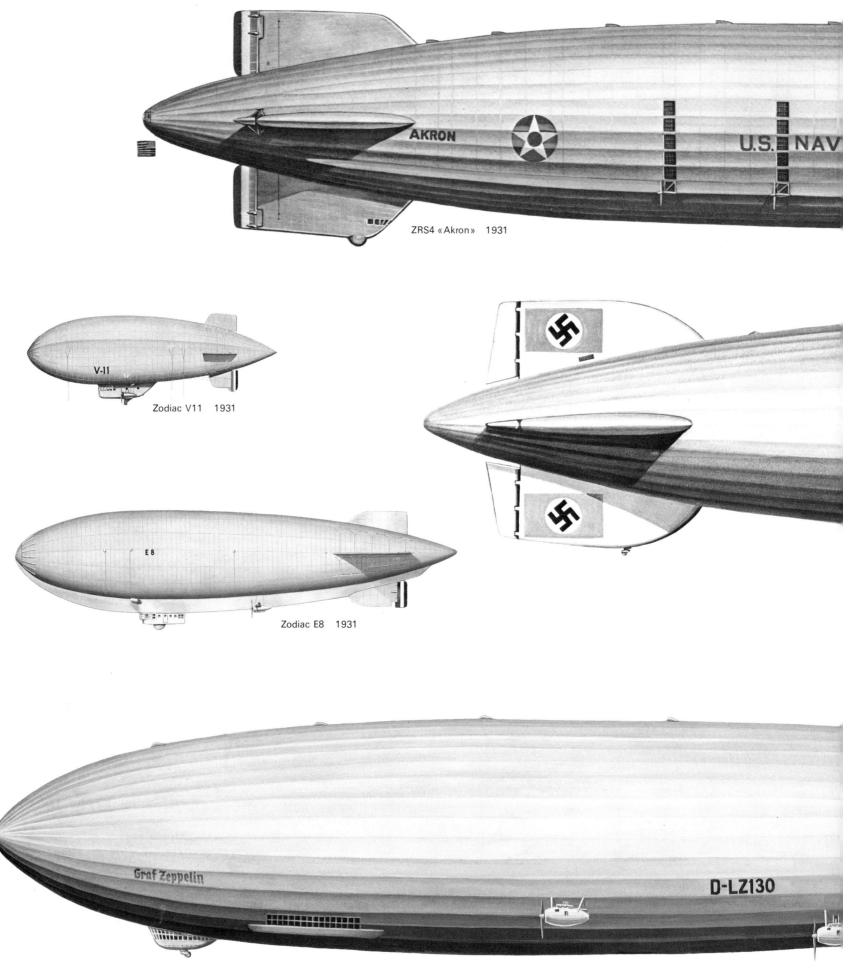

ZRS4 «Akron»   1931

Zodiac V11   1931

Zodiac E8   1931

Zeppelin LZ 130   1938

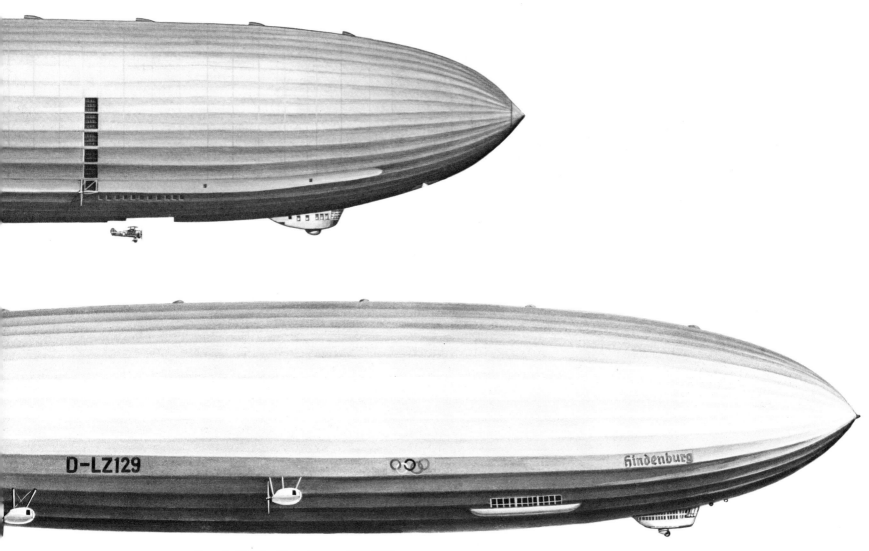

Zeppelin LZ 129 « Hindenburg »    1936-1937

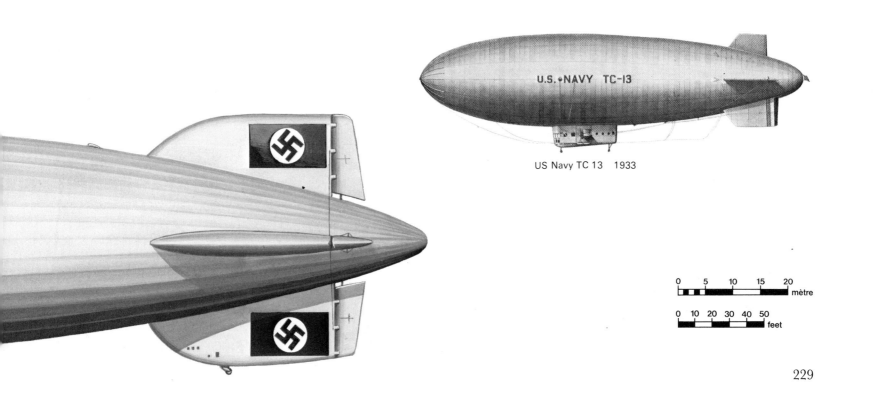

U.S. NAVY TC-13

US Navy TC 13    1933

US Navy K2    1937

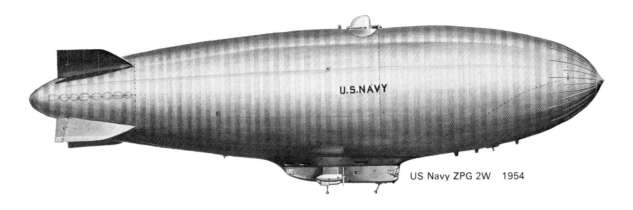

US Navy ZPG 2W    1954

Goodyear « Mayflower »    1964

Goodyear « America »    1969

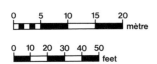

0    5    10    15    20
mètre

0    10    20    30    40    50
feet

WDL « Mousquetaire volant »    1972

# NOTES

# INDEX

# OF AIRSHIP NAMES

# BIBLIOGRAPHY

The list is in order of publication

## SPECIALIST WORKS

FAUJAS DE SAINT-FOND  *Description des expériences de la machine aérostatique*, Paris, 1783

TURGAN, JULIEN  *Les Ballons. Histoire de la locomotion aérienne depuis son origine jusqu'à nos jours*, Paris, 1851

MANGIN, ARTHUR  *La navigation aérienne*, Tours, 1865

SIRCOS, A. & PALLIER, TH.  *Histoire des Ballons et des Ascensions célèbres*, Paris, 1876

TISSANDIER, GASTON  *Les Ballons dirigeables*, Paris, 1872-1885

FIGUIER, LOUIS  *Les Aérostats*, Paris, 1882

TISSANDIER, GASTON  *La Navigation aérienne, l'Aviation et la Direction des Aérostats dans les temps anciens et modernes*, Paris, 1886

TISSANDIER, GASTON  *Histoire des Ballons et des Aéronautes célèbres*, Paris, 1887-1890, 2 vol.

RENARD, PAUL  *L'Aéronautique*, Paris, 1900

ANDRÉ, M.H.  *Les Dirigeables*, Paris, 1902

SANTOS-DUMONT, ALBERTO  *Dans l'air*, Paris, 1904

GIRARD, E. & ROUVILLE, A. DE  *Les Ballons dirigeables*, Paris, 1907

FONVIELLE, WILFRIED DE & BESANÇON, GEORGES  *Notre Flotte aérienne*, Paris, 1908

MARTIN, RUDOLF & SCHACK, GUSTAV  *Von Ikarus bis Zeppelin*, Berlin, 1908

GOLDSCHMIDT, ROBERT  *Les Aéromobiles*, Paris, 1911

DE CARNÉ, CAPITAINE DE FRÉGATE  *L'Organisation de l'Aéronautique maritime (1914-1918)*, Paris, n.d.

WHALE, G.  *British Airships*, London, 1919

NEUMANN, GEORG PAUL  *Die deutschen Luftstreitkräfte im Weltkrieg*, Berlin, 1920

GRADIS, G.  *Les Ballons dirigeables*, Paris, 1923

HOEPPNER, GENERAL VON  *L'Allemagne et la Guerre de l'Air*, Paris, 1924

MONTJOU, GUY DE  *Rapport fait au nom de la Commission de la Marine Militaire chargée d'examiner le projet de loi sur le statut naval (organisation de l'Aéronautique maritime)*, Chambre des Députés, 13e Législature, 1924

PLESSIS, JEAN DU  *Les grands Dirigeables dans la Paix et dans la Guerre*, Paris, 1926

AMUNDSEN, ROALD & ELLSWORTH, LINCOLN  *D'Europe en Amérique par le pôle Nord*, Paris, 1927

LEHMANN, ERNST & MINGOS, HOWARD  *The Zeppelins*, London, 1927

GERVILLE-REACHE, L.  *Autour du Monde en Zeppelin*, Paris, 1929

LOUIS, RICHARD  *30 Jahre Zeppelin-Luftschiffahrt*, Eilenburg, n.d. (c. 1930)

AJALBERT, JEAN  *Le R 101 sur Beauvais, Route des Indes*, Paris, 1931

ALLEN, HUGH  *The Story of Airships*, Akron, 1931

JOUX  *Un dirigeable militaire: L'ADJUDANT VINCENOT*, Paris, 1931

MARBEN, ROLF  *Zeppelin Adventures*, London, 1931

BUTTLAR, BARON VON  *Les Zeppelins au combat*, Paris, 1932

HIGHAM, R.D.S.  *The British Rigid Airships — 1908-1931*, London, 1932

ROSENDAHL, ADMIRAL C.E.  *Up Ship!*, New York, 1932

VISSERING, HARRY  *Zeppelin. The Story of a Great Achievement*, Chicago, 1932

NOBILE, UMBERTO  *L'ITALIA au pôle Nord*, Paris, 1933

SINCLAIR, J.A.  *Airships in Peace and War*, London, 1934

LEHMAN, ERNST  *Zeppelin, The Story of Lighter-than-Air Craft*, London, 1937

MORTANE, JACQUES  *Les Dirigeables tragiques*, Paris, 1938

ROSENDAHL, ADMIRAL C.E.  *What About Airships?*, New York, 1938

CLARKE, BASIL  *The History of Airships*, London, 1961

DOLLFUS, CHARLES  *En Ballon*, Paris, 1962

CROSS, WILBUR  *Nobile au pôle Nord*, Paris, 1963

HOEHLING, A.S.  *Who destroyed the HINDENBURG?*, London, 1962

WYKEHAM, PETER  *Santos-Dumont*, Paris, 1964

ZEPPELIN  *Ein bedeutendes Kapitel aus dem Geschichtsbuch der Luftfahrt*, Friedrichshafen, 1964

ROLT, L.T.C.  *The Aeronauts*, London, 1966

SCHILLER, HANS VON  *Zeppelin, Wegbereiter des Weltluftverkehrs*, Bad Godesberg, 1968

MABLEY, EDOUARD  *The Motor Balloon AMERICA*, Brattleboro (USA), 1969

ROLE, MAURICE  *L'étrange Aventure des Zeppelins*, Paris, 1972

## GENERAL WORKS — AVIATION HISTORY

LECORNU, J.  *La Navigation aérienne*, Paris, 1903

BERGET, ALPHONSE  *La Route de l'Air*, Paris, 1910

DOLLFUS, CHARLES & BOUCHÉ, H.  *Histoire de l'Aéronautique*, Paris, 1932

FLIGHT  *A Pictorial History of Aviation 1953 (by the Editor of Year)*, Los Angeles, 1952

THE AMERICAN HERITAGE  *History of Flight*, New York, 1962

DOLLFUS, CH., BEAUBOIS, H., ROUGERON, C.  *L'Homme, l'Air et l'Espace*, Paris, 1965

– *Le Livre d'Or de la Conquête de l'Air*, Paris, n.d.

## PERIODICALS (passim)

– L'Aéronautique (France)
– L'Aérophile (collection 1893-1914, France)
– The Aircraft Yearbook (USA)
– The Airship (Great Britain)
– Cross & Cockade Journal (USA)
– Icare No. 46, été-automne 1968 (France)
– Jane's All the World's Aircraft (Great Britain)
– L.T.A. (USA)

## BIBLIOGRAPHICAL WORKS

BOFFITO, GIUSEPPE  *Biblioteca aeronautica italiana*, Firenze, 1929.

BROCKETT, PAUL  *Bibliography of Aeronautics*, Washington, 1910

DARMON, J.E.  *Dictionnaire des Estampes et Livres illustrés sur les ballons et machines volantes des débuts jusque vers 1880*, Montpellier, 1929.

DIAZ, ARQUER, G., VINDEL, PEDRO  *Historia bibliografica e iconografica de la Aeronautica en España, Portugal, paises Hispano-Americanos y Filipinas desde los origines hasta 1900*, Madrid, 1930

*The History of Flight. A descriptive Catalogue of Books, engravings and Airmail Stamps illustrating the Evolution of the Airship and the Aeroplane*, London, 1936

TISSANDIER, GASTON  *Bibliographie aéronautique*, Paris, 1887